# Alchemy of Love

## Finding Love, Harmony & Happiness

# Alchemy of Love

## Finding Love, Harmony & Happiness

Michael Samways

AYNI
BOOKS

Winchester, UK
Washington, USA

First published by Ayni Books, 2014
Ayni Books is an imprint of John Hunt Publishing Ltd., Laurel House, Station Approach,
Alresford, Hants, SO24 9JH, UK
office1@jhpbooks.net
www.johnhuntpublishing.com
www.ayni-books.com

For distributor details and how to order please visit the 'Ordering' section on our website.



ISBN: 978 1 78279 116 4



A CIP catalogue record for this book is available from the British Library.

Design: Stuart Davies

Printed in the USA by Edwards Brothers Malloy

# CONTENTS

# Disclaimer

While every effort is made here to present information and advice in a fair and sincere way, you are solely responsible for the way you view and use the information and advice contained in this book. The author and publisher are not responsible in any way for any kind of injury or health problems following use of this book or the advice given in it. Do not attempt to self-diagnose or self-treat for any serious or long-term problems, but rather seek advice from a medical professional or qualified practitioner.

# About the author

Michael has always had an intense love for nature in all its magnificent beauty, which involves experiencing the joys of life, in all its facets, through all the subtleties of the senses and with deep spirituality. He did his PhD at London University, and is Professor in the Department of Conservation Ecology & Entomology, Stellenbosch University, South Africa. He is a Fellow of the Royal Society of South Africa, and a Member of the Academy of Science of South Africa. He has won several major awards and medals for his work, and has published extensively, including eight books. Michael is very involved internationally, especially representing and conserving nature.

# Acknowledgments

This book is a manifestation of collective consciousness among many people. Their resonance, beauty and profound being, are paving the way for a new level of consciousness on our planet as a whole, and beyond. I would particularly like to thank Katharina von Dürckheim for many enlightening discussions and suggestions.

# How to use this book

This book unfolds as a multi-dimensional text on how to find love, harmony and happiness, starting with a philosophical underpinning. It then goes on to practical realities through a wide combination of approaches, which is not normally the case with books in the field of mind, body and spirit. All the points and issues discussed are based on foundations of personal experience as well as researched ideas in science, philosophy and spirituality. References, notes and acknowledgments to sources are given at the end of the book. Certain definitions and concepts are discussed there as well.

The book is intended to be read from beginning to end. The summaries are deliberately extensive and may be read straight away for consolidation of thought, or they can be returned to later. Chapter 15 – *A Personal Guide for Discovering the Alchemy of Love* – is an overall summary with everyday suggestions for life improvement based on all the previous chapters. This chapter is sub-divided according to the previous chapters, and may be read after each chapter, or alternatively, in its entirety after reading the whole book, and as a life coach.

# 1

# How this book came about

*Love fascinated the alchemists of the golden age. They knew that the heart is an organ of perception. When we look at someone we love, we see things other people cannot see, and the initiate who has undergone alchemical transformation has made a conscious, willed decision to see the whole world in this way.*
Jonathan Black

## The overall picture

How do some people seem to get it right! Have you ever wondered how some people just seem be on the right path and find love, harmony *and* happiness? Importantly, they find beauty within themselves. For sure, it didn't happen overnight, or by chance. Those people, like all of us, have been through all the various ups and downs of life, yet have come out on top. You can be sure they have been through some major traumas, whether personal or career, and yet have brought their life path back on track. But let's be real, life does throw curves, and there will be more challenges in the future. So how should you equip yourself to bounce back and be more fulfilled than ever before? How can you find love, harmony *and* happiness? And find your personal beauty within – that alchemical and exquisite tingle where you feel love for yourself and, at the same time, love for all around you? How will you find this grail without becoming a guru, recluse or fanatic, and without sacrificing passion, spontaneity and enjoyment?

The aim here is to provide you with creative ideas for overall life improvement. In short, to light a path towards joy and happiness, for which we all long. This way forward is based on a combination of ancient wisdom and modern research, including that of understanding our deepest roots and holistic thinking, for all aspects of our lives. This book aims to guide you towards fulfillment. It is based on my good fortune of having traveled to many countries in the world, and having met many wonderful people from all walks of life, including mystics, artists and scientists, many of whom have been outstanding life achievers, or rather, and more importantly, achievers of a fulfilled life. It has not been an easy path for them, with wrong turns, dramas and traumas having dealt their share – but who said life is fair? Nevertheless, their darkest times have been illuminated by wisdom, experiences and renewed optimism. They are some of the finest human beings that the world has seen. Not necessarily in terms of their success in their jobs, but rather in the way they have found love and beauty, and consequently happiness. This book is homage to them, and more essentially, as a life guide for you.

## My personal journey

I have seen so much sadness and suffering in the world, much of it having been unnecessary. Life is tough enough physically, without complicating it with unhelpful and even destructive thought processes and actions. In consequence, this book is a personal reflection on how we can make better our lives by recognizing that we have an inner glow and a wealth of beauty that we so rarely tap into. This inner glow is immutable, like the gold of the alchemists. And just as one cannot make gold from base metals, you will not discover love, harmony and eventual happiness through wrong thought processes and inappropriate actions. Finding and following this path involves appreciating life at various levels, from everyday philosophy, to deep philosophy, to understanding physiology, ethology and our deep past. No book yet seems to have weaved these various fields together to bring new insight into the quest for love, harmony *and* happiness. So I draw upon here many fields of discovery which relate to our fundamental biology and psychology on the one hand and current knowledge of our relationship with the cosmos on the other. Detailed notes and references are given at the back of the book.

My earliest memory is of watching a grasshopper singing in the long grass in the afternoon sunshine. It was almost saying that we are all one, you, me and the sun, with all life depending on each other. Growing up in rural England, I experienced many deep and fulfilling experiences, all to do with the sights, sounds and aromas coming from all the facets of nature, from a running stream, to a fresh mushroom and a warm summer meadow. Then the delight of the sight of spring leaves unfurling as the bluebells bloomed in their thousands, while at the breaking of day, being graced by the optimistic song of courtship from the forest birds above. During this time of growing up, I experienced several major satoris, or revelations, where the connectedness of all in nature was so apparent. We are not simply individuals, and, therefore, units, but rather we are temporary points of organization where energy and love ebbs and flows through us. Realization was dawning that we are indeed of the very fabric of *all* nature.

I have always enjoyed oil painting and sculpturing, aside from my professional career in nature conservation. Engaging in and appreciating art is such a wonderful experience that it developed inside of me a profound sense of what I call 'Fern Greens and Serendipity Pinks', which is the interplay of nature, color, art and spontaneity, flying high on the wings of enthusiasm. I learnt how to view an object from all angles and in all lights before painting it, and to use the right tool for the job, a palette knife for steel and a soft sable hair brush for a breast. And then the divine smell of oil on canvas inspired me for life on the joy of touching, feeling and deeply seeing.

Teenage years were one of optimism and occasional delusion, as it is for all of us! I couldn't fathom why so many teenagers had agendas that often repelled love and harmony. Of course as for all of us, such times are one of discovery, among which is the finding out of one's place in the world. But still, why the frequent unhappiness among teenagers? A lot became clear to me when I read the well-known psychologist Eric Berne's book *Games People Play*. It seemed to be that there are two of us: our inner, sincere being on the one hand, and a façade, the ego, which continually tries to dominate all around it, even at the expense of good body health and a sense of well-being. Later years also showed me that we often fall in love with the physical being plus the ego, and we can completely overlook our inner beings in both us and our partner. If only those inner beings could connect without all the interference of the egos!

Then one day, much later, when I was practicing archery and focusing intensely, a strange feeling of 'knowing' came over me. I had been practicing for a tournament in the late afternoons among the beautiful granite hills in savanna South Africa. They were special times anyway, with the sun on the pinkish rocks, peaceful clumps of trees often opening up to a glimpse of an antelope, and a myriad of birds in the long, golden grass, in the bushes and in the air. A strange feeling came over me, as I picked up the bow, drew a breath, saw the swallows wheeling past against the white puffy clouds, as I had never experienced before. The 'I', the ego in me was totally overcome by a cosmic connectedness where the whole world, all the cosmos, all that is divinely beautiful showed me that all is completely connected, with no-space, no-time. In that instant, the bow, the arrow, the target were all one, with an arrow flight so true that my whole being flew with it. The feeling was one of magnificent, explosive, exuberant love, where the whole world was bathed in a golden light. My life that instant changed forever, on discovering that there is an inner glow, an expansive sea of immutable love within us and connected to all in the cosmos. If only we could see it, touch it, feel it, so as to override the strife and havoc caused by our egos.

This then, is a book about finding that path that lies inside all of us. Indeed, finding that path to spiritual well-being and the opening up to our inner being and beauty is where we will find romantic love, family love and a feeling of being at one with all around us.

# 2

# Life's formula

*Imagine you fed all these great works of literature – in fact* all *literature – into a giant computer and asked it the question: What are the laws that determine whether or not a life is ultimately happy and fulfilled? I suggest the result would be a body of laws that included the following: If you duck out of a challenge, then that challenge will come round again in a different form. We always draw towards us what we fear most. If you choose the immortal path, ultimately you will pay for it. A good-hearted belief will eventually transform what is believed in. In order to hold on to what you love, you must let it go.*
Jonathan Black

## Your life plan

Much of all life is about triads, where the balance between two opposites leads to a manifestation. The best known example is that of man and woman, leading to the manifestation of romantic love. These triads resonate, grow and reproduce. Romantic love creates a warm atmosphere and children arise. These triads need to be in harmony, with a man and a woman needing to complement each other in a way that the relationship gives added value to each other's lives. Similarly, the child or children give added value to the romance, and they are happiest when there is harmony between the man and the woman.

Another critical triad in our lives is a set of three realms. These realms are 1) our physical being, its form, senses, motivations and wellness, 2) the egotistical self, which is the self-centered survival mechanism, and 3) our inner being, and gateway and path to higher consciousness. This balance of the triad underpins the triad of love, harmony and their manifestation, happiness

(consciousness, enlightenment). Let's have a look at tl little more detail.

Your physical realm is essentially you as an individua entity, but also as what is known as a physically open s where food, liquid and sensory input flow and keep you and well. In short, our bodies are not a 'something' or 'unit a stopping off point for the flow of nutrients, oxygen, wa energy and love.

Your egotistical realm is more of a 'unit', and is about you an individual, you as separate from everything else. The ego i also about an aspect of you and your mind that is looking after its own survival by bolstering its self-importance, often through competition and strife.

The third part of the triad is your inner self or inner being, the inner you. It is your spiritual realm and the path to full awareness, not just of understanding physical matters, but also of the true *feeling* of spiritual matters as well. This spiritual realm is also a means of achieving full consciousness, where you are totally at one with all consciousness in the cosmos. Your spiritual being is linked with all in the cosmos, as is our physical being, as shown by much modern cosmological research.

The physical realm is maintained in its peak condition as a part of the triad when your physical well-being is at its best. This means doing those things that tune your body functionally, and attune it to the physical world around you. This means enjoying life, feeling healthy, having romance, experiencing good and loving relationships, and surfing life to the full. It is the feeling of 'sensing it, doing it, feeling it, living it'. It is about being fully aware of all the physical nuances, intricacies and wonders of life and nature in general. It is also about eating well, feeling well and having joy. Achieving this end happens through having an open mind, a mind that is creative and lateral. This means dumping past traumas, emotional baggage, hang-ups, and being in the driving seat of your life without you being psychologically

t the mercy of the ego.

Time is of the essence in the physical realm. This is because you wish to squeeze in as much good quality time as possible to tune and attune your body, mind and heart, *all the time.* When adversity is holding you back from your life plan and thwarting your motivation, all you do is simply move around or through the obstacle. You overcome challenges as quickly and as efficiently as possible. This process may mean occasional stepping back to tackle a task and getting it done. Importantly, it is about spending wonderful special time with those you love, and those you wish to love.

It is in the egotistical realm where we meet the greatest challenges and the biggest beast. We need to be alert to this beast, the ego, and be as free of it as is possible. Its currency is memes, which are the forces of influence which spread from one human mind to another. They are not visible but are there all the same. There is continual competition between them, and some are dark (like pitting one culture against another leading to war) and some light (like cultural tolerance and compassion for fellow humans). The ego is a scourge, as it feeds on memes of competition, greed, jealousy and vanity, and sometimes makes us do things that are against our sound reasoning, with us even declaring "How could I have done such a thing!" The ego will drive us if it can, and it will coerce us to gain a competitive edge over other egos.

The ego will even make us do things that are not good for our first realm of the triad, the physical one. We may undertake something distinctly dangerous, such as going through with a dare so as to win what we think is approval or awe from other egos. We think this is about connecting with others. But this is not the case because the ego is a separatist. It does not, in reality, make connections with others. It wants its independence. By allowing us to show off, it tries to make us feel that we are connected with other people. But this is false. The illuminating reality is quite the opposite. Ironically, we have been connected

all along, especially through our inner beings, and it is the ego which is trying to break those connections.

The egotistical realm, like the physical realm, is time and space bound. In terms of our well-being, this egotistical time-space restriction is negative. Time and space dimensions for the ego, the 'I', include winning (the fastest), engaging in greed (bigger the better), and hurt (dominance), among others. The ego is anti-love, anti-harmony, isolationist and aggressive. It thrives on unhappiness, disillusion and revenge and spreads memes accordingly, through the medium of what we commonly call gossip. It is in this egotistical realm that most of us need more awakening, and it is this tough but joyous path that we will explore most.

The third realm, the spiritual one, is your inner being. This is the alchemical gold of pure love that is the anchor for all we do. If only we could feel it all the time, without the ego interfering! The spiritual realm knows neither space nor time and is, 'as is'. It is perennial and immutable, the alchemical gold of love, that has no judgment and is connected with all in the cosmos. We can view it as a glowing golden light that cannot be created or grown by base activities of false love, false sincerity, false coercion, which are stirred up by the ego. It is there, as is, and connected, like invisible and timeless threads throughout all the cosmos.

Using the word being implies some sort of core. While a spatial concept, it is used here so that we can grasp its essence, as it is so difficult for us to visualize, feel or experience 'no-space, no-time'. The closest we get to it is when we put the palm of our hand on our breast and say 'That's lovely!' It is you in residence in you. Your inner being is a glowing core which is a dynamo enabling you to be on your way to experiencing pure beauty, pure love, pure harmony and pure communication. This then leads to enlightenment, which is, in effect, happiness. To find happiness means putting out a hand of love which on the one side connects with your golden inner being and on the other with the great expansive love of all in the cosmos. As neither your inner being nor the cosmos is judging you or anyone else, it is there 'as is' for you to embrace. The biggest challenge of all is that your ego and its agents, the dark memes, will continually interfere. The key is the great 'CL', Compassion and Love, which when you *give* unconditionally, with confidence and commitment, will automatically lead to happiness as that is the currency of your inner being, and is universal illumination. Finding that path is what we shall explore over the following pages.

### Feeling fundamental love

Alchemy is about realizing that there are two 'base elements' in life: the physical realm of the triad (your body and its well-being), and the egotistical realm of the triad (a meme machine). The negative aspects of the ego and its mimetic communication and inheritance (inheriting one set of thoughts from another person) often have negative effects on your physical well-being. This is a treadmill because the more you give in to the ego, often the more unhappiness is created. Working in a manic way simply to accrue more material wealth is an open invitation to the greed memes. These memes are powerful, and as spelt out on a billboard in a world famous shopping mall 'Get all you want here'. What they did not say was that continually getting out your credit card does not lead to happiness. The key to counter-acting these influences is to stay fit and well (through exercise, loving thoughts and eating well) as it gives you more strength to deal with the negative aspects of the ego. We will unpack this in more detail later.

The third realm of the triad is realization that there is an immutable manifestation, the golden beauty of love, which is your inner being. While we often think that love must come from without, in reality it is from within. Alchemy of love is about building on the physical realm of the triad (through a healthy mental outlook as well as keeping fit and eating well), while at the same time discovering the immensity of love and harmony which is already in us and in all the cosmos. This immensity of love and harmony, like gold, is immutable.

We do not aim to change the base feelings of the ego, like base metals, into gold, as that is impossible. It is against all natural laws. Rather, we acknowledge that our inner being and beauty is always there. We aim all the time to associate with it and experience it more and more. We are able to do this by recognizing the activities of the ego, with its negative influences, and dealing with them. This is done by always maintaining a connection with your inner being, and making this connection ever stronger.

In this context, alchemical 'transmutation' is acknowledging and then managing the ego. Ideally, the aim is to dissolve the waste of the ego's activities with the pure light of love, for which the ego, the 'I', has no answer. It becomes mute when confronted with unequivocal, formless, totally unselfish love. It cannot grasp it, and it cannot ever change it. Inevitably, being confronted with such invincibility, it engages in all sorts of diversions to take away any chance of individual people seeing the way forward to experiencing love, harmony and happiness. These diversions promote the individual person, and come at whatever cost. This is seen, in reality, as manifestations of personal competition, greed, coercion to a particular belief system, stirring up aggression and war mongering.

Yet love and harmony can really only grow inside of you and around you when you have actively cultivated the physical base of well-being. So a first consideration is to look after your body, the vehicle of your inner being. It is not easy to give out love when you are simply in basic survival mode. If you are rudderless in the small boat of your body in an ocean of egos, the chances of finding true love and harmony are slim. First of all, respect as well as look after your beautiful body. Give it love, give it good food, fresh air, positive thoughts and lovely sensuous input. Pamper yourself! This is very different from egotistical vanity. There is nothing wrong with treasuring your body, as long as you also manifest its essential partners: kindness, modesty, humility, honesty, truthfulness, physical awareness, sensuousness, spontaneity, passion and discipline. Use time well for this. This means using time for good things, and not letting the ego be able to squeeze its way onto your path of illumination at any time.

On a base of physical well-being, you can then focus on your path to greater awareness, consciousness and enlightenment. You can feel it almost as a 'tickling' or exciting upwelling inside. It is a lovely warm, delicious feeling. This tickling feeling then feeds back into improving your physical well-being and turning up the white light of your love so that it outshines the darkness of the ego.

In effect, the ego cannot bear this illumination. It becomes banished. Like any dragon, it will keep returning, breathing its dark fire, weakening your physical and spiritual walls. Yet the analogy with a walled building ends here, as you are not an isolated fortress. If you are, then you will be starved out by the ego, and conquered. Think of your inner being as a no-place, no any-one-time, and so the dragon-like ego cannot find you because you are everywhere all at the same time, connected with all in the cosmos, giving out love and being loved. No dark fire, no sharp teeth from everyday bites can assault your ever present being, your love, your ineffable beauty.

## How do we know that there is inner being and beauty?

How do we know that there is something deep within us that is our anchor, our guide, our alchemical well, and our future happiness? There is in nature a whole range of polar opposites that enable the cosmos to function and for life to exist. The well-known ones are positive and negative charges, yin and yang, dark and light, good and bad. One of these can only exist in the presence of the other. When these polar opposites are engaged, there is a manifestation, which is a path forward. The key is to find the relative balance of these opposites so that the path to enlightenment (feeling at one with the immutable love in the cosmos) and free will is illuminated and that you are not provided only with the darkness of the ego, leading you forward only for its own survival.

Our inner being is the polar opposite of the drive of the ego. Our inner being and beauty is peaceful, affirmative, loving, compassionate, giving, enthusiastic and immutable. In contrast, the ego is warlike, aggressive, competitive, destructive, selfish, uncaring, demanding, vain and fickle.

Yet there is a spectrum, as light grades into dark. And so there is a spectrum from being ego-bound through to being fully connected with your inner being. We cannot be totally free of the ego, as it is an intrinsic part of our psyche honed by natural selection over the millennia. We can though, recognize it and know what it is capable of. We can show non-reaction to it. This may seem strange, but the ego thrives on reactions. This is unlike the immutable and loving inner being which is, by definition, non-reaction. Non-reaction is the not giving into or, even better, quietly ignoring, the ego's taunts, such as you have got to win over others, you have got to have more material wealth, you have got to be 'ahead' or else you are worthless, or you have got to be recognized and admired.

The main issue in our lives is that the ego is forever striving to dominate. It often succeeds, and at the individual level, this makes us competitive, cruel, vain and pompous, yet highly susceptible to disillusion and unhappiness. It is also a great contributor to shortening our beautiful, vibrant lives. At the social level, these negative egotistical attributes manifest as aggression and wars, often given euphemistic cover ups like defending our liberty when what is really meant is securing our material wealth.

## How do we give out love?

The best way to deal with the torment of the ego is to give out love. Yet it is easy simply to say 'let us give out love'. But what does it really mean and how do we do it? The key is to recognize the triad of 1) your inner being and beauty, 2) the ego, and 3) the vehicle of these, your physical body. The first thing to do is to steer away from the ego as much, and as often, as possible, as it always does its upmost to steer you away from your inner being. We cannot ignore the ego, and it will not go away, as it is part of us, and it had major survival value when we roamed the savannah. The easiest way to view the ego is that it is simply the dark side of us. Firstly, as we have said, you aim to keep well physically, which involves good thoughts as well as right food and exercise, and you practice recognizing when the ego is trying to dominate. When it does try this, all you do is shine the light of your inner being onto it to dissipate its darkness. Recognizing this triad is a fundamental base which makes it much easier for you to give out love and grow towards enlightenment.

One comfortable way to visualize the act and feeling of giving out love is to consider your life as a dance. You do not want to dance in the dark, under the dark shadow of the ego. You feel the glowing attraction of being able to dance in the light, where you become illuminated in all your glorious colors. For your dance, you need to be well, in body, mind and heart. So, you look after your lovely body, as it carries your heart, mind and feelings. You cherish your body and you give it warmth, comfort, good nourishment, and you love it. We will look into all these in detail in later chapters.

Then you need to be well in your mind, which means feeling that you are growing, letting go of traumas, having non-reaction to adversity, giving sincere praise and enthusiasm, and sincerely thinking positively, as well as having immense compassion and empathy. No one is able to pull your strings, and you instantly recognize when psychological game playing is taking place. You also know when to say 'no'. You are confident of your own inner charisma, yet you have humility. These attributes are for you, for those you love, and for others, including other life forms. Again, we will explore these in detail later. Suffice to say that we are just introducing them now.

All the while you are in this lighted area, you are aware that the time for your Earthly course is finite, and that you organize your day, your world, so as to pack in as much goodness as you can, while also surfing the present moment, and living life to the full.

Then there is the light of your heart, which although linked with your mind, has its own special glow and ability to outshine the darkness of the ego. The inner confidence and charisma really comes more from the heart than from the mind because you deeply feel the goodness and love that resides there and emanates from there.

Your physical being and motivational realm of the triad (the triad being your inner being, your physical being, and ego) can actively outshine and dissolve the egotistical realm of the triad through good thoughts and actions. This then automatically moves you to a heart-driven true appreciation and awareness, which in turn, brings you closer to the realm of the triad which is your inner being and beauty. This core of you is of itself illuminated and immutable and connects with all in the cosmos. It is as it is.

You cannot change your immutable inner being and beauty, but you can appreciate and associate with it. You can also bathe in it, largely after having taken care of the physical and motivational realm through activating your good attributes.

Your inner being is always there effectively waiting for you to recognize it so that it can turn up its illumination, so that the darkness of the ego disappears. Your inner being is there glistening in its golden glory before your eyes. This of course is not actually 'seeing'. It is really that wonderful 'tickle' and excitement of love that you feel inside. It is a tickle around your heart and deep inside. It is a feeling that knows, yet does not know either space or time, as it flows into and out of you, and connecting you with the all.

Your inner being and beauty is there, as is, and shining. We view it almost as a place so that we can visualize it, touch it, kiss it and embrace it. And we do so by being continually aware. This awareness is about tuning our senses fully, having a deep understanding of life, and being deeply compassionate. We cultivate these through continual dedication every day.

Your inner being and beauty will continue to glow like golden poetry, with a white brilliance. Yet the ego will always try to interfere with your oneness with your inner being, as it does not want connectedness with others and the cosmos. The ego and its communication lines, which are the memes of ill will that pass around the world, will goad you so as to destabilize your inner peace.

We have to accept the reality that we are fallible, that we do weaken, and that our feelings wax and wane. This means that the light coming from our physical well-being sometimes seems to shine bright and at other times not. Perhaps this is because we are physically unwell or because we are feeling down. In both cases, it is the ego that has got the upper hand. The brighter the light, the easier it is to see and feel our inner being. This means that there will be days where the connection with your inner being is stronger than on other days. This emphasizes the value of keeping well and thinking good thoughts so that the feeling of love will keep you bolstered up as often and as long as possible. Being buoyant like this often puts you on a higher plateau of spirituality, because each time you overcome a setback and an illness, you have even greater chance to grow spiritually.

So, to return to our earlier question of: what is the giving out of love and how do we do it? In short, it is truly enjoying the connection with your inner being and its beauty. It is the outshining of the ego on the physical plane of actually doing and then at the same time, feeling the special 'tickle' and the golden nothingness, the white expansiveness of light, and the total non-reaction of the inner being.

While this waxing and waning is a coming and going of closeness to your inner being, there is, nevertheless, continual spiritual growth. You will find that there are moments and even days when your growth is substantial, while on other days, your growth is minimal, or you may even slip backwards. This slipping back might be because of a sudden ambush by the ego, like someone causing you to get angry (losing your temper-ance i.e. inner harmony). Reflection at such a time is so important. This is not about delving into the past or worrying about the future, but doing a rapid non-reactionary, enthusiastic assessment of what is right and good, what is compassionate and loving, what is lovingly passionate and colorful, and what is not. It is a sort of mental checklist of ticks and crosses. Reflection is the recharging of your spiritual batteries. It is focus on turning up the light of your inner being and especially its beauty in readiness to instantly outshine the ego when it tries to trick you and set you back.

When you are feeling very well physically and the ego is quiescent or is in retreat, and when you are totally aware and you let go of negativism completely, and are also feeling totally non-reactive, you will sometimes experience mega flashes of understanding, expansiveness and connectedness with all of nature. These are satoris, and you will never forget them, and never look back.

Satoris are absolutely and totally life-changing, and you will never slip spiritually to the lower level that you were at before the satori. Yes, the ego will have a shot at pulling you down, particularly unexpectedly and powerfully as it feeds on adverse memes. Yet you have reached a new plateau of spiritual advancement from which you can never come down permanently because your inner being and beauty is in clear view. This is like the parting of a dark cloud. You can now see as far as you feel you can see, and the horizon calls you to journey there for more illumination. There will be times when perhaps physical hardships test the soundness of this plateau, but as it is not physical itself, you will overcome them. It is the illumination through connection with all around you, after which you cannot be reduced to one of your former lower levels.

Depending on your religious disposition, you may call these satoris, or epiphanies, a touch by God. Or you may view them as increasing harmonization with the cosmos. However you describe these experiences, the point is that they did actually happen, and all with unshakable, ineffable, awesome, joyful, love.

So to give out love, is to connect with your inner being and beauty so as to experience illumination. This experience then becomes the 'giving'. This is because its foundation is wonder, non-reaction and non-judgment. It is as it is.

## The path towards full consciousness

In our physical everyday form, we are not either all non-conscious or all conscious. We have relative proportions of each. We are on a path of growth which we can call a path to higher consciousness, or better, a path to greater consciousness, and by the law of polarity, of less non-consciousness. It is a path, a spiritual journey, where there is greater illumination, on the way to full enlightenment, while leaving the ego behind. Yet enlightenment as a form of spiritual self-governance, is as much a beginning as an end, because it is timeless, expansive, and beyond space. It simply is.

This path of illumination is where the light of our living,

vibrant physical body and the linking with our inner being together overcome the ravages of the ego. There are several levels to full consciousness, as understood by masters and seers of the ages, who have viewed our deep humanness as being capable of wonder, ecstasy and laughter. We have it all within ourselves, and we need to awaken to it while we are alive, and to feel the wonderful and delightful sensuous stroke of our inner beauty.

The start of the path to full consciousness is that of physical matter, of material lifelessness, of physical interactions and energy transfer, of starbursts and black holes. The next level is the biological realm, the building of form out of the abiotic molecular milieu. It is the appearance of the negentropic breath of life, a celebration of *responsiveness* to the physical world and to other life forms.

This biological level has three components: variation, selection, and retention. Life is intrinsically variable, and certain life forms are the better adapted than others to physical and biotic life conditions *at any given moment.* It is these which survive and reproduce, with the cycle of variation, selection and retention continuing. The culmination is the variety of life we see today. Indeed, there are more species and there is more genetic variety on Earth today than at any time in the past.

At this point, we need to reflect on where humans stand in this wonder of evolution. There is still today a huge misconception that humans alone are at the top of the evolutionary pinnacle. This simply is not true, and it is a truly sad reflection that our collective mindset is still largely in the realms of egocentricity, so prevalent in the Middle Ages. The reality is that we are just one branch of many life forms that exist today, all of which are well adapted to their current environment and have the right to exist as much as we do. We are not better or more advanced than any other life form, unless we use egocentric language to describe ourselves. Nevertheless, we are certainly more complex than any other life form in terms of our neural networks. In turn, that complexity has allowed life to be conscious of itself and its place in the cosmos. We know we exist, but then perhaps it is a dream, but that does not matter.

Certainly, we are truly one of the most influential organisms on Earth affecting ecosystem processes. Our sheer level of activity means that the future of the planet largely lies in our hands. Risks from major Earth crust upheavals and asteroid impacts aside, the future of life on Earth is for us to determine. We, as humans, must now work as a team, in harmony with other life forms, to secure a future for all of us. We are not so naïve as to exclude biological competition and parasitism, but we also recognize that real progress on this planet came about through mutualisms (working together for mutual benefit) and not strife. Mutualisms overcame many of the great abiotic upheavals and changes that have occurred throughout Earth's history. We now need to see that mutualistic activities pull us and other life forms through to a new world. Mutualisms are, after all, a form of love.

As we have such impact on planetary processes, we must now play a team game for our survival, using humility rather than dominance over, and arrogance against, the rest of nature. For sure, we are the only species that has the mind to be able to do so.

As there is indeed only one certainty and that is change, the Earth will survive, with or without us. We are pushing other species to extinction and we do not know what the outcome of all this will be, especially as every species contributes to some ecosystem process somewhere. We may go down the extinction route of the many species that we have already been sending there. Yet many others will survive, and the biological world without us will continue, but on a different trajectory.

Our survival is now about moving out of the almost unbelievable madness of the egos around the world, where we currently accept war and the spoiling of natural resources as the norm. The future lies between collective egos as the dark polarity on the one hand, and collective consciousness as illumination on the other. It is our choice: sense, sensibility and light, or nonsense, egotism, and darkness.

The next level above the biological one is where the huge complexity of our neural network awakens to our inner being and beauty. We know that our inner being is there within us, and we know that it is the essence of love and harmony. We also know that we should be connecting with it, yet the ego continues to beguile us. Why is that? The reason lies in our deep evolution and the hard wiring of our most primal of survival strategies to procure resources and reproduce at an intensity that worked for us when our population numbers were orders of magnitude lower than they are today. And this strategy worked. We are here today, having pulled through severe genetic and population bottlenecks. The downside is that our overdrive for neophilia, for armfuls of lollipops, and a strong sex drive, is still with us as an evolutionary legacy.

We now need to ease up a little. We need to improve our use of wealth (not our greed), as this leads to decreased reproductive rate. We need to move our craving for newness into discovery of our inner beauty. And we need to cherish the resources that we have by maintaining biodiversity and keeping ecosystem processes functioning optimally. Overall this means that we need to become more spiritually aware and more appreciative of the ethereal rather than the material, and to look after our bodies, our minds and our hearts a little better. It is time to now leave baseness behind, and consider that immutable and lovely gold that lies within us. It means loving our own being, loving others and loving all that is living while feeling the cosmos giving our love transcendence to where it is free to express itself fully.

## You and your connections with all the cosmos

Science and spiritualism continue to converge as we realize that the possibility of life on other planets in the universe becomes a certainty. Whether this life takes the form of life as we know it is another question, but certainly there is likely to be water and carbon based life somewhere, and in all likelihood, in many places. The universe is in all likelihood, sprinkled with life, tiny gold nuggets of complexity in the vastness of mostly nothingness.

While we talk about the future of humankind and its awakening, this is too much of an Earth-centric view. The reality is that we are part of the cosmic awakening that is probably happening throughout the universe. The real joy for us is that we are part of this huge process of discovery, awe and delight.

Still, we have much to do on our home planet and while we may be aware of the birth of a new species as Yatri puts it, or of a new Earth as Eckhart Tolle says, we have a great deal of spiritual work still to do. We are not out of the thick of economic, political and religious conflict yet, with major declines globally as collective egos reign supreme. This does not mean that we must despair, or continue to let the ego dominate everything that we do. On the contrary, it means that there is a great need for more and more people to feel love through their inner beauty. If we all did that, we would all move towards much greater harmony and happiness.

Yet the more we contemplate happiness, the more elusive it becomes. Happiness so often seems to dissolve before our eyes like mist in the morning sun, yet if we are aware, we see that it also gives way to total radiance. Happiness then becomes existence but non-existence, and we catch glimpses of it as we see and feel our inner beauty. The more aware we are the more often we see it, with our goal to be able to see it all the time, in total illumination. Yet when we do look closely, we find out that our inner being is not a node after all, but a great expanse of love that extends forever, everywhere.

As happiness unfolds, it is pure, utter gold and immutable beauty. We can tinker with the base metals and we can change one compound into another, but gold cannot be made. It is as is, our inner beauty. Like gold the metal, which is also throughout the universe, when we smile we see our reflection in it. Golden love and beauty is the mirror which reflects our worth according to the extent to which we have discovered the void. Love continues to reverberate, yet not-reverberate through non-reaction, through being 'as is', like laughter in the cosmos over the absurdity of the ego-mind.

This wonderful upwelling of love is what we experience as a Love Alchemist. We feel that golden emanation that comes from our giving of love, the connecting with our inner being and beauty. Then you realize that happiness actually is very simple, it is the being at one with your inner being and with the cosmos. The realization is simple, yet the path nevertheless is tough. We must now be worthy to progress along this path. We must keep trying, and in doing so will attain.

## On death and delight

Does God exist? Can we assume that He does not? There cannot be simply a He, without a 'She', as this violates the law of polarities. The 'She' is the manifestation of the physical world from stars to starfish. Do we have a soul? Can we assume that we do not have a soul? Perhaps we do: as it is on Earth, so it is in Heaven. 'Soul' is a religious way of saying 'inner being'. Is there re-incarnation? Can we assume that there is not?

All these views are cosmic tongues, like real languages, are framed by where we were born and our experience on Earth from when life was first breathed into us. Actually, it does not matter what tongues we use, as our time on Earth in our current form is finite. There is only one language in both life and death and that is love. It is where there is reduced influence of the ego, no division of form and total awareness. This means being at one with our inner being through total illumination.

As our inner being is part of the greater cosmos and of

universal love, we will, when we die, disintegrate into the great oceanic void of love. This means that there is no reason to fear death. What it does mean though is to delight in life, to celebrate life, as it is love's way of manifesting itself as something we can feel, touch, embrace, kiss, and adore, so as we have passion and peace. Life lets us laugh.

The breath of life entered into us in all its innocence, to appreciate love. Yet we were given the option to accept it, or to let the tyranny of the ego prevail. We were given the option to take joy in the form of our bodies and all their subtle sensitivities and through them to awaken to our inner being and beauty. Together, our physical well-being and our inner beauty brighten the light of being and show us there is nothing to fear, ever. Yet the ego has a trump card, and that is creating a fear of death. Unlike our inner being, which is fearless, timeless and perennial, the ego, being time bound, will create fear to preserve itself.

We will all return to the cosmos as that is our real birth place yet focused on Earth. Our love, our harmony has been there all the time within us and we have a finite time on this planet to see it and to feel it. Our love for our body, for our polar/romantic partner, our family, for humankind, and other life on this and other planets is simply the physical manifestation of our love within the cosmos. We will return to the cosmos to complete the polarity of love within and love without. That is where harmony lies, in life and death. Happiness is enjoying that great big smile of universal, passionate, cosmically romantic love that is forever calling us.

* * *

***Life's Formula*** We are a triad representing 1) our physical being, its form, senses and motivations, 2) the egotistical self, and 3) our inner being and beauty, our gateway and path to higher consciousness. Our goal in the physical realm is to improve our well-being. Besides improving our functionality through looking after body and mind, it also means enjoying life, having romance, having good and loving relationships, and experiencing life to the full, especially through having an open and creative outlook on life. This also involves letting go of past traumas, emotional difficulties, and psychological blockages through taking charge of and deflecting the negative activities of the ego.

Time is of vital importance in the physical realm, as our life on this planet is short and we aim to squeeze in as much physical quality time, exciting action, and good loving as possible. We also aim to overcome challenges as quickly and as efficiently as possible so that there is more time to focus on the lovely things, including spiritual growth.

The challenge overall is the tyranny of the ego, which manifests itself in a whole host of ugly ways. The ego does its best to divert attention away from the third realm of the triad, our inner being, as it does not like the harmony and the connectedness with all that resides there. The ego even taunts us, through competition and vanity, to do things which jeopardize our physical being. Egos when viewed from the outside may seem to bond beings, as at sports meetings. But instead of bonding, these egotistical activities only serve to separate us from each other. Real bonding ability resides with our inner being, and its ability to connect through love.

The egotistical realm is highly time-bound, and thrives on the fastest, biggest and best, dominance and pride. The ego is anti-love, anti-harmony, isolationist and aggressive. It also thrives on unhappiness, disillusion and revenge, and spreads its tentacles through the media and gossip.

Our inner being and beauty 'is as is' and timeless. While we can view it as a 'place' within us, it is really a connection with universal illumination. Yet we feel it in our breast, often as a sort of divine, sensuous and exciting 'tickle'. Alchemy of love is about building on the physical realm of the triad, while at the same time feeling the immensity of love and harmony in and around us. This great love, like gold, is immutable.

Through realizing and dissolving the strong activities of the ego, as well as feeling goodness in the physical realm, there is connection with our inner beauty. This then outshines the ego and makes it mute, as the ego has no answer to love.

The possibility of feeling love is greatly enhanced when we focus on our physical well-being, both body and mind. By treasuring ourselves, which is not vanity, our path of love, harmony and illumination becomes more open. The manifestation of the connection between our physical selves and inner beauty is the 'tickle' inside. This is the white light of love dispersing the darkness of the ego. Inner being and beauty, which is immutable and timeless, as well as being connected with all, cannot be pinned down by the ego. The ego simply cannot grasp love as it has no means of being able to do so, and love is too ethereal and strong for it.

Nature functions through laws of being, and that of polar opposites is one of them. On the one hand there is the ego, which is warlike, aggressive, competitive, destructive, selfish, uncaring, demanding, vain and fickle. On the other hand, its polar opposite, our inner being and beauty, is peaceful, affirmative, loving, compassionate, giving, enthusiastic, passionate, spontaneous and immutable.

There is a spectrum, from being ego-bound to being fully at one with our inner beauty and being illuminated. While we cannot be totally free of the ego, we can move away from its influence as much as possible, especially through non-reaction to it. We need to be aware that the ego tries to dominate, and often does so when we are least aware.

Giving out love first requires recognizing the antics of the ego and instantly having non-egotistical thoughts in alignment with our inner being. These thoughts, when converted into deed, then become capable of outshining the darkness of the ego. These thoughts are literally colored with good intentions, both for our own physical well-being and that of others. This positive approach is also about being able to let go of trauma or disillusionment, and giving out compassion and empathy with enthusiasm. In practical terms, to do so also means organizing our day for maximum efficiency of well-being activities.

Our inner being and beauty cannot be changed, as it 'is as is'. We can though, bathe in its light, especially after we have taken care of our physical well-being and motivated ourselves to give out love and compassion. It is, in effect, the turning up of the light shining from our inner being so that we always metaphorically see it, touch it, kiss it and embrace it. This is often hard to do because the ego, being goaded on by memes of ill will, will always try to deflect awareness away from our inner beauty.

There will be days when we are feeling physically and emotionally more able to relate to our inner being than on other days. During the down times, or less aware times, it is essential to think positively and constructively with love and compassion. With those thoughts, coupled with deeds, the tickle of love will start to be felt again. In the end, it is all about giving our love, which is the same as truly enjoying the connections with our inner being and all around us.

The path of growth is not continually upwards because we are fallible, and our well-being or awareness slips. This is why it is so important to reflect on what is colorful, loving and wonderful, and what is not. These reflective times, which are not the same as letting the chatter of the ego fill the mind, are a way of re-charging the spiritual batteries. This returns the spiritual strength needed for constant awareness and vigilance so as to be able to deal with the activity of the ego.

When the ego has dropped its guard, and there is a feeling of wellness and non-reaction, as well as a feeling of being alive and in love with the world, flashes of insight appear. These are satoris and may be small or large. They are spiritual growth spurts where we become illuminated from within. They are life changing, and like the parting of a dark cloud, life's destination becomes clearer and the feeling of love inside becomes immensely strong. There are also strong feelings of harmony with the cosmos. It is a feeling of awesome, joyful love.

In our physical living everyday form, we are neither all non-conscious nor all conscious. We experience varying and changing proportions of each. The key in life is to move into more consciousness and less non-consciousness by leaving the ego behind. It is about awakening our inner being and beauty so that we have greater capability of wonder, ecstasy and laughter. It is to enjoy the tickle coming from inside us.

The path to full consciousness began with the base world of material lifelessness, which is the case throughout most of the cosmos. Then the next stage was the breath of life, which is responsive to the world around it by maintaining its complex form. Life changes through the triple process of variation, selection and retention, where genetic foundations and physical expressions of life forms continue to change over time. Humans are part of this variety of life, and are joined in this celebration of life by a whole host of other species that have also remained in the evolutionary game and are highly adapted to the modern world.

While there has been much emphasis in the past on natural selection being 'red in tooth and claw' we are now beginning to realize that many of the great leaps in life have come from mutualistic interactions between life forms. By working together, there has been the emergent property of totally new life forms. As there is only one certainty, and that is change, we need to think more in terms of a mutualism between our physical body, including its thoughts, and our inner being, and our link with all the cosmos. Our future is in our hands, with the possibility on the one hand of collective egos creating an even darker world, or on the other, our collective consciousness awakening a whole network of inner beings.

While we continue to try and connect with each other and with the cosmos, the egos still continue to beguile us. This is because of our ancestral hard-wiring to procure new resources and reproduce as much as possible. These intense dispositions have left us in biological overdrive. We now need to ease up a little and reflect on making the effort not only to look after natural resources but also to love each other better.

The certainty of life being on other planets is now upon us. We are probably not alone, which is encouraging us to move away from our Earth-centric view and to start to think cosmically. Yet we also have only one home planet that we need to cherish, and we have much spiritual work still to do while we are on it. For our future survival, more and more people need to connect with their inner beings which will lead automatically to much greater love with others.

Happiness seems so elusive because it is not a 'thing' but a path, an essence, a 'tickle', after having given out our love and found harmony. Golden love and beauty is the mirror which reflects our worth according to the extent to which we have discovered the void, the gateway of which is our inner being.

This feeling of the 'tickle' coming from our inner being is there all the time. We feel it and can revel in it when we give out love and harmony. The 'tickle' is a tangible reflection of love being returned to us.

However we perceive the cosmos and whatever words we use to describe it, our relationship with it has literally come from the locality on Earth wherein we were born and grew up. There is really only one language in both life and death, and that is love. This happens when the ego is literally managed. In the process of doing this, the world begins to seem to have no division of form. Through total awareness, we then begin to feel total connectedness with all. This is another way of saying that we are becoming one with our inner being, and on our way to becoming fully conscious.

Fear of death is the ego's last stand, and its trump card, so as to stay alive itself and to perpetuate the gossip of ill will. The ego's tyranny is overturned when our physical well-being, through linking with our inner being, brightens the light of being by outshining the fear created by the ego. We will return to the cosmos, from where we came, to discover that love and harmony has been within us all the time. In turn, happiness is the great big smile of passionate, cosmic love shining back at us.

* * *

# 3

# A strategy for getting on track

## Better to have done it than never tried

There are no practice runs or dress rehearsals for life. We have only one chance, and so we should surf its wave of opportunity and never look back, as there is no future in dwelling on the past. Each second that arrives is a new opportunity, a new adventure, a joyous adventure. That is hopelessly too optimistic and head in the clouds, you may say! But why not make every moment count… count towards making our lives rich and fulfilling. Moments can be fulfilling even when they sometimes hurt, as it is a time of growth. Added together, all these moments make up our whole life, our one and only life.

Let's never have any regrets, and give life our best shot. Yes, we will trip up, make mistakes, and go in wrong directions. Yet these setbacks are messages to move on to something new. It is comforting to know that we have all made mistakes and have all taken wrong directions. It really doesn't matter that we have made a mistake, small or large, with the real issue being how well we dealt with it and successfully overcame it. What matters most is that from a mistake, or even a disillusion, we found a wonderful new wave of opportunity to experience. The point is, when things go wrong, at least we tried, and now we are on course again.

Part of this process of inner growth means being at peace with yourself, cutting yourself some slack, and accepting your imperfections at any one moment. None of us is perfect, and we all need love, affection and security. Yet finding an emotional balance and mental harmony is not to be rushed. It involves a gradual letting go of emotional blockages based on insight, compassion, consideration, wisdom and discipline. As Mahatma

Gandhi said, there is more to life than increasing its speed. It is about quality, especially quality of the present moment, quality of achievement in growth, and quality of future vision. After all, quality is enjoyment. This is where you invoke your no-regret strategy: you did it, you overcame obstacles, and you set your new course. This must be done with absolute honesty and openness to yourself. This leads to the following question.

## What sort of person are you, really?

As none of us is an island, you need to ask where are you in the bigger scheme of life? This comes down to asking yourself: what makes me tick? Leaving career ambitions aside for a moment, what sort of person are you really, deep inside? What are your interests? What makes you feel happy? In your eyes, what are your perceived strengths and weaknesses? What is the social environment that you really enjoy?

These questions are partly answered by reflecting on your achievements and moments of happiness in the past. But you must be ruthlessly honest with yourself. So, while it is essential to live the present moment, and enjoy everything about it, this present moment sits on a foundation of the setbacks and successes you have had in the past, how you overcame the difficult times in the past and how you moved forward. Life is a roller coaster ride of ups and downs, with the key being to move the overall trend in your life upwards. This means building on the ups and letting go of the downs.

You can imagine yourself on this chart of ups and downs, and say 'I am at this point right now'. And maybe that point is at a dip. The key is then to say that this doesn't matter, and that the curve will go upwards next. Accepting those ups and downs is a crucial first step to the process of letting go of setbacks and inhibitions, and emotionally capitalizing on the next upward swing.

The trend line of your life is about defining those features that give you deep and honest satisfaction. This line upwards is a choice tree where you continually make new and small choices that steer you onwards towards fulfillment. In turn, deep fulfillment starts with loving yourself and caring for your body, physically and emotionally. You can then move forward with a sense of giving, especially the giving of warmth and compassion to others. This creates a feedback cycle of positive good feeling. Only with that sense of good feeling, can you then make the best decisions for your life trend, based on knowing who you are.

This knowing who you are cannot be forced. It trickles through to you once you start on your positive feedback cycle: start with a little bit of love of yourself, give some love to others, and feel the illumination of who you are. Once you have started with these loving thoughts, go on then to feel more love for yourself and more for others. Visualize your feedback cycle as a wheel with decision branches.

## Our deep roots

Anthropologists point out that we are 'anatomically modern humans'. Seen another way round, we are humans that evolved in a natural world but have to live in a modern world of geometrical shapes, mechanical tools and electronic communications. The key to developing a life strategy is to recognize our roots, yet adapt to modern living. Our species has seen the coming and going of ice ages, and scarcity and abundance of food. Survival meant working as a team and the sharing of scarce resources in times of hardship. This sharing involved love and caring, as well as sharing of tasks. It also meant reading the signs in nature, and knowing when different foods were available at different times of the year. These foods were variously nutritious, with a variety of trace elements and proteins, and an abundance of fiber.

There are two important points here. Firstly, our senses have been honed to appreciate nature, its wildness and its variety, which is one reason why we have excellent color vision, enabling us to see fruits and the state of freshness of potential food. Today our well-being depends on experiencing nature, from fresh air on our faces to the smell of the wet earth after rain. Secondly, we evolved in a co-operative social context. Working well together meant that we survived together. Helping each other meant thriving together. Without social interactions that promote mutual survival, we have a feeling of being lost. It is what today we call loneliness. Our ancestors probably only rarely experienced loneliness, as their family bonds and friendships were so strong. Those strong and caring bonds were also essential for a good life. Our forerunners spent time experiencing nature, exploring nature, and socializing among nature. This tells us that we must always be returning to experiences of nature, both as individuals and collectively, so as to harmonize with our inner being and to feel a sense that we are moving towards a fulfilling life.

The key here is to recognize that we need that varying complexity of wild nature to better enable us to tackle the challenges of modern life. We also need a partner, a family and true friends; as did the bands of early humans, where frequent communication, kindly interaction and regular touch forged bonds of well-being and compassion. Indeed, compassion, which was strong in early humans, is a first step to finding mutual love.

*In his relations with others, the sage loves kindness*
Lao Tse

## The Mexican fisherman

There is a famous story of an ambitious American businessman on the pier of a small coastal Mexican village when a little boat came in with a fisherman on board. The businessman commented on the quality of the fisherman's tuna catch and asked how long it took for the fisherman to land them. "A little while," replied the fisherman. The businessman, then said, "But why didn't you stay out longer to catch more fish and make more money?" "But I have enough for my family's needs," said the Mexican fisherman. "Then what do you do with the rest of your time?" asked the businessman. "I sleep late, fish a little, play with my children, take a siesta with my wife Maria, and stroll into my village in the evenings, where I sip wine and play guitar with my friends," replied the fisherman. Then the businessman said, "Why don't you spend more time catching more fish, then buy a bigger boat, and work towards having a fishing fleet? You could then even open up a cannery, and have a main office in Mexico City and eventually a Head Office in New York." The Mexican fisherman then asked, "But, senõr, how long would this take?" To which the businessman replied, "Ten to twenty years." "But then what?" said the fisherman. "Well, then you could sell your company and make millions." "Millions, senõr, then what?" The businessman replied, "Then you could sleep late, fish a little, be with your children, take a siesta with your wife Maria, and stroll into your village where you could sip a little wine and play guitar with your friends."

This story tells us that the important essence of our life strategy is about finding ourselves, enjoying life, and finding love, harmony *and* happiness. The arrival is within ourselves, not simply through accumulating vast material possessions, many of which we then have to worry about maintaining and securing. This does not mean that you must let go of all material possessions. It does though, mean focusing on material possessions that are love enhancing as well as life enhancing, such as a finger ring with special significance. Such special body ornaments are deep within our psyche, as seen by necklaces, bangles and survival-securing devices, such as bows and arrows, found so often in the burial mounds of early modern humans.

We are reminded of the Mexican fisherman's philosophy in the familiar adage that no one on their deathbed has ever wished they had spent more time working in the office.

*Rare and valuable possessions keep their owners awake at night*
Lao Tse

## Beauty, and passion too

There is a story of a medieval Japanese archer who could split a cane while shooting an arrow from horseback, and also split a cane after being blindfolded. When asked by a novice how he was able to develop such a skill, his reply was that he was still learning. Such insight and deep understanding, coupled with humility and grace, goes a long way towards a sense of holism and a connectedness with all of nature. Harmony then becomes central. We so often stress ourselves too much to maintain our social status and accumulate possessions that we do not even have the time to use. This leads to disharmony as we get stuck on the ultra-materialistic treadmill, while not growing spiritually.

Developing a sense of wonder and joy for beauty is core to living a fulfilled life. In turn, beautiful thoughts are one of the best foods for inner well-being. Beauty begets beauty, as it is the full appreciation of life as it is in this special moment, with its challenges on the one hand and opportunities on the other. An appreciation of beauty even helps to enable us to overcome many of life's challenges. It is an important antidote when feeling emotionally down. This means that learning to appreciate beauty, all around and within us, is an important part of our daily activities. Even the process of *learning* to see and feel beauty can be a joy, because each step in our accumulated development is a step to increasing fulfillment.

The insight from beauty is not the same as simply accumulating knowledge, but more akin to knowing with immense insight. It is the weaving of life's experiences into a tapestry of well-being and fulfillment, through absorbing the good, and learning from the bad. You can then go on to harnessing beauty. This means going beyond the passive activity of appreciation of beauty, to the active flavoring of your life with a little passion.

This is having a passion for life itself, as well as passion for what you feel is interesting, right and good. Yes, you might say, but passion only leads to desperation in the end. But we need to recognize that we are emotional, feeling beings. With some passion, we gain fulfillment out of love and harmony, which when well-directed, leads to happiness. By all means think and learn, but make sure that you feel the essence of beauty too.

## What we can learn from Helen Keller

There is always going to be someone who is going to be better looking or richer than you or me. So, a good starting point is to accept who we are. This goes for health too.

One of the most inspirational characters to ever have lived was the deaf/blind Helen Keller. Born in Alabama in 1880 and living to the grand age of 87, Helen contracted a disease when she was a baby, leaving her without sight and hearing. This didn't deter her, and after being the first deaf/blind person to earn a Bachelor of Arts degree, she went on to become a prolific writer, and even politician and fund raiser. In 1887 Anne Sullivan, herself visually impaired, became Helen's instructor, teaching Helen by spelling words in her hand. Anne then taught Helen the word for 'water' by running water over one hand and spelling it in the other.

What this biography tells us is that with the right frame of mind and motivation, no matter what your physical challenges, you can achieve something meaningful, not necessarily in the great, wider world, but definitely among your own family and friends. Indeed, at least part of the success of Helen Keller seems to be that she grew up in a caring environment, and that ability to care she passed on to others in later life.

## The 50 percent rule

On this roller coaster ride of life, a good basic philosophy is the 50 percent rule. Rather than going on vacation and thinking all is going to be great all of the time 'because I deserve it', think that 50 percent will be good and 50 percent will be not so good. It is a strange phenomenon that we often feel everything should go right, and yet we go on to magnify the occasional bad happening. If a meal in a restaurant turns out to be not quite as good as you were expecting, just say to yourself, that that is part of the 'not so good 50 percent', even if you do challenge the restaurateur, and so you should. Growth and the giving of love is not just a fluffy and accommodating activity. It means that you must also stand firm on your good values, and interact with all, including your lover, on a fair and firm basis. You choose and affirm your values, and then stand by them. With this 50 percent rule, disappointment is avoided, and the good 50 percent starts to become the bigger portion.

This 50 percent rule also applies to people that you meet. Often we have the expectation that everyone is going to like us. But when you apply the 50 percent rule, and say, "well never mind that is one of the 50 percent of people who do not like me" then the rest becomes easy. The next person may well like you very much. This is more than a coping strategy. It is a part of a positive feedback cycle where the negative is released, letting positive feelings and insight automatically gain ground. Then combine this letting go with simply giving out sincere loving and compassionate thoughts. The end result will be that it will be well over 50 percent of people will like you, and you are well on your way to love, harmony *and* happiness.

* * *

***A Strategy for Getting on Track*** We have only one shot at life. What we get out of it, is what we put in. Our putting-in is not just about effort, which is important, but about our giving love, reaching harmony, and letting happiness flow. Nevertheless, we need always to *try*, so that we can continue to move on and upwards. Should a small step not work out, simply move on anyway, with no regrets. While we must live for the present moment, we need to grow from our past, and develop a life strategy for the future.

When we give true love, we will in time receive it, maybe not right now, but it will come. This reciprocity is based on our ancestral survival roots of the deep past, and on cosmic balance. Some personal, meaningful materialism is not bad, but with materialism to excess, the road to love, harmony *and* happiness is lost.

Whatever our physical disposition, we can find happiness, as long as we *feel* love and *give* love and *maintain* harmony. It helps to have a 50 percent Rule: half our time will be good and half not so good, and half the people will like us and half perhaps not. No worries, these proportions will change for the positive as love, harmony *and* happiness grow.

* * *

# 4

# You are free to choose your path

*According to Buddhism, human beings have free will, and in the exercise of free will they engage in self-determination. In a very real sense individuals create themselves through their moral choices. By freely and repeatedly choosing certain sorts of things, an individual shapes his character, and through his character his future.*
Damien Keown

## Time of ages

The Great Pyramid of Giza, Egypt, is the only surviving mega-structure of the original seven ancient wonders of the world. Not only has it survived, but it is in remarkably good condition despite the ravages of time and humans. This amazing stone edifice is of great antiquity, having endured five millennia, with most of its internal structure intact. The Great Pyramid is not just about its bulk, it is also about its exacting architecture and its internal complex network of sophisticated passages. Much of its design is related to astronomical phenomena. Yet its passages are not ordinary corridors but loaded with numerical symbolism written into the arrangement and dimensions of these passages and various other features, including ceilings, steps, pits and bosses. We can only wonder at the durability and intricacy of its structure, and why the builders went to such great lengths to write a message to last through the rise of history. We cannot escape the fact that there must be a profound message in this numerical stone coding. It seems it was designed to last and communicate earthly and divine messages to humankind over the millennia from its construction and into the future, at least for a few thousand years more.

Whether or not the Great Pyramid was used for actual initiation of novitiates we may never know. Yet it does seem that its message was left for elevation of humanity into higher consciousness, through advice in stone to individuals. The builders of the Great Pyramid clearly thought this to be sufficiently important to have built the most enduring of all structures on earth.

The archaeologist Peter Lemesurier decodes the Great Pyramid in his book *The Great Pyramid: Your Personal Guide*. In his illuminating account, he deciphers the code in the passages both for individual lives and collective consciousness of humankind towards harmony on the planet. While this is not a view accepted by many historians, we cannot escape the fact that the message as relayed by Lemesurier is paralleled in spiritual knowledge from other philosophical and spiritual systems, most of which have also endured millennia.

So, you may ask, what does this have to do with love, harmony *and* happiness? Well, the message of the Great Pyramid is that in life we have choices. The ultimate aim is to illustrate that there is a path to light and higher consciousness, so that we are at one with the cosmos at the end of our life. We should aim to take the right turns, when the various opportunities arise, to move from the brain's left-hemisphere, egotistical materialism towards giving love and harmony. Of course, this is no easy task, and it is the path of a lifetime, where we must try to make the right decisions whenever we can. According to the Great Pyramid, doing so will give you wholeness, or what we call today happiness. The point here is that happiness is the reward, not the goal. It comes from continuing to make small corrective steps throughout our lives.

Lemesurier's reading of the Great Pyramid suggests that there are various times in our life where choices in the path we take are particularly crucial. Age 12 is an appropriate time to awaken dormant energies of adolescence, and while we may be past that, at least we can teach our children the opportunities arising from bringing out more right-hemisphere intuition and creativity, leading to improved development. By about 19, sexuality, self-assertion and potential aggression would have come about, with the important message that they need to be channeled into healthy and creative forms of expression. Age 21 is then an age for exploring wider interactions – physical, intellectual, social and commercial, with deep-felt humility and selfless love ideally taking place at 24.

By 28, and building on earlier experiences, speech expression, whether involving the expressing of experiences, teaching, giving advice or commanding for the common good, becomes important. With continual development, through trying, various spiritual and psychic abilities start to dawn, preparing our way for final gaining of cosmic consciousness from the age of 49. Even after that age, we still have opportunities for correcting our path towards final integration with the cosmos. This path to final integration and enlightenment involves development of humility, which often comes from overcoming traumas and setbacks. It also means dealing with disappointments which, virtually by definition, are dents to our ego. Growth towards enlightenment is feeling our inner, loving being, without the ego setting us back.

## Who said life was easy, or even fair

It is intrinsic to the behavior of most animals to undertake great physical activity only when really necessary. This is the rule of parsimonious use of resources, where exertion only takes place to procure food, a mate and shelter. This is because resources are, by and large, scarce in nature. Animals are adapted to getting what they need, and then resting. This also means avoiding predators. But then you may say, what about play? These apparently recreational activities, common among the young, have a more survivalist reason for being. Play hones physical co-ordination of brain, hormones and muscle, with the result that the animal is then more successful at finding those resources. Play is also important for bonding among mates, as with pairs of soaring eagles. Sometimes though, play does seem to take place simply for the joy of it, even among ravens, which will roll around in the snow, seemingly just enjoying it. Whatever the case, play does feel good, and that is why we must make time for it. It is the reasoning behind the concept that we must make sure that we are always a happy child throughout adulthood.

What this means for us, with our basic biology, is that we are naturally equipped only to undertake physical exertion for our basic physical needs. Yet we have a large brain. Because of this, and stemming from our self-awareness, we have to literally work through the choices outlined in the Great Pyramid by means of making a huge physical, mental and spiritual effort. But that effort does not come easy to us. That is why those people aiming for spiritual enlightenment, such as Buddhist monks, must go through discipline and focus. While we may say 'nothing ventured, nothing gained', we may also say 'nothing really given effort, nothing really gained'.

Peace of mind really only comes after exertion, mental and/or physical, and also after the release of any bad thoughts. The Great Pyramid says this loud and clear. So to avoid the pitfalls of a materialist, left-hemisphere brain, we must go that little extra distance, in understanding what it takes to open up the creative, right hemisphere. Life, a fulfilled one, is indeed not easy. To tackle this, means to think and act not just in terms of giving our all, but always trying that little bit harder. When we do so, the rewards are enormous.

This is where play comes in. It is complementary to exertion. Play is the polar opposite of exertion, and in the scheme of a triad, together they build character and stimulate spiritual development. Walking on the beach, rolling around in the sea, squelching along a footpath, and stroking our loved ones, is important for tactile-induced well-being. Yet we also need time to reflect. With reflection, in a quiet place, the psyche is opened up, as long as this does not involve dwelling on the past and worrying over the future. This dwelling, also known as vertical thinking or the mind treadmill, is what Buddha called listening to the chatter of monkeys. It is essential to deal with this 'chattering' by focusing on the here and now and living present experiences, such as being aware of all sounds, sights and smells around you, even above and behind you. It also means being aware and enjoying your own body movements and expressions.

Another misperception is that we often think that life just isn't fair. But nature does not work on fairness, although the ego does. We can think of fairness in individual transactions and regular interactions involving the egotistical 'I', but we cannot in terms of our whole life, as that is simply not how it works. Furthermore, fairness is like human rights, which pertain to us as egotistical individuals, not to us as a species. So the sooner that we let go of our outlook over what we deem to be fair, the sooner we are free to deal with the choices that we need to make for our spiritual development.

## Dealing with downers

Life does deal blows. This is the trial of life. It is a natural reaction when there is a disappointment or failure for us to declare 'why me?' This is the trap of feeling victimized, or more really the ego being affronted. The first practical thing to do here is to assess the magnitude of the setback, and sleep on it. Yet there is also a positive side. Out of setbacks there will come recovery, opportunity and even success, so long as you think of giving love and being resilient. Indeed, it is essential that you *resolve* to be resilient.

A disappointment or failure feels that way as it is really the ego that is being dented, not the inner being, which cannot be. Losing a sports race is a case in point, and it is the mirror image of the elevated ego that comes with winning a race. Yes, we need motivation to win a race. Yet in the greater scheme of our whole lifespan, this is a mere blink of the eyelid in the experience of life. It will not lead to enlightenment. We see this with archery. Western competitive archery is about hitting the gold centre of the target, but traditional Japanese archery, *kyudo*, is focused rather on the mental and physical, particularly breathing, in preparation for releasing of the arrow. The target is of lesser significance. The significant feature of this approach is the form, such as stance, posture and hand position, practiced to such an extent that the whole exercise becomes automatic and enlightening, rather than competitive.

Other setbacks, such as loss of a major possession, require a plan either to recover the possession, replace it or mentally let it go. If you have lost a camera, it is not likely to be threatening to life or a relationship, and in such cases, where recovery, say, through insurance, is not possible, it is the ability to let go that is important. Letting go is one of the least practiced of all our activities in the modern world. One of the reasons for this is that our lifestyle is so geared to accumulation of material goods that we forget the art of letting go and moving on. So, as with competitive sports, there is a downside to the activity of accumulation as well as a perceived upside, and this we need to know from the outset.

Loss of job is of course in a completely different league from loss of a sports race or a camera. As with all loss, there is always initial shock, as your livelihood is threatened. After receiving the bad news, job loss often leads to worry, and this must be dealt with immediately. The point is that job loss leads to strain on all the family, and even friends. Surprisingly, job loss is one of the least discussed topics in trauma management, yet it is such a widespread phenomenon.

A plan must be put in place where you can recover. The first reaction is often one of panic, and if this is the case, one of the first things to do is get exercise, whether it is walking, cycling or any other activity that suits you. Exercise with fresh air is the best, as you are then getting nature therapy through taking in the natural healing essences that are all around you in the non-human world. Then, the key is first to think long term rather than short term. Ask yourself where you would like to be in so many years from now. Then consider your strengths and weaknesses, and then seek opportunities, making sure you always keep up the physical exercising meanwhile. Think long term, with loving thoughts, and tell yourself you will get out of this downer. Indeed, you will. It is just a matter of time and healing. Meanwhile, it is crucial to look after your body chemistry, through continuing to eat well and getting plenty of rest and sleep, as well as exercising.

Loss of a loved one, especially a family member, is the greatest trauma most of us will ever experience. A loss may also be associated with the tragic news of a pending divorce, or even news of one's own imminent death. In any of these situations, we usually go through a grief cycle, which is a set of natural emotional reactions. These were originally researched by psychologist Elisabeth Kübler Ross in her landmark book *On Death and Dying*. The stages are 1) Denial, where there is a conscious or unconscious refusal to accept what has happened, a disbelief, 2) Anger, where the griever is angry with themselves and/or others, even their own loved ones, 3) Bargaining, where there is negotiation with one's God, or in the case of divorce, asking for at least the friendship to continue, 4) Depression, where there is a gradual acceptance of the fate, with concurrent feelings of fear, regret, sadness and uncertainty being common, and, 5) Acceptance, where there is self-reconciliation with the circumstances, and in the case of one's own death, sometimes a sort of letting go of the life force. These emotional steps are not necessarily mutually exclusive, with often a transition back and forth between them.

With loss of a family member, this may take many months, if not years, to overcome. The recovery period depends on the personality of the person involved. The recovery is linked to their inherent emotional reactions, and even how involved they are with various other life activities. With a divorce, it is usually best not to enter into a new relationship until the broken one has been resolved within one's self, which may take up to two years. Such major traumas may also require intervention by a skilled medical practitioner or trained counselor to help cope with the personal loss.

The point here is that your life will have downers at some time. Knowing that time is a good healer, and with the help of friends and family, you can move on, and in all likelihood grow from the experience, albeit a sad one. During this healing process, it is vital to make the effort to *give* love and harmony to those around you. This involves engaging for example in just some little thoughts and actions, such as touching someone close and saying thank you for being there, or preparing a beverage for someone else. You could even get involved in doing some charity work. This may seem contradictory, when you may, sometimes desperately, say that you need love yourself. Yet it is a fact of life that the process of you actually doing the giving is one of the best healers that will enable you to reconnect with your inner being. Giving will also set you on the path to enlightenment or happiness, and your life mission of seeking fulfillment, simply because you are taking action that is steering every part of you away from your selfish and essentially destructive ego.

## Big knocks, small steps forward

*Failures are the pillars of success*
Traditional saying

The knocks and setbacks of life may seem devastating, and the future may look bleak. While time is an important healer, there are nevertheless some strategies you can put in place to help with the recovery process. Like dealing with any pressure in life, the first goal is to not just think but also to *feel* recovery, and to resolve that you will indeed recover. This will happen in steps, with negative thoughts and upsets coming back now and then, but on an increasingly less regular basis and with less force.

The first of these steps in the healing process is to let go. This involves actually deciding to release the trauma and the negative feelings by sending them out into the universe. The best way to let this happen is to bring in good and positive thoughts which will, in time, literally edge out the bad thoughts and feelings. Any feelings of guilt and loss should be firstly recognized and then released. Doing this is not always easy, and the way to help you do this releasing is to let go of parts of the stress, almost like chipping away at the edges of the feelings of loss.

This letting go is partly holistic in the sense of having a general feeling of letting internal energy flow, but it also involves focusing on specifics. This means identifying some of your past issues, especially family ones, being honest with yourself and letting them go. Identify what it is that you might be clinging onto and what might be holding you back. Perhaps you are working very long hours because it was expected of you as a child to work hard. It is important to recognize such past pressures and to deal with them. In the case of work, what you are really aiming for is effective and enjoyable work, which then becomes no work at all but an enjoyable pastime. Effectiveness is then achieved through balancing and focusing during working hours, and then having a complete change in activity and some rest for you to freshen up. The point here is to intensely focus and then really rest up, actively or passively.

During this process of letting go after a trauma, it is important, hard as it may seem at the time, to increase awareness of your surroundings. This involves seeing, listening, experiencing touch and even tasting. This experience of surroundings is best done by being in nature, and if you live in an urban environment, find trees to look at, and clouds. It is the complex, fractal characteristics of these features of nature that play a role in scrambling obsessive and vertical thinking. They reduce the 'chatter of monkeys' in our mind.

Sounds of birds and children playing also help dispel those negative thoughts and feelings that seem to keep closing in around us. Even spend a little time touching and exploring leaves and flowers. The reason why this experiencing nature works is because it is in the natural environment where we evolved. It is where our complex brains were able to freely roam all the complexities and subtle changes of shade and sound taking place in nature. In a way, these experiences of nature distract the chattering or distraught mind from the vertical thoughts of bereavement.

The point is that the healing process is about going up steps, one at a time. There are activities you can do to help you with this. The emphasis here is on *activity*. The ideal is to combine experiencing nature with actual physical activity, because this activity 'burns off' the neurotransmitter epinephrine (adrenaline). It is the compound that is largely responsible for the 'fight-or-flight' response in us and many other animals. This is why running up and down stairs just before exams works so well, as the adrenaline is being used up. The body is in fight-or-flight mode in anticipation of the exam, and exertion has a releasing feeling.

Walking is one of the best of activities, particularly walking in nature, where you can combine the sensual experience with exercise so as to release the feel good neurotransmitter serotonin, and with more vigorous activity, endorphins as well. Walking along the beach is particularly good because the ozone in the sea air, the sight and sound of the waves, and the massaging effect of the sand on your feet, are all effectively healing you. When you are feeling a downer, go for a walk and play by the sea.

## Living the moment

The past is gone and the future is yet to arrive. There is only one moment, and that is the present one. The letting go is largely about releasing past experiences. This does not mean that you should forget about them, but the mind is a good sifter anyway, with good experiences generally being cherished while bad ones are forgotten, or at least moderated. Experiencing the present moment goes hand in hand with going up one step at a time towards greater awareness. Seeing, hearing, touching, smelling and tasting are all present moment experiences. It is these here and now experiences, however small, that are such wonderful healing elements that accumulate positively, which seek to harmonize with your inner being. These experiences also lead to more and more cherished moments.

This living for the moment does not of course exclude planning sensibly for the future, but it does mean that the mind is being taken off dwelling on the past. Every little moment, every pleasurable sensation builds you up, a step at a time. This is, in effect, enhancing the process of developing awareness. It is a path of spiritual growth, not hedonism, because you will be giving thanks for small life experiences. Look at a reflection in the water, hear the rustle of leaves, catch the scent of a flower, and then eat an orange and not a hamburger. Enjoy all those little instant moments, and let them enrich you, let them inch out the bad feelings, and let them heal you. They are, after all, comforting psychological strokes, and when you can combine them with physical strokes, like the touching of hands, then you are well on the way to experiencing the present.

The 'now' is relative in terms of our senses, perceptions and reactions. While our reaction time to a warning signal is virtually instantaneous, such as braking hard in the car to avoid an accident, our conscious perception of the world takes at least half a second to process, with our minds evaluating the various sensory inputs against past experiences and even possible future events. Then, for most input to be stored, it needs a few seconds of conscious remembering to really sink in.

Where the input is particularly meaningful to us, whether positive, such as a special glance from a loved one, or negative, such as the witnessing of an accident, only a brief amount of time commits the experience to memory. The point here is that the more something literally grabs our attention, the more readily we absorb it, and the more it shapes us into the future.

Yet our mind, even when performing the most absorbing of tasks, frequently wanders, simply because we are not being 'mindful' as the Buddhists say i.e. focused. Nevertheless, the greater the interest we have in something, the more mindful we are. This translates into increased awareness and motivation. These in turn sit on a foundation of discipline. While certain things intrinsically interest us, others may not, and this naturally differs substantially from one person to another. In those cases where we feel less motivated or interested, we will benefit from calling upon a little more discipline to reap the awareness rewards.

As our everyday consciousness is so full of chatter, mostly about relatively meaningless and egotistical issues, it is important to be active, as such activity enables the mind to experience more and dwell less. This activity should be undertaken now, through instantaneous discipline. By being active, this does not necessarily mean always being physically active, but it does mean being mindful. This can, for example, come about through a passive activity such as meditation, which although sounding simple, does in fact require much practice to reduce the intrusion of arbitrary thoughts, reduce heart rate and improve breathing. Nevertheless, with discipline and practice, it is possible to reduce the mind chatter.

The aim with meditation, and any other positive activity, is to let go of negative thoughts, especially those which cause negative inner reactions and emotions. The letting go also means bringing in positive, loving thoughts, a sense of wonder, joy and even curiosity. This tuning in to love and warmth then leads to love coming to you, or in the words of the famous pathologist Louis Pasteur "chance only favors the prepared mind".

## Experiencing love, giving love

Present moment experiences are in effect giving love to the universe. This is because awareness is being awakened in you. It is the opening up, like a flower to the morning sun, enabling your inner being to become one with all around you. This is part of the step-wise reconciliation of your being with the universe. The awakening of higher consciousness is the development of love. It is the growth of the love experience, and it is moving up one small step at time, that leads to a feeling of harmony. As that sense of love and harmony develops, then you will feel you are more easily able to give love. The giving of love, even just thoughts of love, then develops into a positive feedback cycle, where growth of consciousness becomes ever more accelerated and ever greater.

This process of experiencing the present moment, the development of awareness and the feeling of love cannot be hurried, and it must be left to flow, while opening your mind enough to let it flow. There will be times when doing nothing is an essential part of developing your higher consciousness. The doing nothing is a resting on the step, before you take the next step upwards, however small. It is the time for reflection, consideration and consolidation, which is very different from dwelling on the past and being anxious about the future. Reflection is, as the ancient Chinese believed, considering the space in the cup, and not just the material cup itself.

This doing nothing is also a holding process, which you can use instead of letting negative thoughts and hurt creep in. So reflect and do not dwell. See things exactly as they are, with no emotion and no judgment. Even practice thinking of nothing, and where this seems too abstract, simply look, hear, smell, taste and touch, and experience the instant, that small instant. See if you can grasp its flavor.

This may all seem rather vague, but it is the philosophical grail that sages have been expostulating for millennia. It is, in effect, the finding of your being, which is there anyway awaiting discovery. But this search does not come to us easily. It requires practice, discipline, and the taking of action, with the search in time then becoming elevating in its own right as awareness increases and illumination begins to appear.

This returns us to the steps, small ones, one at a time, which take us along the path to awakening. Enjoy taking one step at a time, and do it regularly, and then more regularly. You can do it while traveling, sitting in the train and even while shopping. Simply notice everything around you, and practice seeing first, as it is our dominant sense. Even say to yourself, I noticed that, I saw the leaves were light green, the flower was a pinkish red, and the two birds were flying in tandem. Then spend a little time hearing, and recognizing any different sounds, and feel the texture of as many natural products as possible, while all the time never judging. And in the case of people, just say to yourself that you saw her wearing a red dress and not that you didn't like the red dress.

This experiencing the present moment, without judgment, will cultivate the sense of love in you, and once those present moment experiences start to develop, you will then start feeling your sense of actual giving love developing more and more. It is the awakening of your inner awareness, your inner being and inner beauty.

### Never too late

It is never too late to take a first step. Start it now, and then add other steps, reminding yourself that each positive step counts. Then add more small steps, enjoying every one. As you reflect on each step, perhaps a step towards healing, it is moving closer to complete awareness. Reflection during this process is important because this is the consolidation of experiencing the present moment. Say to yourself, yes, I saw the clouds today, I saw that flower, as I looked out of the car window, and I felt the breeze on my face as I walked along the sidewalk. But remember that there must be no judgment, no 'I don't like cloudy days', 'weeds are such a nuisance', and 'brrr, I don't like the cold'. Just observe and experience, and enjoy doing it. Fill yourself with a sense of love and growth, and continually say to yourself that you are harmonizing. The sooner you start with this experiential outlook, the sooner you will feel more at one with all around you. Once this development starts, positivity will gravitate towards you more and more. And then, as your experience of love and harmony increases, you will eventually feel a profound sense of happiness.

* * *

***You are Free to Choose your Path*** Ancient insight suggests that our life is charted out, yet we are given choices throughout our life. Our choices are also our freedom, and freedom is love and harmony. Our ultimate aim is to continue to seek the path to light and higher consciousness for a sense of wholeness and happiness. This spiritual path involves embracing humility, without the ego setting us back. To do this, we need to overcome setbacks, disappointments and traumas, all of which are an integral part of our developmental path.

Life is not easy, and we may perceive it as sometimes unfair. We can partly deal with this by recapturing the sense of play we had as a child, with its sense of rapid forgiveness and pure optimism and discovery. Yet as an adult, this involves our rising to the challenge by letting go of bad thoughts, opening up creative channels, avoiding the pitfalls of obsessive materialism, giving love, and giving with determination and enthusiasm. This comes about by aiming at completeness from within, focusing on the present moment, letting go of the past, and not worrying about the future.

Life does deal blows, which is the trial of inner development, as so many ancient texts tell us. These blows are usually dents to our ego, or the loss of material goods, the penalty of accumulation. Sometimes though, these blows are shocks to our system and trauma in our lives, whether loss of a job or a loved one. Our reaction to such loss follows a natural pattern of recovery. Yet we can help ourselves recover by taking small healing steps at a time.

Starting to let go of the shock or trauma, by releasing it into the universe, is the first step we can take in the direction of healing. This letting go is enhanced by developing a sense of awareness of our surroundings. This can be done in steps involving seeing, hearing, smelling, touching and tasting. It is essential to experience all around, especially the natural world, where healing elements reside.

Along with developing this awareness, we need to engage in physical activity, as this stimulates the well-being chemistry of the body. Walking in nature is the best of all, as it leads to deep breathing, and awakens the senses and improves general well-being. Walking is a time to take notice of all around, and it is important to enjoy doing so. Each mini-experience then becomes one small step to recovery.

Present moment experiences, which equate to going up the developmental ladder step by step, then begin to turn into feelings of love. Sensing all around us then starts to take us along the path of giving love, especially when the senses are honed by feelings of love, even from the smallest of experiences of nature. This then leads to a sense of harmony, which grows through a positive cycle of revitalization on the path to greater consciousness.

This process should not be hurried. It will start to flow of its own accord, with letting go of any bad or hurt, and when reflection begins to replace mental dwelling. The key is to reflect on the beauty all around and in all its form, and non-form (the space between form). See the spaces between the trees as well as the trees themselves. Reflection is thinking of nothingness, which while seeming abstract, is simply experiencing and enjoying without judging.

See, hear, smell, touch and taste, without judging, one small step at a time. It is never too late to take these small steps of non-judgmental experience. More experience leads to more positive steps being taken. These in turn, lead ever more to feelings of love and harmony, along the spiritual path towards happiness.

* * *

# 5

# Finding your life path

## Having a clear picture of your spiritual goal

Choosing your path in life begins with imaging your goals as a crystal clear image. It means having a clear sense of where you will arrive spiritually. As you have decided to take this path, small steps at a time, and all the while developing a sense of giving, with determination and discipline, you will inevitably arrive there. What this first requires is imagination, one of the greatest attributes we as humans possess, yet rarely use to its full capacity. You imagine yourself glowing with love. This is love for your own being and for all those around you. You can see yourself on earth and in the cosmos embracing all of nature. You imagine yourself with charisma and confidence, glowing, smiling, with arms outstretched. You practice seeing this image of yourself, you see yourself as no-space, no time, and free from the shackles of the ego. This means feeling good about yourself, cherishing yourself, while being compassionate towards all people and other life around you. For now this is an image, a visualization, which you know for sure will one day become a reality.

We can start by looking at this concept of visualization in a down to earth, practical way. It is no good simply saying "I want to be a millionaire" as this is a selfish, ego-ridden concept. The thought must instead be "What service could I provide from which people will really benefit". "How can I make the world a better place." Notice that these are really statements, rhetorical questions, and not actual questions. Such statements are a declaration of faith in yourself and for you to imagine where you wish to be. This means deciding on your target, which is the visual image itself. Imagine yourself as having already arrived at the point you want to be. You then start to take the steps that carry you along this path. Learn to recognize when you are wandering, and take immediate steps to put yourself back on track. Also, if you are becoming too obsessed, take time out to relax and to focus on something completely different for a while.

The visualization needs, for vividness, to be a picture in your mind. In terms of the way our minds work, this visualization should be in color. See and feel yourself actually in the picture, and see yourself in the context of the world around you. This does not have to be hurried, and you may wish to see different glimpses now and then (reruns) before you decode on the ultimate image. If you are lonely and feeling down, visualize yourself with family or friends, chatting and laughing together. This is not a still picture but a dynamic one. See yourself interacting, and most important of all, see yourself giving. This giving is about giving love and giving harmony to those around you. This sense of giving will then lead into a feedback cycle where love and harmony flow back to you. Yet this receiving must not be the goal, it is the reward.

The visualization process needs practice. It is something you will grow into, step by step. The way to start is first to see a color, whatever one you are most comfortable with, and this will change and morph as your visualization is practiced. Best to start in a quiet spot, where you are warm and comfortable, having had a modest meal and are not thirsty. This comfort platform is essential as it is our first level of need, and once satisfied, then enables you to progress with a free mind. Then embellish your visualization using your other senses as well. Imagine aromas, sounds and even tastes appropriate to your visualization. Together, these various sensory imaginings are mutually reinforcing. Yet, the visualization needs to be more than just any image. It needs to be one that you can feel excited about and really feel motivated to make happen in practice.

The next step is the all-important process of active follow

through, which becomes so much easier when you have a clear picture. This follow through should be done enthusiastically and creatively. Think of all ways with which you are comfortable to move towards this visualization. Enthusiasm, which is the pursuit of higher goals, with no looking back, is profoundly powerful. It cannot be disputed. It is 'as is'. It washes away so many small, everyday issues that can so easily clog our path. Enthusiasm is a light of goodness that shines out all doubts, all inhibitions. It also enables bonding through inspiring others. It is healthy, it is full, and it will carry you along the path to enlightenment, which is the path of love and happiness.

Let the images morph around and always see them as happening right now, actually taking place. Cast all bad thoughts, negative thoughts, and any harmful thoughts, out into the universe. Visualize warmth, kindness, and giving. Practice this on a regular basis, whenever you can. Build on your visualization, especially when you see and experience positive things and positive interactions. These might be something in nature, such as a colorful flower or a bird singing, or a child playing. It might be a lovely piece of art or design. Do not dwell or judge, just absorb.

Revisit your visualization whenever you can, wherever you are. Continue to sharpen the focus of your visualization, and let it change color and forms, so that bit by bit, it builds up an increasingly warm picture in your mind. Also focus in and out. Focus up close to parts of your picture and all the interactions taking place in it. Then focus out, rising up above the ground, then into the sky and then above the Earth, and then practice seeing your image among the universe as a whole. It does require practice, and it requires perseverance, yet the rewards are enormous.

## Positive thinking, with sincerity

Thinking positively with intrinsically good thoughts is an

important part of well-being. It is the guide along the path to enlightenment and happiness, with love and harmony the cornerstones. Always deflect negative thoughts, which may be dwelling on the past, or they may be to do with envy and even jealousy. Yet all the while, never judge. Never think of any harm to anybody, or even to any animal or plant. Always greet a friend, smile and chat, even briefly. Reply to a negative comment with a positive one. When someone says "What an ugly, windy day", say, "I like the wind on my face, it is invigorating". And always smile, but smile inside too, as it is not just about a facial expression, it is about inculcating a sense of well-being, and imparting that to those around you.

Always do your best to see the funny side of things, as a sense of humor and laughter is an amazing healer. It is just the way we are made, and laughter is a manifestation of our consciousness which scrambles obsessive thoughts. While on this theme, it is always a boost to positive thinking to remember funny stories, incidents and quips. Recall them as often as possible, and relish them. Watch a funny movie too. Grab every moment you can to smile with joy, and to laugh.

Then of course there are also fond memories, those halcyon days, wonderful days of laughter and color. Recall them. This enriches living the present moment, because our mind is an amazing filter of the past, remembering the best of times. The present moment experience then becomes synergistic with the positive past moments. The two then meld well-being.

Positive thinking is about your moving forward, step by step, with every positive thought banishing bad thoughts. It is about practice, whenever you can. This may even be while driving, but they come easiest when on a walk, when meditating, or when simply observing the world around you, especially nature and all aspects of color and beautiful form. Positive thinking is also about finding solutions rather than being stumped by obstacles. We are talking here of the little obstacles, not necessarily the great big life obstacles. Let's say that you have to finish a work project, and yet you have promised to spend time with a friend, a lover or your child. Rather than feeling stressed, just leave all the other daily tasks and focus on the meaningful relationships right now. Think positively about it, and feel the joy of being creative and constructive, and you will find the project is done efficiently and you enjoy to the full your time with those you cherish.

> *"At this moment, my mind is creating a very deep crevasse, master," the prince murmured.*
> *"And my mind is creating a very strong bridge," the lama replied.*
> Isabel Allende

Some of the earlier writings on positive thinking were about how you might gain something, essentially at someone else's expense. This is not a healthy approach, because inevitably this involves negative feelings and thoughts, which always misfire in the end.

Positive thinking only really works when it is coupled with a sense of giving, loving and harmony. Such thoughts also only keep you on the path to enlightenment when coupled with humility. In other words, you need to think positively, without arrogance and without allowing interference from your ego. Think in terms, not of the egotistical 'I', but of your inner being, which is connected with all around you. Then *visualize* those connections clearly in your mind and *feel* them at the same time. This activity will help you onto a sincerely positive path. It is about thinking and feeling the connection between your inner being and all the good vibrations in the universe, over and above the more practical, and the thinking of good things instead of bad. Abstract as this may sound, it does work, and it does so because all in the universe *is* connected, much more than we normally realize. This connection combined with a positive feedback cycle, where more positive and good thoughts make you feel better, and in turn, lead to more positive energy, enables you to find a steady path upwards. This then leads to a point where the discipline of engaging positive energy becomes more familiar, but not necessarily easier, as there is always an incline. The outcome for you is that you will not be put off, because the spiritual view along the incline becomes clearer with every solid, positive step.

## Know yourself

'Know thyself' surfaces in many religious texts. It is borne out of long standing wisdom, from days when people had more time to contemplate the peacefulness around them without interference from the intense flow of information and incessant noise of our modern age. Reflecting on who we are and our place in the universe is an important feature of being human. This links with positive thinking in that it enables us to evaluate who we are, our strengths, our weaknesses, our connections. But often, the so-called strengths and weaknesses are a perception rather than a reality. This is because they exist only in context. Strength in one situation may be weakness in another: the quality of witty repartee at a party may well be in contempt of court in the courtroom.

Positive thinking leading to positive action must be for the good of all, otherwise it will not work. This again is because all is connected, and if the ego is left to unbalance you relative to the rest of the world, the benefits of positivity gradually evaporate. That is why positive thinking must go hand in hand with compassion.

With a continual sense of giving, of love and of harmony, you will find that the perceptions of yourself will change. These need only be small gestures and acts of kindness: a touch, a warm smile, a small act of assistance. These small positive steps create the feedback loops, where even just a small step forward of compassion rewards back to you as a small tickle of loveliness. This positive growth comes about because you are beginning to relate directly to your inner being which is immutable love and beauty. These small gestures of unequivocal kindness, tenderness and compassion override the selfish and egotistical 'I'.

In this process, it helps to firstly go back one step and simply say "I like myself". But then you may well say that there is an 'I' in here. The point here is that you are persuading your ego to accept and even like your inner being, the real you. The ego has to accept this because you have visualized compassion, thought and felt positively, and given compassion. And the more that you reinforce these first steps with more love and kindness, the more your inner being and its beauty will be awakened. Indeed, it *will* happen, and this then leads to your saying 'I feel that delicious beauty within', which is ever more powerful and self-reinforcing, putting you on a positive feedback cycle taking you along the path to enlightenment.

You will then find that you will begin to deeply love the space within you more and more, and then find it easier to love those and all around you. It will then be a natural turn of events that others will feel that love, and return it. It is just a fact of life that the more you love, the more you will be loved. This comes about from your action begetting the same action in others. Your aura will become enhanced and this will be detected, subliminally through subtle sensitivity, by others. It is perhaps too the underlying reason that the most fulfilled person in a romantic relationship is the one that gives the most love.

"But it is impossible to be doing this all the time" you may well say! Then go quietly on your own and stamp your foot, and shout "ughh", then breathe in and out deeply. Or if that is not possible in the circumstances, just mentally deflect the infringement on your path, and just cast it out, and by all means use your hands to underscore your thoughts. You can then return to a sense of balance because you have *responded* and not *reacted*. In other words, you are in control the whole time.

## Recognizing your talents

On your way to constructive engagement with the world, and your path to love and harmony, leading eventually to happiness, there is an important action that you must take: recognizing your talents. Make a start by not dwelling on what you feel you might be not so good at. Instead, capitalize on what you have to offer the world and, in terms of your path to enlightenment, of what you have to offer for your and others' spiritual growth. This is not a selfish approach, but a step to feeling love emanating from you and being returned to you.

Recognizing your talents also involves not weakening to boasting. Rather build up quiet self-confidence as your talent begins to express itself. Tough as it may sound, there are always going to be others that are more talented than you, at least at something, which reminds us to be modest.

Recognizing your talents and developing skills is a physical growth process. It is at the same time a spiritual growth process. As you develop a skill, whether a sport, meditative activity or a pastime, it is tuning your body and mind to greater perfection. It is the development of greater awareness of what is physically around you, while at the same time, also developing a greater feeling for the essence of life, the vibrations of life. In short, it is the developing of aliveness. In all likelihood, you will also start to realize that you had talents that perhaps you hadn't even dreamed of before. This works because developing a sense of aliveness deflects vertical, non-creative thoughts. New creative avenues open up. Where you thought your talents only lay in sports, academic avenues, art or music, you then discover that your talents also lie in other areas, such as caring, conflict resolution, enabling people to see beauty, natural leadership through compassion, and a whole host of other things. As you may develop a perfect activity (which needs to be done without becoming an obsessive perfectionist) you will experience along with the growth of technique, a growth of confidence too. This is a feeling of unwavering growth. When this growth is then coupled with humility rather than arrogance, there is, at the same time, spiritual growth. This spiritual growth comes about because on the one hand you are developing perfection but not becoming a perfectionist, and on the other, you are becoming very good at what you are doing but not letting the ego use it as a tool against others.

Being proud of being able to outperform in any particular skill is to appeal to the ego. By traditional wisdom, this leads to downfall. In other words, to unhappiness, as pride is transient. If you do happen to be good at a sport, enjoy passing on your skill and wisdom to others, especially children.

But then you may say, "Well, I still want to be good at something." Let's imagine for a moment that you would dearly like to be an opera singer, but then you say "I could never be an opera singer, I don't have the talent!" This does not mean that you cannot appreciate opera singing, or indeed love it. You can appreciate a talented singer, without necessarily being that person doing the performing.

This acceptance is part and parcel of recognizing who we are, and being really honest about recognizing where our talents lie. It is, in fact, an irony of life that we all have the talent for love and finding harmony, yet we get side tracked into channels that can frustrate and disappoint us. So, the first step to recognizing your potential talent is to link it with developing your ability to love, be loved, and achieve harmony. And this is how.

During your talent development, it is essential to dispel any thoughts of failure and envy. In other words, have courage. Then reflect on your visualized path, sharpen your visualized image and give out love. If you are really not in the mood to give out love, then simply reflect by looking at a view, or stroke an animal, or touch a leaf. Better to be neutral and reflective than to be negative. Then reflect too, on what a marvel the human body is, and how lucky you are to be blessed with this wonderful thinking, feeling apparatus that is such a rich tapestry of thoughts and feelings. Think too, that you are really going to enjoy every moment of being alive and excited about having this experience of being alive on earth!

No talent is too small to assist you along the path to enlightenment, that is, the path to happiness. We all have talent at many things, from being a loving parent to being an acute observer of the changing seasons. We do not, for sure, all have to be talented performers. That is for the few that enjoy being in front of others. They are certainly not necessarily happier.

Your growth through developing a talent also means traveling the path with others, metaphorically, and even literally, hand in hand. Perhaps you are good at, and enjoy, flower arranging. This is something others can share with you and appreciate. This is a pastime that, among many others, is under appreciated in this fast moving world of ours today. Yet it gives so much joy to so many. How much more lovely a table in a restaurant looks even with one flower in a small vase.

Recognizing your talents, and developing them, soon begins to bring out other talents. Perhaps you are a businesswoman as well as a lover of flowers. Then why not start flower arranging classes, or a florist shop. Perhaps you enjoy photography and enjoy writing, in which case you could produce a book on creative flower photography.

If it is a business you wish to develop, then it will only truly grow when there is some sort of giving, which in this case would be good service to customers. While this has been said countless times, the point here is that your business and personal growth is not just about service as a cold 'you get what you give', but involves genuine customer care. On the other hand, you may not be interested in business. Perhaps your talents lie in a different field, such as cooking. Then cook a really interesting and enjoyable meal, and prepare it with loving thoughts, in every ingredient. This means drawing on your creative talent to make the dish look attractive. Eating together in harmony is a fundamental feature of human culture across the world, and there are few people who do not enjoy a lovingly prepared meal. A delightful meal will inevitably lead to appreciation, which will trigger at least friendship, which, who knows, may also trigger love of you. Go on, be bold and invite someone you would like to get closer to for a lovingly prepared meal, which means paying attention to detail and preparing with true care.

## The envy trap

The British writer and historical commentator Jonathan Black points out that we have forgotten much ancient wisdom and have been bewitched by materialism. To correct this, he says, we need now to use our imagination to reach back into the cosmic mind. We as a species, together with many other organisms around us, are heading for possibly the biggest environmental crisis since the end of the Cretaceous, 65 million years ago, when a 10 km diameter meteorite hit the planet. That impact enabled the diversification of mammals, including ourselves, by ending the 150 million-year dynasty of the dinosaurs.

We do not see and, by and large, seriously react to, the impending environmental crisis because we are simply not hard-wired to do so. We react to a rock fall, a poisonous snake and an aggressive animal because that is how we have been honed through natural selection. But we are not fundamentally equipped to deal with a global environmental crisis unless we employ a collective consciousness to seek environmental sustainability, and financial alternatives, to move out of our current way of thinking and behaving. Of course these issues are being addressed, but fundamentally we are living a heyday on bygone sun energy which powered the organisms which give us the fossil fuel we use today.

What has all this got to do with love, harmony *and* happiness? It has to do with the envy trap. Envy in our deep past had important survival value. When the total human population was small and there was some minor competition, envy was an integral part of our behavior. It was a motivating factor for sculpting better tools and finding more valuable natural resources. This in turn led to greater possibilities of finding a true partner. Furthermore, our mind sees the grass as always greener on the other side. However, in the last 200 years, when many people in the developed world have become accustomed to a lifestyle of freedom and luxury only experienced by royalty 200 years ago, envy has, to put it bluntly, got out of hand.

This envy drive has been fueled by the media, which emphasizes that our worth is not just about what we have, but what we should have, and what we should consume, just so that we give the appearance to others of being better off. We are shown pictures of glamorous cars, big houses and exotic holiday destinations to satisfy our childish lollipop syndrome of being grinningly self-satisfied, and being falsely happy. This is underpinned by many people, when asked 'who are you?' replying not in terms of how they feel or how spiritually aware they are, but in terms of their indirect material worth: a Chief Executive Officer, a successful broadcaster, a best-selling author, and so on. That is what they have got, not who they are, and certainly not how happy they are.

This envy drive may well cost future generations dearly. In any room where people from the developed world or from the wealthier segment of society from other parts of the world are gathered together, their lifestyles would require 4 planets to sustain them if everyone on earth lived at this level. Of course it is about population levels as much as it is about population consumption, but the message is clear: we need to change our outlook on how we consume resources by overcoming, at least in part, the envy trap. This is a contribution that all of us can make towards a more loving and sustainable future.

Translated into everyday thought and activity, this means not being concerned that we do not have as many material possessions as our neighbors. The new world will be much more environmentally conscious, spiritually aware and socially harmonized, which involves letting go of the envy trap and growing our talents in keeping with this new, and inevitable, direction for humanity.

## Setting goals

Ok, so you have now decided on letting go of the bad, the past and the ugly, and you have visualized yourself as a loving human in harmony with all around you. You are now also thinking positively and you have recognized your talents. Now what? First of all, we recognize our earlier point that all will be done in small steps, with persistence and with good intentions. But there still needs to be actual goals, both long and short term. You need first to step back from yourself and ask "where would I like to be where I will find happiness". That happiness of course will only come when you have given of yourself love and compassion, and not simply because you have simply attained some material goal. There is no harm in having a material goal, so long as it also involves benefit to others, and preferably some benefit, no matter how small, to the future of the planet.

Material goals are not a prerequisite for happiness, so long as you have enough on which to live. There is nothing wrong with generating wealth, as long as it is directed to your spiritual growth and connecting with your inner being, as well as for the well-being of others. Being thoroughly minimalistic is not easy for us in this technological age, although it is practiced by Buddhists and other ascetics.

We modern technological humans are well able to understand material prosperity. Yet in contrast, we have to work hard at being philanthropic so as to grow spiritually. Unfortunately, philanthropy usually engages the ego, as most people like to be seen to be giving.

A further consideration is that the generation of prosperity must not cause any human hardships or environmental damage. In other words, generation of wealth must be good in its own right, and not a manifestation of greed. By 'good' we mean here to improve human and planetary well-being, and not static accumulation of material goods and currency.

Where the long term aim is happiness, that can only really come through giving love and harmony, which is your short term goal anyway. Both the long and short term goals should be finding the path, and staying on it, to enlightenment, to higher consciousness. This also involves appreciating the rules and regulations of the democratic society in which we live. You may not agree with all the laws of the land, but as countless people have learnt throughout history, to flout them is to do so to their own detriment. Yet there are times when an egotistical tyrant determines the rules, and it is only when this person is deposed and democracy prevails that enlightenment can begin to grow.

This means that our path to enlightenment has distinct boundaries, and these are often enshrined not just in the laws of the land but also in the religions of the world. Many of these are standards for decent human behavior, and include well-known rules for the common good. These include activities such as not to kill other humans (and other animals out of malice in some cultures), commit adultery, or steal. These in one form or another are common to many societies.

Then there is a whole host of other rules and regulations, that to violate, only leads to unhappiness. The most common of these is over spending, and as Mr. Micawber says in Charles Dickens' *David Copperfield* "Annual income twenty pounds, annual expenditure nineteen pounds nineteen and six, result happiness. Annual income twenty pounds, annual expenditure twenty pounds ought and six, result misery".

Yet there are a multitude of much smaller boundaries which are not enshrined in laws and regulations but collectively are very important for guiding you on your upward path. Among these are gossip, disparaging comments, and swearing in place of a more articulate description (but as Mark Twain says in *Pudd'nhead Wilson* "When angry, count four; when very angry, swear"...so as to let off steam). Yet all these behavioral traits apparently have basic survival values, with the point being that you wish to use them as guides to rise above the mundaneness of everyday life, because your path is one of greater illumination.

On anger, philosopher Francis Bacon tells us "Anger makes dull men witty, but it keeps them poor". Indeed, to rise out of bottom feeding survivalist strategies, you should not even have thoughts of anger; as such thinking is as real, and as inhibiting as doing. Consider the famous words of philosopher René Descartes "I think therefore I exist", where the ego and thought are linked. Interestingly, by noting the two 'I's', one could translate this into 'my ego is active and my ego is all'. This is why the path to enlightenment is about developing intuition and all-giving love to overcome this egotistical arrogance, difficult as it is sometimes. The ego feeds on unhappiness, and the best we can do is to overcome it. Dealing with anger is certainly helping us do that.

## Being in control of your own destiny

It is your life, your destiny, your choices and your path. So, how do you continue on your path towards enlightenment and happiness, step by step, with love and harmony, when there are so many pressures on you? The starting point is to firmly re-affirm to yourself that it is you who is in the driving seat of your own destiny. It is up to you to make those choices that will always guide you back to the right path. Let no one else grab your steering wheel. They may touch you, comfort you, and even boost you along your path, but the bottom line is that sometimes you will simply need to be brave. When you have dependants, whether children or parents, you are still always free, and especially free to make inner choices. Your little lifeboat on the sea of life will be rocked by those on board, and the key is to keep on course regardless.

Strange and ironical as it may seem, staying in the driving seat often involves being compassionate. As we all know, being compassionate is not always easy in the current competitive world. The key is to keep your mind strong, and to ask the question "Am I being manipulated?" This manipulation can often come from people closest to you, friends and family, and not necessarily intentionally. The whammy is that the manipulation (e.g. 'you don't really love me') affronts our ego and so is especially hurtful. This is where you need to gather your inner strength and call upon your deeper insight and harmony. This of course is a tough call, and the game play of everyday life. 'No worries', you say to yourself, as you are on the path to greater enlightenment. And at the same time, you say 'These everyday trials will not deter me from that path'.

The key here is to recognize when game playing, even by those who love you, is taking place. Recognizing and understanding those games is half way to dealing with them. Then truly smile inside and move on. There is also nothing wrong to saying 'no' to something that you feel is not right or not good. To be able to say 'no' like this also empowers your inner self. This ability to say 'no' also deals with dilemmas, even small ones, which may be intrinsically stressful. You may for example, be asked to make a contribution to something which you may suspect will take away a great deal of quality time with your family. By saying 'no' you then have more time to devote to your loved ones. This is not a question of saying 'no' every time that there is an outside request, but it means understanding how to balance your life in a way that you are efficient, full of energy, and above all are in a position to give focused love and compassion. Allied to this, is the ability to forgive those that 'know not what they do' as Jesus said, as often it may be their egos which are driving them, with little compassion attached. Such people may be demanding and even unkind. It is not easy to forgive under these circumstances but it is important to keep trying to forgive, especially through understanding the motivations behind the demands or unkindness.

This path of strong mindedness does not mean that we can indulge in selfishness, but it does mean standing firm on what you believe is for a higher cause based on feeling the love that is inherent within you and which is connected with the cosmos. It also means making a determined effort to listen to other points of view, and synthesizing those other viewpoints. Let those around you speak their part, without you butting in. You don't have to be right, as that is the ego interfering. Rather reconcile your thoughts with those of others, and compliment the thoughts and ideas of others. Life is about team work, with the more sharing of thoughts, the more it becomes reconciliatory and progressive. This also means that life becomes more enlivening for all. And the more you will enjoy the social interaction because of these connections.

This progression also involves your ability to be non-reactive. You do not have to defend yourself or to react to all that is said. Rather, just digest it and learn from all circumstances. Even in everyday situations, such as someone being difficult. Smile and understand their perspective by simply asking yourself why they should be so obnoxious. Perhaps they are just having a bad day, or perhaps they are defending a rule put in place by their manager and they are simply bearing the brunt of public frustration. Then just say 'This just is not important in the bigger scheme of things'. Same applies to inconsiderate drivers on the road. Why should you let them pull your strings, it simply is not important. Your non-reaction is your strength.

This acceptance is not the same as giving in and being mushy. It is about you building your inner fortitude in the face of minor frustrations and challenges that are inevitable in everyday life.

Stand firm and know that you will not be put out of phase by these arbitrary intrusions on your inner peace. Just deal with them, and then let them go. This also means being fully aware that parasitism and predation are a fact of life that biologists have studied in great detail. So while you give out love, understanding and caring, it does not mean that you are being naive.

Where you suspect predatory or unfair dealings, simply move on, breathe deeply, and do not react to them. Revenge will only reduce your vigor and retard your spiritual growth. It is one of the least rewarding yet energy sapping of all activities. This is where you bring in your power of non-reaction. It is a way to deal with adversity without your upward growth being deflected or stunted. Do not react, but rather seek to understand, and aim to move on.

Also, when you feel anger, let it out on your own by stamping your foot in private, but do not voice it to others. The reason for this is that anger generally cannot be bottled up, but it can be deflected. Yet with spiritual growth you will feel anger being ever increasingly replaced by compassion and a genuine smile. The key is not to internalize or personalize an affront, but rather wrap it up and let it go by casting it into the universe. The same goes for blame. As blame can weaken you, wrap it up into nothingness, as it is not important, and move on.

## Your beliefs are important

Physicists R. E. Davies and R. H. Koch have calculated the connections throughout the universe. In particular, they have shown that the whole of the observed universe has contributed to life. As you give love, this will resonate with the universe and you will never be alone. Belief in this resonating omnipresent love underpins our sense of harmony and our ultimate feeling of happiness. This is because we are spiritual beings as well as physical ones. We need beliefs because they nourish us as much as food does. Your primary belief is in your being, and who you are in the world. Our sense of place is usually well honed, because where we physically reside is where we feel we belong. This is why physically relocating can be so traumatic, although sometimes making a change can be exhilarating. That exhilaration though, can often lead to a downer as time goes by and realities of living and senses of 'not quite belonging' come into play. This is particularly acute when moving nations and even more so when a different language is involved.

All these feelings of being an outsider are perfectly natural as that is the way we are made, essentially tribal. It is under these circumstances of change of place, like dealing with a traumatic loss, that you need to call upon your inner resources and determination, as well as also on your spirituality. Belief leads to hope, a first step in positive thinking. Yet this first step cannot simply be left there. It is essential to regain your whole path, and to continue up through more steps by practicing awareness and reinforcing your well-being.

So, what is spirituality? It is not the same as a traditional religion which is largely social, involving groups of people and a set of doctrines appealing to and loving a God. The two are not necessarily mutually exclusive, but spirituality is more your particular path to enlightenment and consciousness, and may or may not include your religion. It is a personal journey that is yours alone, yet with everyone and all the cosmos connected to you. It is your belief in your inner being, and developing the keen feeling that you are not alone. Indeed, you are never alone, although you may perceive yourself as being as such. It is a question of awakening to the fact that you are not.

The key to spiritual development is changing that perception of awareness, and awaking your consciousness to know that you are connected to all in the cosmos. Then by giving love out to the cosmos, including through giving love to those around you, you will enhance your path to oneness with all.

* * *

***Finding your Life Path*** Defining life goals involves clearly imaging these goals. This must be done with sincerity and a sense of well-being for all. It also involves giving out love and being of service. This encompasses enthusiasm, which means divine inspiration and revelation. Enthusiasm sweeps away much of the everyday negativism that hinders our inner growth. Visualization of the path of spiritual growth involves practice, and the conjuring up of dynamic and colorful pictures in the mind.

There must be high motivation and real belief in this path. We can visualize ourselves walking along it, with positive, good thoughts, joy and determination. This focus requires that we give out love and harmony to those around us. One key in this process is never to judge, and to see the funny side of things. We recall magic moments in the past, and smile on them, while never dwelling on the negative. We aim to turn a problem into an opportunity. While we are visualizing, as well as thinking positively, we also have humility. We think in terms of our inner being and the fact that it is connected with all around us. This means not thinking in the groove of the egotistical 'I', which continually steers us away from our positive path.

This process of visualization and growth is an essential feature of our journey along our path to higher consciousness. We need to reflect on our place in the greater scheme of things. We aim to feel an ever increasing connection with our inner being and beauty. This can be felt as an upwelling of love within, which is the same as giving out love. The more love we give (the more spiritual upwelling from within), the more love we will receive.

There are also practical issues that we need to attend to, such as recognition of our talents. It is not a case of how good or bad we are at a task, but how we can direct our talent towards growth by recognizing it for what it is, and as a way of seeing our own inner beauty.

We recognize skills and positive attributes in others, and enjoy their abilities. As we relate our talents to those of others, we begin to feel connectedness, and a sense of wholeness in the world around us. This dissolves the impact of the ego in favor of our inner beauty through the growth of love. This also involves actually doing loving and creative things for others, especially those people who are special to us.

Envy today has got out of hand. It is fueled by the advertising media. It tweaks the ego, and the ego thrives on it. This is because it is largely about what possessions we have, or should have. It is about consumption, not love. It is crucial to overcome the envy trap. The converse also applies. Turning away from wealth does not on its own mean that you will find love and harmony. By all means have wealth but share it, so that others can grow too.

We have to live within the rules and regulations of a society. Depending on the particular society, we will perceive some rules as fair and others as not. Nevertheless, there are basic ones that are fundamental to all decent societies, such as not to commit adultery. To flout these basic rules of society is a fast track to unhappiness. We need to keep within reasonable boundaries. In addition, we should also avoid financially overstepping ourselves.

We are in control of our own destiny. We are in the driving seat whatever happens around us. Hand in hand with this is that we must learn to recognize instantly when we are being manipulated by other egos. And then we stand firm on what we feel is right and good. Nevertheless, we listen to other viewpoints and reconcile the good in them with our thoughts and direction in life.

There is no need to react to adverse behavior and comments. We smile, we ignore the badness, and we move on.

In short, we respond, but we do not react. Reacting to them is letting the ego get the upper hand. Same with frustrations. We accept them and know that they are little challenges to overcome which enable us to grow. Acceptance of challenges dissolves them, and then they become easier to overcome. Similarly, revenge and blame have no place in our spiritual growth. They are just other ugly faces of the ego trying to deflect us. There is also no need to internalize or personalize. The conceptual ideal is to parcel up all this negativity and cast it out.

Our beliefs are important. Faith is the partner of spiritual growth. It gives a sense of belonging but not necessarily to a particular place but to the beauty of the cosmos. This is so because all in the cosmos is connected, as shown by research in astrophysics. As we give love, this will resonate with the universe and we will never be alone. Belief in this resonating omnipresent love, which we may call God, will give us a profound sense of being at one, feeling harmony, and ultimately, having happiness.

* * *

# 6

# Becoming aware of your inner being

*In order to activate the sleeper of the heart we must first distinguish our ego from a true sense of Self. The ego is a marvelous fiction. It is our normal image of what we are, but it is a false mirror. This ego is a novel written by ourselves about ourselves and the very first step on the Quest is to disentangle ourselves from its seductions and to dis-identify with the manuscript we, and the collective consensus around us, have managed to create.*
Yatri

## Be content with yourself

One of the first steps to finding love, harmony *and* happiness is to feel good about yourself. This does not happen all at once, but in small steps, any one of which builds on the previous one. This does not mean that you have to look like a superstar to feel good about yourself, a myth fired by the media. Magazines in particular are largely geared to stir up envy and advertise products that are purported to make you slimmer and look younger. This is a cruel treadmill that often challenges you to be an almost impossible combination of everything: a good partner or wife, a good mother or father, a good cook or handyman, a good homemaker, a good career person and so on, and so on. Yet you, as a woman, do not need to feel compelled every moment of the day to look as if you are about to be photographed by a glamor magazine. Although, if by being chic and well-groomed, you feel well, that is fine too, so long as it is your own decision not because your strings are being pulled by the influence of the media or other people. Nevertheless, being physically well-toned and of moderate weight is important for your overall health and well-being. This attainment of physical attributes that make you *feel* good is a step in the process of actually having well-being. In a way, it is about showing responsibility for yourself, making sure that you are of a weight that medical practitioners have emphasized is appropriate for your height and age. Maintaining yourself within that norm means that you are at least physically free to connect comfortably with your inner being, especially as your body is the vehicle for your thoughts and feelings. But even if you are not in that best weight bracket does not mean that you will not be able to feel good about yourself. Then having the optimal weight means that it is likely that you will have most energy for self-development. The key is not to dwell on exactly what you *look* like, but on what makes you *feel* physically well and spiritually fulfilled, every minute of the day.

Feeling good about yourself is also about building confidence and creating a charisma about you, based on thoughts of warmth and love, and even more so when based on giving out love and warmth. This giving out of compassion starts with recognition of the pressures that impact on you, and then knowing that you can deflect them. You can start with simply thinking about giving of love and compassion, without necessarily putting it into practice immediately. Let the good thoughts fill you with warmth and then you will know when it is time to give love and compassion. As there are so many everyday pressures, and even torments, in everyday life, you cannot, at least at first, be giving out good intentions all the time. Start small, with a few small kind thoughts and acts a day, both towards those close to you and the occasional stranger, even if it is simply a kind word.

This giving out of love and compassion sits on a foundation of loving yourself. This comes once you are kind to yourself and reasonably content. In reality, this contentment is a feedback cycle, with a sense of being comfortable with who you are (a special person in your own right), which links with loving yourself. In other words, contentment along with loving yourself go hand in hand, and are mutually reinforcing. This cycle is then linked with the bigger cycle of loving others around you, also creating a feedback loop of ever increasing joy.

Where the cycle of self-development grows most actively is when you focus your attention on your inner being, and not on issues of pride, greed, competition and other manifestations of the egotistical 'I'. In other words, you should reflect on and focus on your deep inner space, and not on the superficial ego. This is the same as aiming to grow with humility, warmth, enthusiasm, and particularly compassion. The difference between the 'I' and your inner being is easy to see: the 'I' is absorption in the impression you see in the mirror, while your inner being, which is inner beauty, is the deep feeling of compassion and joy you feel when you put your hand on your chest.

## Your universe

We are connected with all about us. We are not islands, and the food we eat, the liquids we drink and the air we breathe are all a manifestation of our connectedness. This is brought home when we consider ourselves as, what biologists call, 'open systems'. In other words, energy flows through us, and that is what sustains us. This flowing through also applies to energy fields that resonate across the universe. With that, the mind and heart, being part of the vast connectedness, gather and impart energy from and to those fields. This gathering is analogous to eating well. We become what we take in, what we perceive, and what we build upon. This is a two-way process, with giving out, as well as taking in. When the body is well looked after, and the mind and heart are of good intention, there is a resonance with positive aspects of the cosmos.

Our bodies and our existence are essentially receptors and resonators, and we choose whether we build upon goodness and well-being, or not. The universe is big enough for us to release bad thoughts into it, which the universe knows are destructive and deals with them. This is so because life is part of an evolutionary process and there will always be changes in life forms towards something better adapted and often more complex. This process appears not to be some sort of lifeless lottery but has purpose. It seems almost that there is an ultimate cosmic plan, but that is not yet proved by science. The universe appears to 'pull' as well as to 'push' through the agency of so-called attractors, which are not yet fully understood. When we engage with these, we are taken along both a personal path and a collective one. As individuals, we need to ensure that we steer ourselves towards a better developmental path where we attain greater connection with our spirituality. In other words, we need to tune into the cosmos' creative activity by becoming aware of our own inner illumination, our inner being and all its beauty, and allow ourselves to spiritually evolve in keeping with the great attractors in the universe.

Yet what is certain is that there will always be change. So you can tune in to the universe's disposition for change by taking in the good energies that will enhance your and other people's life. Accepting these energies is a first step to tuning in to your inner being. This is the same as loving yourself and others. Loving, quite simply, is tuning into goodness, beauty and loveliness.

This tuning in is also about sensing your place in the universe. It is an exciting exercise to actually visualize yourself from above, from the side and from below. Practice seeing yourself, across the room, from the ceiling, from afar, from a hilltop. This means looking not just at the physical you, but also the inner you, your inner space, your inner beauty. Focus in and out, and imagine traveling up in the skies and looking down, then move around yourself as if you are the universe looking at and loving you. Feel love flow back and forth as you travel in your imagination. This is not a vain exercise because you are exploring yourself, trying to see the beauty within you, from all angles. As you do this, your level of awareness will increase enormously.

Looking down from high above is particularly effective,

because the ego fades into a little insignificant spot. By doing this, you also start to experience your inner being in relation to all the processes taking place on Earth and around it, which then become increasingly clear, and more meaningful.

You can add to these wonder travels by also imagining your place in time, relative to both the distant past and the far future. Visualize the awe of transcending time, and all the while feel the warmth in the universe, that all-present love and goodness. Imagine the universe's warm hand holding you and loving you, while also giving you back loving thoughts throughout the arrow of time.

## Deflect pressures from the ego

Our ego's excesses are our worst enemy. The path to enlightenment and consciousness, where there is love, harmony *and* happiness, comes about by first recognizing the relentless activities of the ego, and then managing them. While doing this, we can also practice developing connections with our inner being, space and beauty. Every step you take along the path of spiritual development is being more and more tuned to your inner being and beauty while recognizing the activities of the 'I' and deflecting them. This is a step-wise process of growth and development that comes about with practice.

It is the human ego that has caused so many problems in and among societies over the millennia. The ego continually tries to steer our course away from higher thoughts and inner peace and beauty. The key is to recognize when the ego is steering you away from higher thoughts and feelings. Promoting self-importance and pride are among the challenges with which the ego beguiles us. So why do we have such a strong and influential ego?

Deep in our past, when we lived in small hunter-gatherer bands, the ego had strong survival value when dealing with all the difficulties facing us in the natural world. Ego is associated with cohesion within small groups of early humans, where factors such as pride and determined procurement of animal resources led to risk taking and ultimately to more successful bands with more births. But as civilizations have grown in size, complexity and technological power, the ego has begun to overwhelm us. We see this with the internet, where the flow of information by people, about people, is set to swamp us, mostly because this huge electronic traffic is being driven by egos, and rarely from inner peace.

Every moment that you can embrace humility, life and warmth, while at the same time, releasing ugly, selfish thoughts, will be another small step to enlightenment, well-being, love and harmony, inevitably leading to happiness. So, learn to recognize the ego trying to dig its sharp claws into you. No need to *react* to it, because that is exactly the route it wants you to take, with the result being competition and eventually conflict. The key is to deflect it, to cast off its taunts, so that you are not drawn in. Every time you deflect that 'I' in favor of your inner being and beauty, the closer you will be to finding inner peace.

## Value the quiet moments

Information-flow in our world has reached almost intolerable levels. So much of that information is someone, somewhere, making a statement of some kind and demanding of our time and inner resources. Much of it is masked, and seemingly made respectable, by appealing to our ego. We prefer any contact or communication, even if demanding and sometimes even hurtful, than no communication at all. These communications cause us to react, as the ego has been tweaked. They too, are often spun to taunt our conscience or pride. "Surely you care about your children don't you? If so, then prove it by buying our product!" "You can only be a happy family and all smiling (the two adults and the predictable two children aged about 6-10) when you buy our new family car!" "Exercise on our home gym and you will soon look like a six-pack, grinning superstar!" We must always be alert to these highly professional persuasions and not let them cause us to deviate from out spiritual path.

To keep on this path to higher consciousness, and eventually happiness, also means taking time out to reflect, so as to begin to understand and to realize. Reflection does not mean *dwelling* on past events and throwing thoughts back and forth, but rather harnessing the present. It is about exercising your imagination and visualizing your being comfortable and at one with the universe. It is also about recalling little cameos of life, like a smile on the face of a friend, watching a chef preparing sushi with exactness, the wisp of a cloud, or a funny incident. These thoughts embellish our present moment.

As life is so fast, it is essential to find quiet time. This may be once a day, and may be active, such as practicing yoga, either alone or with a teacher. It may be to stretch all parts of the body and open the mind, through a good walk, a swim, or a workout at the gym. The point is that this quiet is about not talking, not even listening to conversation, and just 'being', just letting the physical oneness of you with the universe wash through you. It is also about letting a sense of goodness flow through and about you, as if it is a warm sea washing around you, calming body and mind. A long soak in the bath with bubble bath does the same, and while soaking, stretch and let go of any harmful or ugly thoughts, let go of the taunts from the ego, and simply revel in the thought of how good life is, and how wonderful it is to be alive.

Simply enjoy the physical sensation, while gradually letting the mind move into a non-thinking, non-dwelling nothingness realm. Very passive quiet is also valuable, especially through meditation, but also through simply enjoying a good book where there is no bombardment of voices. A good book enables you to stretch your imagination in peacefulness, while television for example usually does not; it simply bombards you.

## We make the bed that we lie in

As we think, so shall we be. Our destiny is defined by the way we think, and not just what we do. After all, the doing is only an extension of our thoughts. Always think good, think loving and harmony, as this is on the path to happiness. This is so, as it is a rule of the universe that as we give out, so it is returned to us. We may believe that our thoughts are private and ethereal. The reality is different, and our thoughts are as tangible, in terms of love and harmony, as much as the physical doing.

The thinking of love and harmony must be absolutely sincere. It is the equation of life, that what we intentionally cast into the universe so will it return. So there cannot be bad thoughts or intentions or else they will return in one form or another. This is not the same as the letting go of, or the casting out of bad thought energies into the universe, which is a type of dissipation in favor of the good. The point here is that it is not so much *where* these thoughts, intentions, and even feelings, are actually going, but *how* you are dealing with them in your own mind. This means that if you are actively seeking sincere love and harmony to come to you, it is essential that you give out unconditional, loving thoughts. In other words, these thoughts must be coupled with non-judgment. Simply give, and give with feelings of beauty and warmth, give with a tingling inside. Then, to really make love and harmony happen, give with joy, enthusiasm and an inner smile, a smile that envelops you and all around you. That smile is one of contentment and inner well-being, and the more you exercise it, the more it will build you up from within, and put you on the path to enlightenment. At first, do it in small steps, one at a time, now and again, and then do it more often and with greater intensity. You will then reach a point where it is virtually instinctive, and then chance events of a positive nature, what you have always truly wanted, will of their nature gravitate to you.

While thoughts may seem to be a private affair, they do in fact drive our emotions. There are a series of reactions arising from how we perceive an event in the world around us. After perception, there is then a process of thinking about it, which in turn determines how we react to it. Sometimes this chain of events can happen very quickly. If we are not aware of these events around and in our bodies, there can sometimes be very fast and adverse reactions, as in the case of road rage.

At other times, we bottle up the negative thoughts, which compound over time. When they are negative thoughts, this has an attritional effect on our bodies because of the powerful influence of the egotistical self. The associated negative emotions then gnaw at the inner balance in our bodies. In contrast, when you actively think, feel and imagine linkage with your inner being and its beauty, coupled with the casting out of negative thoughts, this then redresses the balance within you. The increasingly good balance then enables you to cherish good and harmonious thoughts, which puts you even more in touch with the alchemical balance of your inner being. This positive feedback loop then continues to strengthen you physically and spiritually.

## If it's not working, move on, now

Much as we may set goals, long term and short term, and much as we may think in terms of goodness and harmony, sometimes the strength of our outgivings and their direction may not result in us receiving love and harmony straight away. These are the big steps in life that we still must climb, so as to move on and up. These are the challenges that life development will always hold for us, and they are an integral part of the path to enlightenment. The key here is to *believe*, believe in yourself and the strength and beauty of your inner being, so as to help you overcome the challenges. And never quit.

Moving along the path means meeting the challenges as they come, one at a time. It is in effect making sure that you climb each step, and then consolidating your emotional and spiritual ground. While reflection and developing well-being may involve letting go of bad or hurtful thoughts, there are also life's obstacles to overcome. Some of these you may well straddle with ease, but others may keep coming back to plague you. You may not yet be ready to deal with these, or the step you are trying to take is too big in one go. Recognizing that there will be these challenges, whether small or big, is an important part of your growth process.

Recognition is one thing, while dealing with them may be quite another. The challenges that you can take on, even if through a small step at a time, are footholds on your progressive path forward to spiritual awakening. Other challenges may not be so easy to tackle. Dealing with this is a three-phase activity. Firstly, the challenge must be acknowledged and the steps for overcoming it assessed by you as to its magnitude. Always take a small step at a time, and consolidate your sense of well-being. Secondly, hard as it is sometimes, a challenge can only really be dealt with through self-discipline. This discipline though, is not to be thought about too deeply. Just do it, just make it happen. Sit quietly for a moment, or go for a walk, read a good book for a while, and give a little time to sending out warm and lovely thoughts. Then tackle it with speed, determination and certainty. Thirdly, there is re-assessment. Simply ask yourself how well you are doing. When you start feeling that success is coming your way, it means that you are on the path to enlightenment, higher consciousness and happiness step by step. Problems then start to fade away automatically.

Apparently insurmountable challenges require two approaches. There are those that must be dealt with, and if not, then in all likelihood, they will return at some other time. Then there are those challenges that are either so great, or, on reflection, they are not really relevant after all. If something simply is not working out and the challenge intrinsically too big, perhaps it was just not meant to be. Tell yourself that this is not a problem, and just let it go, and move on. No point in banging your head against a wall, as you will be the only one that will get hurt. Move on, and move on now. No need to look backwards. Yet a significant challenge for you and your spiritual growth, even when large, must be taken on and overcome. If you do not take it on, it will, in all certainty, return. Reflection is again the key, and you may well decide that this is not the right time to take on the challenge. You may need to harness more inner strength, which may take more time and more gathering of inner fortitude. There will then come a moment when you will instinctively know that you are ready to take on that challenge. That is then the time to move forward with a renewed sense of optimism and enthusiasm. Future challenges after that will, in all probability, seem not so big. You have become practiced.

Remember too, when you are feeling down in spirit, it is often the ego that is taunting you. Indeed, you will find that the more you let go, the quicker will the seemingly insurmountable challenge fade away. And the more you do the letting go right now, at this moment, the quicker will be the fading of the frustrating challenge.

When you do let go, and let go now, the more and sooner will new and exciting opportunities present themselves. This is all seemingly part of the greater scheme of the universe and its resonance. This is encapsulated in the Chinese word for 'crisis' which not only means breakdown, but new opportunities as well. This surmounting of challenges through non-resistance, letting go, and finding new direction is what the ancient Chinese have described as water flowing through bamboo growing on the hillside. You just need to flow like water, flow between or around any unnecessary obstacles.

## Carpe diem

Carpe diem is Latin for 'seize the day'. Have a look at the clock for a moment, and watch those seconds, minutes and hours ticking away, never to return. We have only the one shot at life, and the time to get it right is disappearing as you see that time ticking away. Carpe diem is about living every moment to the full. It is surfing every moment in life, and living moments on which to reflect with a smile.

But you may say "I have to get up early and make breakfast every cold, winter morning". Yes, true, but just do it, no grumbles, no judgment, and no negative feelings of self-sacrifice. Enjoy the getting up by thinking some truly positive thoughts, like doing breakfast in a different way, taking a good sniff of the fresh coffee, and giving thanks that you do indeed have a breakfast to eat. Then think of some fine little thoughts of how you are going to have carpe diem that same day. You are going to make someone smile, or even better, you are going to make them laugh. And better still, you are going to make them feel loved! You are going to notice some really good things today, however small, be it the sight of children playing, the lovely colors in a flower, the freshness of the breeze, and even the joy of rain on your face. Seize them all, and more importantly, seize the joy.

Ok, you have to do your tax return today, then just do it, get it out of the way, and then seize an opportunity for joy as your reward. Get a bunch of flowers for the home, give yourself a small treat. Much more important is to experience some giving, especially the giving of inspiration to those around you. Let them share your joy, even if it is just being joyous, even if it is being bold, but be kind in what you say. Carpe diem at its best is when you stimulate carpe diem in others.

Seizing the day is one of life's most fulfilling experiences, and it grows inside of you, attracting love, simply because the joy you are feeling gets experienced by others, and you are all the while giving out love. This growth of joyful experiences lodges in the warmest parts of the mind and heart, where a sense of really being alive grows and grows.

The accumulated carpe diems lead to very fond memories,

and that delicious feeling of halcyon days. These days remain with you forever, and are the consolidated ground along the path to spiritual awakening. But then you may say that this is not living the now, the present moment. Yet it is a fact of life that these experiences are not one-dimensional. You are living the now, the present moment, with carpe diem, while at the same time growing your inner strength and color on good-life experiences. Enjoy all the facets of life, and grow.

### Happiness is a reward, not a goal

The meaningful, special moments are happening in the present, as you seize the day. Each of these moments accumulate and continually move you back onto the path of enlightenment, onwards and upwards. As you give out love, and love returns to you, harmony within yourself and with the universe, continues to grow. All this takes place within the bounds of everyday life's normal reasonably decent living, without violating the basic rules of good human behavior. This does not mean that you should not have a lot of fun and even take on some stimulating goals that you wish to achieve. Indeed, taking on challenges, overcoming fears, having a fulfilled and exciting life, make up the growth process.

The magic ingredient is to give all that is good to those and the world around you, which inevitably leads to a sense of wonder and joy, with love coming back to you. Out of this two-way process of love flowing in both directions, will arrive harmony. This harmony will be both within yourself and with your whole world, physical and spiritual.

Yet the growth will not be linear, with times of good growth and inner consolidation, and other times of setbacks. You will then shrug off those setbacks with renewed vigor, drawing on your inner resources of love and joy. You will be doing this step by step, and knowing that some challenges will take a little time to overcome, but you resolve to be patient and let time also help you over any major setback or trauma. Your growth will then continue, because you instinctively know that there is a solid spiritual core that gives you strength and encouragement. It is just a matter of always remembering that alchemical inner being is there for you, to enable you to grow.

"But I just want to be happy!" you may say. First of all, bear in mind that 'want' is not a healthy word. As the old adage goes 'I want, never gets'. So first of all, you should 'give' rather than 'want'. Give out love, give out goodness. And then you may say, what about happiness? Well, let us be very clear that happiness is not a goal. Aiming for happiness is unworkable and untenable. It is a reward. It is a return that comes only from you giving love and finding harmony. It is largely an automatic return on your growth policy of the giving of sincere, non-judgmental, non-agenda love. It comes too, from giving joy, simply because as you give joy, so joy will come back to you. Happiness will start to appear as you grow along your path to enlightenment. It will at first come in small, almost passing, feelings, which then become fuller and more intense as you continue along your path. These happiness events will then loop and emanate from your inner being, as you connect with this alchemical 'center'. Each small encounter with your spiritual being and its beauty will make you feel that you can give even more love, and so the positive feedback cycle will continue.

*If peace, order, and the pursuit of happiness are invisible things, obviously they cannot really be obtained by visible means.*
Lao Tse

## Knowing your loyalties

'Loyalty' seems such an old-fashioned word, almost dull and restricting. Yet strange as it may seem, it is borne out of fundamental biology. The most obvious sense of loyalty is to our family, which has strong biological and genetic underpinnings that have been well researched. Historically, our 'tribe', the extended family, also requires loyalty, simply because we are co-operative beings for mutual survival of individuals in the tribe. Yet today, in our larger society, such loyalties have become blurred at the edges. Nowhere is this more evident than in the hire and fire mentality of the corporate world, where all is about competition and material accumulation, wherein lies so much stress and unhappiness. Nevertheless, even in this materialistic world, there should be loyalty, but it must be two-way. If not, then move on. Move on to a zone where you start to experience two-way loyalty.

'Loyalty' is closely allied to 'faithfulness'. Yet faithfulness must first rest on a sound foundation of openness, transparency and truthfulness. In terms of personal love of an intimate relationship, there needs to be a complete sharing and mutual understanding of what faithfulness means to each of the pair. This is where it is essential to discuss these boundaries with your partner, and then keep within them.

Every relationship will be different, and your physical and spiritual place in that relationship needs to be determined. As emotional feelings vary and change over time, they need to be periodically re-assessed. This re-assessment would not of course be cold and dispassionate, but done with joy and genuine mutual understanding. Perhaps you do not mind your partner admiring another woman or man, but then perhaps you do. Whatever the case, it is essential to share those thoughts, before bad thoughts and feelings accumulate and aggravations start.

Perhaps the best compromise is to occasionally agree to disagree, while recognizing that there is a basic biology, honed by the millennia, which cannot be denied. By all means look and admire another person, but agree that taking that admiration further by touching will almost inevitably lead to discord. So talk about it, get it out in the open, and give out trust as part of giving out love.

By sharing, understanding and trusting, harmony will grow, and happiness will ensue. This trust goes hand in hand with transparency. Indeed, it is openness that leads to trust, and in turn, to companionship, which then grows as that trust and transparency is maintained.

### Stand back and look at yourself

We mentioned earlier the importance of reflecting where you are physically and spiritually both in your local world and in the universe in general. You would have practiced seeing yourself from the outside as a means of appreciating yourself. And now we have brought into the equation some extra elements, like transparency, loyalty and trust. It is important to keep practicing these activities and character-building approaches. Now and again briefly do a self-check on how well you are doing. Ask yourself whether you are being honest, loyal and trustworthy, whether to your partner, family, friends or the world at large.

But first of all: ask yourself whether you are really being completely honest with *your own self*, loyal to what you think, feel and do, and are you in harmony with these. This is not a simple exercise, as there are many issues that color and cloud our perceptions. Ask too, whether you are fully in charge of yourself? Are you in the driving seat? The key ingredient to dissolution of these questions is to *give out* love and feel harmony based firstly on a love of your own physical, emotional and mental being. Give without having any doubts, letting your inner being do the giving and not the 'I'. Inevitably, this giving of honesty, loyalty and trust will be returned to you. In other words, give out warmth from inside of your being, and never expect any reward.

"Yes" you may say, "but that is naïve, I will get hurt". First of all, notice it is the 'I', the ego that could get hurt. Then, naivety is about not having all the facts and feelings before you. This means that a more thorough assessment is needed, a weighing up of all the possibilities and outcomes, and this can only really come about after the sharing of thoughts and feelings with those who are close to you.

Chat with your partner or friend about what it is that means so much to you. Also chat around ideas and opportunities, and do it with non-judgment. No need to engage in catharsis, where emotional trauma is unleashed. But then you may say "I have done that and my partner/friend has let me down!" Have you tried with sufficient love, honesty, loyalty and trust? Have you shared thoughts and feelings often enough that there are no misunderstandings? Perhaps you have not, in which case share some more. If you have, and the relationship reaches stalemate, then move on, and move on before there is more commitment. Let go, be brave, and find your true love and true friend. Perhaps that person who you thought was so close to you, simply has not grown as much as you. It is all your choice after all.

## Dealing with your bad thoughts

Not one of us is perfect. We all have foibles, some idiosyncrasy, and occasional dark thoughts. It is the nature of us. These are not in isolation but in the context of where we live, the structure of our personal lives, and the society in which we live.

Yet what may be considered, by you or anyone else, as strange, odd or dark in one context or place may not be the case in another. The way people greet or touch each other is a case in point. Different cultures have different perspectives on what is acceptable and what is not. It is unacceptable in public to show physical affection in many Eastern cultures compared to in the West.

Yet there is a fundamental fabric of norms common to most societies across the world. These often relate to what is good and what is bad. Sadly, they often break down in times of war. This general breakdown is intrinsically uncomfortable to us, hence we use the term Ministry of Defense, and not Ministry of War.

When is behavior good versus not good? Bad behavior is

essentially when there is deliberate intent to hurt others, including other organisms. That doing hurt arises from thought processes that have caused us to stray from the path of enlightenment. This is partly sculptured by what we as individuals perceive to be bad, as compared to what is actually societally bad.

Physically hurting someone else is not acceptable in society as a whole. Personal bad behavior may be, for example, eating a pile of doughnuts. It is not intrinsically bad, but you may view it as 'bad' relative to your individual norms, goals and standards. This personal wavering away from your good path must be identified, and scrutinized, so that you can deal with it, so as to keep on track for your own well-being.

Whether harmful for you or for anyone else, any thoughts of ill-will must be cast out, and released into the universe to dissipate beyond harm. Like thoughts and feelings of setbacks and traumas, the key is to practice letting go. One way to do this is to practice instantly recognizing when a bad thought or feeling is creeping in and change it around to a thought of goodness, love and warmth. If a jealous thought comes in, cast it out straight away, and replace it with a positive, good thought. Then support the thought with an action. To take jealousy as an example, if you feel jealous about someone, chat to them, smile with them, wish them well, and enjoy doing it.

With practice in turning situations around, soon you will find that the bad thoughts will gradually fade. That fading will apply to a whole host of bad thoughts and feelings, simply because you will be giving out love which will dissolve any badness. In short, deal with your bad thoughts and feelings by flipping them around, radiating goodness and well-being, and letting go of any ugliness.

## Dealing with obsessions

Obsessive thoughts and behavior are a displacement activity. They come about through the ego being thwarted, and trying to derail your growth to spiritual enlightenment. It is the continual slipping down the steps of the onward and upward path. It is the locking into a negative feedback cycle.

The way forward is to break this cycle. But how do you do this? Recognition of what is an obsession, with its negative connotations, is a first step in dealing with it. It is really only intrinsically bad when it is loaded with a sense of hurt either to yourself or to others. An obsession about a thing or a person is the lack of ability to let go, often also associated with a need for immediate self-reward.

Having recognized that an obsession is pulling you off course from a fulfilled life of love and harmony, the next step is to begin to overcome it. Deflection of the thought before the behavior even begins is the first strategy for you to adopt. As soon as the obsessive thought appears, think and preferably feel for an alternative that is good and positive. At first, this may be to visualize simply a color, a color that is comfortable for you. Then couple this with a fond and warm memory. "But" you may say "the obsession is about fond memories, and it is the loss that is the obsession, I can't get over it." Notice first of all, the 'I', to the neglect of the resonance coming from your inner being. Think and feel those good times, and cherish them, and recognize how they were nourishment for you. If those times are totally irretrievable, then you must practice letting go of thoughts of them. Be friends with your inner being and all its ineffable vibrancy, and know that those good times are there inside of you, never to be taken away.

This process of letting go will take time, but each time you do a little bit of letting go, the closer you are to healing, and the closer you are to moving on, continuing your journey to spiritual awareness and to all-embracing love. We can only grow from these setbacks and traumas, through the letting go of obsessions. As you connect to your inner being and bypass the pressures from the ego, an obsession will automatically be nullified. You are then able to continue your journey to greater enlightenment, where there will be more challenges, but also more opportunities for growth. You need to know that in reality you will be ok, because you are looking after yourself. This will all come about once you have let go and sealed off any obsession that is holding back your growth.

### Your no-regret strategy

The whole letting go process, which is central to your growth, is tightly linked with having no regrets. And of course 'regret' is very different from 'remorse'. We have all done things which have either hurt ourselves or others, or both, and we are sorry in our hearts for that. This apologizing to the cosmos is a letting go, and is remorse. It is a feeling that helps us on our path to greater consciousness.

Regret, on the other hand, is a non-decision and a continual recycling of a negatively impacting past issue. It feeds the ego, and is tied in with dwelling on the past, which is not a healthy way forward for your spiritual growth. So start now with your no-regret strategy, and tell yourself that you are not going to think or do things that lead to regret, which could otherwise hold back your progress to higher consciousness. Yes, we all make mistakes, and when this occurs, apologize openly, and treat it as a learning exercise towards the higher path.

Where there is remorse, it should not be considered dark or heavy. It is a clear cut, bright recognition of where we went wrong, where we deviated from the good path. Once recognized and dealt with, remorse should then be coupled with the parallel process of thinking positively, thinking goodness and thinking love. The bright colors will then always outshine the dull ones, and steer you back onto the path of enlightenment. Recognize a wandering from the good path, then package it, paint it with color, and move on, without any regrets whatsoever.

Viewed another way round, this also means thinking proactively, anticipating where your path might deviate into the realms of unhappiness. This returns us again, to the issue of choice. Be in the driving seat, make positive affirmations and choices which pre-empt wrong turns, which otherwise might lead to regret.

## You are still learning!

We are all forever learning, and that is a motto for life. Life is about practice, while realizing that there is no trial run. It is for real, and there is only one shot. Saying that you are still learning, and always will be, lets you tip the scales in favor of your inner being and its beauty rather than for the egotistical 'I'. It also inculcates humility, one of the greatest of all your allies for growth to enlightenment. Strange as it may seem in the West, humility without sanctimoniousness is strength, not weakness. Furthermore, there is nothing wrong with making mistakes, we all do.

The key for growth is to treat mistakes as integral to your path to higher consciousness. Mistakes are a way forward to grow, and overcoming them goes hand in hand with joy, wonder and opportunity. You need to know that dwelling on mistakes and reacting to their impact is simply a dent to your pride, to your ego, to the ugly 'I'. Having that awareness, makes tackling mistakes a matter of course for your growth. Additionally, it is a clear fact of life that learning is youthful. To admit that you are learning is to say that you are resilient enough to still keep vigorously growing, which is a wonderful feeling. Enjoy it!

* * *

***Becoming Aware of your Inner Being*** An essential step in spiritual growth along the path of love and harmony is to feel good about oneself. This is done in small steps, and is about building confidence and charisma. It is fine to look and feel good physically, but it is essential to grow inside at the same time. This means maintaining a good lifestyle, feeling comfortable with, and loving, your physical body.

We are what we take in, whether healthy food, clean air and good energies around us. Loving is about tuning into the universal well of goodness and beauty. This means letting imagination transcend space and time, so that it is possible to visualize being anywhere in the cosmos and at any time. This is part of becoming aware. This process helps shed the pressures from the ego, which will always try its best to stifle our connection to our inner being.

Quiet moments are so valuable for reflecting and connecting with our inner being and feeling its beauty. These moments are not dwelling on the past, with the chatter of monkeys in the mind. These moments are also not speculating on future fright. They are times for us to smile with our inner being, and feel a warm upwelling inside, and washing over us. These are moments when we feel we are floating, connecting, enjoying. During these times, the apparently real world of egos sometimes seems like madness.

It is not just what we do that makes us what we are, but also the way we think. Our thoughts must always be sincere and loving; otherwise the chances are slim that sincerity and love will be returned. And we all need love returned. These loving thoughts and feelings must be allowed to flow and grow in steps over time. This involves overcoming challenges by letting spiritual growth develop through thoughts of love and harmony. These good thoughts let your inner being carry you unimpeded, like water around bamboo stems. Like the water, we are flowing on. We feel no resistance, just more light.

Time is valuable but we are not slaves to it. We make a point of enjoying every moment. Where enjoyment is not an option (having a tooth drilled) then we accept. We aim to enjoy every little task of daily living so that we can grow while doing the everyday chores. We are not just seizing the day, but the second as well. We are surfing life.

With a sense of wonder, joy and enthusiasm for the world, time becomes beauty, and a feeling of expansive love and harmony develops. Happiness then becomes a reward rather than a goal. It comes the more we overcome the manipulations of the ego, by giving out love. The wellspring of love is within us.

Our love needs to be constant. This translates into being loyal and faithful to those we love. This includes being loyal to our own being, which means feeling our inner beauty, and not listening to the taunts of the ego. This does not mean that there will not be disagreements. We can find solutions by agreeing to disagree, by being honest and transparent. This also means reflecting on life now and again, but not dwelling. It means making sure we are in control of our reactions by relating to our inner being and not to the ego.

When disagreement and differences are left to become magnified by the various egos, hurt is the inevitable outcome. Jealousy is close on the heels of rift. And close by are obsessions. Jealousy and obsessions are the ego engaged in churning issues around and around, destabilizing our inherently good natures. These bad feelings must be released and cast aside.This means not dwelling on them, and having our own no-regret strategy where we think only on the good memories with a smile which comes from our inner being. This requires humility, side-stepping the egotistical power struggles, dissolving pride, and moving on. It is all a delicious learning and growth process to illumination, and something to really enjoy!

* * *

# 7

# Love your body

## Self-image and appreciation

Life is a journey, a wonderful, exciting journey. Nevertheless, it is a journey of ups and downs, of rejoicing and sadness. Your aim always is to overcome challenges, both physical and emotional, and move on and upwards to ever increasing enlightenment and fulfillment. The more you travel and the higher you go, the more will you be able to give out love, and it will be returned to you. You can have confidence that this will happen as there are attractors in the universe steering you there when you tune into them through your inner being.

It seems that our mind is physically and spiritually connected with much around us. While the center of the ego is in our brain, the center of our being is within the whole of our body, especially in and around the heart. The heart is the place of infinite bliss and splendor, which appears to be of a vibratory nature rather than a material entity. Recognizing this heart glow, this vibratory inner being, is an important part of realizing our connection in the universe.

This signals the importance of more than just recognizing, but also appreciating, the glow of your inner being. Self-image is not about your superficial appearance, as that is the language of the ego, the 'I'. What is important is your spiritual center. The ego must nevertheless be recognized and managed effectively. This means that when you improve your self-image, you need to resonate with both your physical well-being as well as your inner being, both of which tune into each other. Your outer appearance needs to be what you are comfortable with, and what is in harmony with the immediate physical world around you, as well as in keeping with your lifestyle. You can view this as your outer shell. Yet this shell is permeable, and how you think and feel determines the extent to which your inner beauty shines through.

The glow of life from within you, emanating from your whole being, especially the heart, is what interplays with your physical being and gives you your persona or charisma, which is vibratory in nature. Being able to let your inner glow shine through involves reconciliation between the activities of the ego and the resonance from your inner being. This comes about from tuning yourself, first by thinking and then by doing, into acts of goodwill, compassion and love, all the while being fully aware of the pressures from the ego. In normal everyday life, the ego tends to dominate our lives, which inevitably creates a lack of balance in our self-image, which then swings from disapproval of our looks and enormous efforts to correct it (an enormous expense on such things as excessive buying of clothes or slimming pills) to disappointment and even despair when the looks we want to achieve do not satisfy us. This can also lead to excessive vanity, which interestingly is despised in almost every human culture, as it is closely related to greed.

The key here is not to focus on narcissistic self-appreciation, the 'I', but on appreciation of your inner being and its intrinsic beauty. Tuning into the good vibrations from your inner being will build your sense of connectedness with all around you, which also reflects back as love and appreciation of you. We need this reciprocity as we are not islands. We cannot be thinking loftily all of the time, and we are still essentially primates with a great need for love and affection. This cycle of giving out and then receiving, with sensitivity, is growth along your journey to a more fulfilled life.

## Being brave

Bravery is a very interesting concept which we normally associate with physical activities, especially in wartime. Bravery is about a trade-off between risk to the physical self and the receiving of rewards and recognition, in other words, feeding the ego. But, you may say, heroes did what they did for the country. Then we need to ask what, actually, is a country? It is a purely artificial, political entity, often united by language, one of the great divisive features of humankind, organized (or disorganized) by leaders with massive egos.

True bravery is connecting to your inner being, and moving along the path to enlightenment. It is the giving of love and harmonizing with all around you, including humankind and all of nature and all in the universe. Bravery is making a commitment to cultivating your intrinsic beauty while dissolving the power of the ego. Truly making the effort to feel the love emanating from your inner being, loving humankind, loving nature takes much more bravery that fighting for a cause. The reason for this is that to create disharmony, chaos and hurt is much easier than creating harmony, constructive engagement and warmth all around the world. It is also an everyday, all day, life-long bravery, and not just a single event like most ego bravery.

## Hygiene and health

Maintaining hygiene and health is fundamentally important. The reason for this is that the body is the vehicle for the inner being. Without looking after that marvelously integrated and immensely complex vibratory form we call our body there will be disharmony. This discord has an interconnected physical and spiritual component, with being 'dis-heart-ened' leading to being unwell. The discord manifests itself both as a solely internal disease, and as an infection caused by a pathogen that can spread to others. In both cases, we are not contributing either to the betterment of ourselves or to that of humankind. This means that we must first be aware that hygiene is so important for stemming infectious disease, by far the biggest killer ever of humans.

Hygiene is not just about washing regularly and making sure water and food is fresh, but also about tuning into your inner being. When you stop giving out love and harmony, and engage in egotistical activities which cause stress, inner discord then develops. This then invites infectious diseases so well known to us, for example, as various forms of colds and influenza. When such discord, often coupled with unloving thoughts, is prolonged, an intense, more serious and life-threatening diseases can develop. But, you may say, the disease is in the family, it is genetic. Yes, partially, but it can be triggered and made worse by continual stress and disharmony.

## Appreciating the chakras

'Chakra' is Sanskrit for 'wheel', referring to the wheel-like vortices of life force, or 'chi', around the body creating an aura. There is not yet a scientific explanation for chi, but it does seem to exist, as seen in the martial arts, where for example chi is harnessed by skilled practitioners to prevent damage to the body.

There are seven major chakras and several minor ones, which are believed to harness energy from the cosmos and distribute it around the body. This life force has two facets, yin and yang, which require balance for tuning into and resonating with your inner being. Yin and yang represent the continual flow and change in the universe, and are two polar opposites in a continuous whole, with natural harmony and creativity being a balance between the two.

Yin represents receptiveness, contractiveness, responsiveness and sensitivity, while yang represents expansiveness, overtness and dominance. Often yin is considered feminine and yang masculine, but the point is that everyone has both yin and yang, and the dynamic balance of the two makes for harmony. Disharmony comes from a lack of balance between the two, most often because yang is too strong.

The seven main chakras, from the base of the body upwards, are 1) The base chakra, located at the bottom of the spine, and wherein lies 'kundalini', an energy force that can travel up the spine to the brain, and when awakened, for example, through appropriate yoga practices can trigger an awakening where the body feels bathed in light, and a state of exaltation and happiness results, 2) The sacral chakra is located around the sex organs, and is not simply to do with sex, but enables self-realization through sensual love in the rhythmic dance of yin and yang, 3) The solar plexus chakra is located above the navel and influences the pancreas, stomach, liver and gall bladder, and affects the emotions, 4) The heart chakra is located in the center of the chest and governs the heart and the circulatory system, and awakens unconditional love, 5) The throat chakra is about audible sounds and communication, associated with the search for truth and creativity, 6) The brow chakra, known as the 'third eye', is in the center of the head between the eyebrows, and associated with the pineal and pituitary glands, and relates to highly-tuned senses and imagination, 7) The crown chakra is situated on the top of the head, and is often represented in medieval paintings as a halo or a dove, and brings enlightenment and cosmic consciousness when all the other chakras are in harmony.

Being aware of these chakras is an important step towards loving and being loved, whether sensual, familial or humanitarian. Loving and being loved is about awakening these chakras, and letting the chi, the cosmic life force, flow through you, and connect you to all around you, both close by and across the cosmos. The more that this energy force washes in and around you, the more enlightened you feel. This enlightenment comes from feelings of love, awareness, forgiveness, acceptance, compassion and enthusiasm. These are creative and spontaneous dispositions, and the more you feel them, the happier you will be.

*The throat chakra is the organ of the formulation of spiritual wisdom. It connects the heart chakra with the brow chakra. In the physiology of an initiate, currents of love stream up from the heart chakra through the throat chakra to light up the brow chakra. When this light streams up on to the brow chakra, it opens up like a flower in the sun.*

Jonathan Black

## All things in moderation

Reduced calorific input, especially when coupled with intake of chromium picolinate and selenium, can promote well-being and is said to increase quality longevity. Also, reduction of intake of animal fats while increasing intake of fiber and amino acids, through quality vegetable and fruit intake, also improves well-being. There is a simple biological reason for this. The context in which we evolved was one of hunter-gatherer, where we were sustained by fibers and berries, with only the occasional meat feast. The essential issue here is about moderation, and not just moderation in diet, but moderation in all we do. Now, you may well be thinking that moderation is dull. The key to overcoming dullness is to have variety.

Our bodies have evolved to go through lean times, and also to have variety, both on a weekly basis and throughout the year. It is one of the facts of life that having sameness all the time, even the perfect temperature, perfect surroundings, and perfect but continuous diet leads to what biologists call 'captivity ennui'. It seems that we have an inherent drive in us to seek variety, in all we do, in what we see, we feel and we experience. We are alive!

We are also driven to search, and this applies to love, harmony and happiness. Often the search, and even the anticipation, is more exciting than the arrival. This seeking novelty is what biologist and philosopher Lyall Watson has called 'neophilia'. It is intimately tied in with motivation for survival through continually searching for optimal conditions, and is built deeply into our psyche.

What this all means on a daily basis is that we must vary our routines, which is tantamount to enjoying the exploration, but at the same time knowing the boundaries. To illustrate this, let us consider brief encounters with the opposite sex. It is inherent in us to flirt, and unless we are on a mission of denial, it is something most of us enjoy immensely. We even have social conventions dedicated to it, such as dancing. We all enjoy that brief smile, a brief touch, a kind word, from someone who appeals to us. How much further we take this encounter depends on our social context. If we are happy with our dedicated partner, then that brief encounter is the end of it, fleeting and beautiful as it may be.

The key here is to recognize what is good and life-enhancing through providing variety as opposed to what is not. We need also to identify what are, and the extent of, any temptations that might cause us to wander from our path of illumination. Such serious wanderings, such as having a romantic affair, while apparently enjoyable in the short term, usually lead us in the end into a zone of discomfort and disharmony. This is just what the ego bargained on, to use vanity to break a formerly sound romantic relationship by an affair. Sometimes affairs are for the best of all, but this is rarely the case, and the relationship foundations of all four players must have already been shaky. The old adage that affairs are 'playing with fire' is in most cases very apt, and in some cultures, catastrophic for the woman.

Small challenges within the realms of moderation are one thing, but letting obsessions develop is quite another. Some of the challenges may actually be very large. You may feel, for example, that you wish to take on a challenge that really stretches you physically and intellectually over some time. You may decide to climb a mountain or do a college degree. This is perfectly fine, but inherent must always be the ongoing giving of love and compassion at the same time. This will not reduce motivation, and may well increase it.

Even better is to make your path to enlightenment your backbone in life, and then you build the challenges around that backbone. This is making discipline, mental and physical, a basic cornerstone around which you build on the challenges you wish to undertake. This backbone analogy for appreciation of the path of love and compassion has even deeper implications given the role of the chakras. As we saw in the last section, it is within the base of the backbone that lies an important chakra that, when awakened in the right way, can lead to illuminating happiness.

## Little treats

While certain gurus may believe that denials of various sorts are integral to their path to enlightenment, it is not a natural course for most people. This is because of our evolutionary heritage, which has made us exploratory by nature, and to seek and be rewarded. This has several levels. The first level is to have enough quality food to feel and be healthy. The second is to feel safe and secure. Until most recent times, we were very prone to predation by large carnivores. This of course is still the case in certain parts of the world, but today the threat has largely subsided without us realizing it. The awareness of such a threat still lingers as a behavioral legacy within us.

Then there is the drive to seek love and companionship, which is not just about emotion, but also about survival. So, while we talk about the higher elements of love, it is nevertheless also fundamental to our survival through deep-rooted behavior. Coming together and loving, and having a family, and linking with a group of friends, is the same as forming a band of hunter-gatherers, where there is protection and mutual survival. We are made to *need* companionship and love.

So how do little treats fit into this? It is tied in with our avoiding ennui, sameness, and to have change. There is also another facet, and that is about bonding. It is intrinsic in our makeup to give and receive. At one of the most basic levels, it was Paleolithic human behavior for males to bring back the bounty from a kill, protein in particular for women and the young. It was also the role of the females to complement the animal protein with gathered fruits and ground roots, for essential fiber and amino acids. Both genders felt content to be giving their contribution to the common good. When times were good and food resources abundant, perhaps coupled with a new discovery, such as a new flint deposit, there were ensuing feasts. These festivities were, and still are, binges, but essential ones for variety.

These behaviors say to us that we are actually made to enjoy occasional treats and feasts. By all means moderate during the week, but there is nothing inherently wrong with the occasional binge among friends. This is a natural thing for us to do. In addition, we still need variety during the week. This may also involve having something different occasionally, such as 'fish on Friday', which has become enshrined in Christian religion because it also has important survival value, the intake of omega 3 and 6 fatty acids, so essential for our well-being. Even small chocolate treats, particularly of dark chocolate, is a joyful and purportedly healthy way of overcoming sameness.

Other clues from Paleolithic humans tell us that it is natural to give artifacts, for the man to give a woman a shell necklace or bead bracelet originally crafted lovingly with his own hand. For a woman, a sure sign that a man loves you is when he gives you a gift from the heart, and a man feels cherished when it is appreciated. Yet there is a balance here. When the gift is too big, such as a large diamond ring, then it is the ego giving it, and acceptance of it is effectively greed, as encapsulated in actress Zsa Zsa Gabor's famous words "I have never hated a man enough to give him his diamonds back".

> *...in the case of wanting more expensive possessions,... eventually you'll reach a limit...; you'll come up against reality. And when you*

*reach that limit, then you'll lose all hope, sink down into depression,... So that's one danger inherent in that type of desire.*
HH Dalai Lama and Howard C. Cutler

## Your physical environment

Throughout the universe there is ongoing and vast creativity leading to evolution and form. Stemming from the smallest elementary particles, throughout the cosmos there are vibrations and resonances that create these forms. Appreciating this is important for our well-being, through what the ancient mystics called the order of place, the order of things. Muddled and indecisive thoughts lead to a muddled and confused life. This means that you need to create order around you. Yet this does not mean that you must frenetically tidy up all your belongings, but it does mean knowing where all your meaningful things are positioned. Of course, the less you have the easier this is.

Most of us would probably not go as far as the Indian leader Mahatma Gandhi and cast aside all material possessions, but too much accumulation of items is a physical manifestation of a feeling of inadequacy and not being able to let go. The more we hang on to yet more material possessions, the more frustrated we will get, simply because accumulation has the frustrating downside in that there is always more to accumulate. What this means is that by all means have things untidy, at least at a superficial glance, but at least know the order in that untidiness.

Create around you a sense of ordered beauty, a sense of knowing, and a sense of loving. Put love into all you have around you, and enhance it occasionally with something special, from a traditional ikebana flower arrangement to a work of art.

*The antidote of greed is contentment. If you have a strong sense of contentment, it doesn't matter whether you obtain the object or not; either way you are content.*
HH Dalai Lama and Howard C. Cutler

## Vive la difference!

Well-known primatologist Desmond Morris in his fascinating book *The Naked Woman* gives an account of not only the beauty of the woman's body but also its functional role in sexual attraction and natural selection. While some aspects of the woman's body were in all likelihood selected for non-sexual survival reasons in our distant past, some aspects today clearly have a secondary role in sexual attraction. These non-sexual primary roles, which are often to do with woman's survival and that of her infant are articulated from an essentially feminist perspective by Elaine Morgan in her book *The Descent of Woman*. The truth probably lies somewhere in between, for evolution has taken place not just on males but on females too, with woman the nurturer, fruit gatherer and pot maker, and having been as equally important as man the home protector, hunter and tool maker. Then there has also been selection of infants for survival to reproductive adulthood.

It is important to recognize the sex differences ('vive la difference') with our technological age being dominated by yang (expansive, extrovert, and demanding). We need, as physicist and philosopher Fritjof Capra says, to move much more towards yin (contractive, responsive, conservative) to urgently find much more Earth harmony by appreciating not just the yin and yang within each of us, but also among us.

This all needs to be viewed against the background that at times in the past, human populations were at very low levels. During these times, sexual selection and survival of infants within the family group were critically important. This suggests that early men must have respected women more than they are sometimes given credit for. In all likelihood they were not brutes dragging the woman into a cave but caring and sharing partners. This must have been so or else we wouldn't be here today.

Much of that respect must have come from appreciating and protecting women, as well as the infants, simply because men find women so beautiful. This beauty is a clever way of managing testosterone in males for best reproductive advantage in women. Much of this appreciation of women by men has dwindled with the onset of settled agriculture, development of territorial imperatives, and the onset of large-scale warfare. Settled agriculture has led to an enormous increase in conflict among humans, when in the pre-historical past, it was the environment (climate, resources and predators) that were of most immediate concern.

So let us now start with looking at why men find women so attractive, leading to mutual love. The dominant sense here has been that of sight, bearing in mind also that sexual attractiveness does have an individual bias based on genetic and developmental tendencies. There are also other factors that play a role, such as social interaction, including mollifying soft speech and song, and the production of pheromones (a chemical factor that triggers a response, and secreted from the skin).

Another factor that plays an enormous role, yet rarely discussed, is that of hygiene in an evolutionary perspective. Being clean and fresh has probably had an enormously influential evolutionary role in the pre-historical past, especially as it is associated with good health and hence survival. This in turn, goes hand in hand with maintenance of family groups, security and physical well-being. So it is not surprising that men find women's attractiveness enhanced when the sexual signals are combined with good grooming. This has led to men being perfectly accepting of women taking the time out to 'get ready'. Similarly, a hygienic man is intrinsically more attractive to a woman than a man who is not for deeply survivalist reasons.

Desmond Morris points out that humans are essentially neotenous, with women more so than men. The word means that juvenile features are retained into adulthood, and is an evolutionarily advanced feature. Neoteny has the remarkable ability to bring out protective instincts in men.

A good example of physical aspects of this neoteny is the subcutaneous fat layer, reminiscent of a baby, and is proportionately twice that in women as in men. It would have had important survival value in the past when resources were scarce. Similarly, women's voices are higher pitched than those of men, again eliciting a protective response, especially when combined with cuddling-up body language. This also goes for the face, with a woman's face being essentially baby-like, often with the eyes emphasized by mascara and the nose minimized, just as we see a baby. This is highly attractive and attracting for a man.

Long or voluminous shiny hair is immensely attractive, and is even a signal at a great distance. Feminist and writer, Elaine Morgan believes that even our early ancestors had long hair, and its purpose was for infants in a proposed aquatic/marine phase of our history to be able to hold onto as it drifted around in the water. Hair certainly can grow about 15 cm a year and in some women can be over 4 m long. It has been subject to decoration and adornment throughout at least the last 20 000 years of human history.

While short hair in the modern era is symbolic of the business environment or sports arena, attractiveness from most men's point of view comes from length, coupled with good hair care. The sexiness of hair has often been enhanced at various times in history by lightening it. Dying it blonde is again neotenic as it is associated with infancy, with hair tending to darken with age into young adulthood. When blondness (which is associated with high estrogen levels) is combined with volume and shine, it is a powerful signal of sexiness and care. Volume and shine are also powerful signals of sexiness and vigor in the case of black or auburn hair.

## Beautiful body signals

When a man talks to a woman, he sees an overall picture of the head, neck, shoulders and breasts, essentially a portrait. In contrast, a man talking to another man sees mostly just the eyes and body language. This portrait perspective of a woman is strongly influenced by the body adornment that a woman wears, as well as the style and health of the hair.

Ears play an important role in this messaging, with earrings drawing attention to the neck. The slenderness of a woman's neck is highly attractive, and attracting, with long, dangling earrings inviting a kiss on the neck. The same applies to a necklace, which often provides a complementary half circle from one earring to the other, drawing attention to the suprasternal notch (the small indentation below the throat between the collar bones) and the cleavage.

The circle is completed with the eyes, which are enormously powerful in communicating not just attractiveness, but also health and well-being. In turn, a small nose, with its neotenic message, is often described as cute. The portrait is completed by the mouth, which is a strong center stage, conveying invitation for affection.

While the full lips of a woman, especially when adorned with reddish or pinkish lipstick, have been described as overly sexual, the message is really one of invitation for affection, with the lips strongly enhanced by the teeth. What is really attractive is the softness of the lips, and enhanced to look enticingly wet with lip gloss. Brightness and straightness of the teeth also convey good health and are powerful if sometimes subliminal attractors.

This sensuous attractiveness is derailed when bright red lipstick is used, which conveys the message of not to be kissed, else it will be smudged. Prostitutes wear bright red lipstick because kissing on the lips, ironical as it may seem, is considered too intimate. Bright red lipstick in the case of a prostitute is to enhance attraction to the body, as it is usually combined with overexposure of the body above *and* below, at the breasts and legs, advertising sex and not affection.

In turn, a stage performer wears bright red lipstick as part of the glamor, with the physical distance from the nearest man, as well as the intense social context, precluding lip kissing. This is verified when a woman performer is kissed in congratulation after a performance where she puts out her cheek and not her lips to be kissed by a man.

Elaine Morgan suggests that the breasts were developed to enable the infant better chance of being breast-fed when held in its mother's arms. Yet of course they also give out a strong sexual signal, especially when pushed up to mimic the buttocks. But again let us be clear on what is overtly sexual as opposed to what is invitational to affection. As we saw above, a prostitute will often expose many parts of the body at the same time, cleavage, belly *and* legs. This is overt sexual invitation, which is different from esthetic invitation by, for example, overt exposure of just the cleavage, as in the eighteenth century when décolletage was combined with long dresses to the floor.

Similarly, attractiveness can be a short skirt, as long as the breasts are not overt at the same time. In turn, exposure of the belly is attractive, as long as there is not overexposure of legs and breasts. This line of argument can also be applied to the back, with a halter neck combined with a plunging backline being invitational to affection, but invitational to sex when combined with an excessive exposure of the breasts, bearing in mind too that the smoothness of the back is a neotenic feature creating a feeling of affection in a man.

The legs are much more openly sexual than the upper body for the simple reason that they focus attention on the genital area, hence their being covered up in many societies. It is interesting why legs per se are so attractive, and enhanced by high heels, which emphasize the calves and make the feet look smaller. This is probably related to bipedalism, and a look of healthiness combined with neoteny through smoothness. Healthy long, straight legs, besides being immensely esthetic, echo ability to move, quickly and efficiently. They emphasize that a woman is not confined just to the home but able to move fast, and a potentially good breeding partner for sons, who in turn, need to move fast on the hunt.

There is one other feature that is crucially important as regards signaling from the female body, and that is, the waist circumference relative to that of the pelvis. The pelvis of course is wide to enable the large-brained human infant to pass through. Also, it is the width of the pelvis that gives the female walk its enticing swaying movement. While many women are concerned that their buttocks are too big, the more important issue is the front view width of the pelvis relative to the waist. The greater the ratio of pelvis to waist, the greater is the level of sexual attractiveness. Also, large buttocks are a sign of good health and a healthy resilience to scarce resources. So, from a man's perspective, sexiness is not just about the bums, but the proportionate narrowness of the waist too.

A woman's arms are also neotenic, being smooth and soft. In turn, the hands are about grace and fineness, and are always noticed by men, as they are the hands that craft and touch. Nails are another feature of great significance, with well-groomed nails being a sign of good health and hygiene, and indicative of a good diet, albeit virtually subliminal.

Finally, all these features are enhanced by good body posture. A fully upright stance is of substantial evolutionary significance, as it signifies high capability for holding up loads in the hands in front of the body. The eye of the observer subliminally detects when the spine is in an upright and comfortable position as opposed to an uncomfortable, bent posture which would carry risks to the health of the spine. This is also related to the fact that so much of the life energy flows through the spine. A straight spine also begets tallness, which also indicates health, and is why many performers, from trapeze artist(e)s to Cossack dancers, end their acts with their posture tall, chin up and arms outstretched, often doing so on the tips of their toes to confidently enhance the appearance of good health. Yet notice that they also end with a bow, a mark of humility and graciousness that emanates naturally from a truly great performer.

* * *

***Love your Body*** The beauty that resonates from our inner being is associated with infinite bliss and splendor, and is particularly vibrant around our heart. Recognizing this heart glow is realizing our relationship with the universe as a whole, where resonances maintain what is good and creative. These resonances are therefore gateways to higher consciousness where all of similar forms are connected. This means that giving love will resonate to receive love, like tuning forks vibrating together. Our body, with its glow, is our vehicle of love. We can view our body as our container of good health as well as home to conscious resonance in association with our inner being and beauty. This container can be viewed as permeable, where resonance within us is linked beyond time and space with like resonances in the cosmos. It is for us to tune in to those resonances. A starting point for doing that is to care for our body.

While care of our body is essential, this is not the same as vanity, which is closely related to greed. Vanity and greed are tools of the ego. It is feeling good that is important, not simply looking good, although feeling good *through* looking good is just fine.

Bravery for nationalistic or other group causes is bravery of the ego, as national and other boundaries are political, egotistical entities. Real bravery is making a commitment to resonating with our inner being and beauty. This is enhanced by giving love and compassion to others wherever they are and whatever their tongue.

Maintaining hygiene and health is fundamentally important

for enabling spiritual growth. Discord, drummed up by the ego, nibbles away at our healthy bodies and allows infection to infiltrate, with disease being by far the bigger killer of humans. Increased disease also goes hand in hand with increased conflict and disasters. The key is to reduce stress and find harmony through increasing resonance with our inner being. This is done by being in the right frame of mind, which is always about love and compassion.

The energy of life, chi, flows in wheel-like vortices, or chakras. There are seven main chakras which harness energy from the cosmos and distribute it around the body. The life force has two components, yin and yang. These are polar opposites, with yin representing contractiveness, responsiveness and sensitivity, while yang represents expansiveness, overtness and dominance. Everyone has yin and yang, and for spiritual illumination, we need to complete the triad, with balance of the two, leading to the third point of the triad, which is manifestation of this balance.

The seven chakras are aligned along the body from the base of the spine to the top of the head. Being aware of *all* these chakras is a major step towards loving and being loved, through letting chi flow. The more we feel this energy flow in its contractiveness and expansiveness, as waves of beauty, the more we feel happiness grow.

It is essential to moderate in all we do, from diet to organizing our lives. Yet we, as humans, are evolved to seek variety. We innately search for this variety, yet often, as soon as we think we have found a perfect situation, we want to have more. We continuously need new things and new experiences, which is a treadmill, without end. So long as we crave these things and experiences so as to satisfy our human fallibilities, we will forever be pulled away from the path of illumination. Yet we cannot deny our deep biology, so we can indulge in new things and experiences as long as they are only now and again and in moderation. This requires listening to and resonating with our inner being, through discipline and practice, and as often as possible feeling the tickle of love.

A man who loves a woman really enjoys giving her heart-felt gifts and, in turn, a man feels appreciated when the gifts are cherished. The key again, is moderation, as well as putting love into all that we do.

A woman's soft voice and song has a mollifying effect on a man. A woman's attentiveness to hygiene and good health are also very attractive to a man. The reasoning behind this is that in the distant past they played a role in how men selected women. Health and vitality in a man, in turn, stimulated selection by women. Female attractiveness is also associated with the fact that women have specialized and highly-evolved neotonic (baby-like) features that make men instinctively feel protective of them. These features include a soft, smooth and sensitive skin and a fine layer of fat under the skin, giving it its soft quality. A woman's face has proportionately large eyes and a small nose, both very attractive to a man, as is long, healthy hair. Blondness is associated with high estrogen levels, hence its attractiveness. In the case of black hair, its attractiveness is its volume and shine.

When a man talks to a woman, he sees a portrait of the head, neck, shoulders and breasts. This is not the case when a man talks to another man. A woman's ears, as emphasized by earrings, convey strong signals. Earrings play an important role in emphasizing the neck, and necklaces highlight the breasts and throat. At the focus of this portrait of a woman, besides the eyes, are the lips, also soft and baby-like.

There is a balance between the amount of skin exposed by a woman and the message conveyed. Some skin exposure, such as the cleavage or the knees, is attractive. Too much, especially of the upper and lower body *together* is too overt.

The circumference of the waist relative to the hips is what is important to a man, not simply size on its own. While women often think that their bums are too big, this is generally attractive to a man as it signals well-being and sexiness.

Well-looked after hands and nails are also attractive to a man, as they signal gentleness and good health. The same also applies to good body posture. The man perceives all these subtle aspects of the female form subliminally. This subliminal attraction is reinforced with body language, facial expressions and skin aromas.

* * *

# 8

# Feeling beauty and finding enjoyment

*The Beloved is devoted to its lovers for how else can it be Belovedness? Each and every Lover is the Beloved: each and every Beloved is the Lover. Love longs for Beauty; Beauty thirsts for Love. The Absolute Unity, which is the Absolute Beauty and Absolute Love, loves its Beloved so intensely it leaves not a trace of themselves. For in reality there is only the Beloved, only loving.*
Meher Baba

## The breath of life

The instant we are born and take in the first breath, we take in the life essence of the universe for, and of us, as an individual. At the same time, that first breath links us with all around us. We then glow with chi (our aura) and essentially we are in a state of perfect innocence. This first breath is not simply about taking in oxygen, which actually continues to burn us up our whole lives. Yet our body, with its life essence continues to defy this erosion, at least for a few decades. Life as a whole seemingly defies this natural process of breakdown, known as entropy, by harnessing a life force that is probably resonating throughout the universe, beyond space and time.

While oxygen is harmful for our tissues, long ago animals learnt to harness it to enable the regular metabolic processes that sustain us today. Breathing then, is a two-fold activity, where we take in oxygen to keep us going, and we are able to connect with the life force.

Bearing all this in mind, means that practicing breathing is an important part of finding a harmonious life, and for tuning into the resonances around us. This is clearly illustrated by spiritual leaders who have practiced breathing for years, whether for meditation or the martial arts. Eugen Herrigel illustrates this well in his book *Zen in the Art of Archery*, where as a westerner, he trained with a Zen Master for six years, and having to master breathing first and before releasing an arrow. His Master pointed out that breathing binds and combines, and by holding the breath, it makes everything go right, and loosens and completes by overcoming all limitations. By breathing well you discover spiritual strength and feel the life force flow more easily through you.

Practice regularly either sitting or standing upright, with your spine as straight as possible. When you sit, do so in a yoga position with your knees apart and your hands held out in front with your fingers apart and comfortable. Depending on your mood, let the tips of the fingers of each hand just touch the corresponding fingers of the other hand. This allows chi to flow. Sometimes though, you will feel that you want your fingers to remain free, which is good too. If you are not comfortable sitting on the floor, even on a cushion, then sit on the edge of a chair, so long as your spine is straight and your chin up.

Take a slow deep breath, feeling the inhalation expanding your ribcage, and imagine that you are breathing in the life force deep into your lungs. At the same time, imagine that the air is entering the upper outside of your arms, through the sacral dimples either side of the base of your spine, and through the twin areas either side of the spine between the shoulder blades. Then hold your breath for a few seconds, and then let out your breath slowly, imagining and feeling all the time your connection with the universe, and feel the life force flow. This whole process should not be hurried, and should, after some practice, take up to about 20 seconds, or whatever amount of time makes you feel comfortable.

It is the brief holding of the breath, for three seconds or so, that enables the thorough exchange of oxygen in and carbon dioxide out. Do this three times in a position where you have quiet, and repeat the triple process, if you can, several times a day, focusing each time on the present moment. You can even do this sitting on a train, cryptically switching off from the rush of everyday life. You can also do it while standing up in a line. Do not do this while driving, because you will find that your road awareness may temporarily decrease and you will automatically shut your eyes and reduce concentration on the road. By all means do it as a passenger.

## Water love

> *Water teaches us how to live, how to forgive, how to believe. If you open your ears to the possibilities in life, you may just be able to hear the sound of the pure water that flows through your body even now. It is the sound of your life – a melody of healing.*
> Masaru Emoto

Our bodies are about 70 percent water, and composed of billions of cells, most of which are not actually our own, but all the little micro-organisms that make up our body fauna. This is a manifestation of our long evolutionary heritage, with even the mitochondria, the energy power houses of our cells, being an alliance between our body and ancient bacterial cells for optimal survival of both. This emphasizes again our connectedness with all around us. We are not what we may seem. We are not one, but many.

Water is one of the most extraordinary substances in the universe, and is essential for life as we know it. We can live without food for many days, but when our body loses water, we must replenish it, with a 15 percent loss starting to become lethal. Water is so essential to us, it is virtually us.

Water has many special properties the best known of course being that it expands when frozen. Even water molecules are in a perpetual play of movement, one momentarily touching another and then moving on to the next, giving water all the wonderful forms and movements seen in its dancing movement and wave action. It gives and receives vibrations. Water's molecular flexibility is one reason that it is all about us, flowing through the air, soil and deep into the earth. It is in continual flux, and in its vaporous form in the air, seen by us as clouds across the planet. It also reminds us of so-called 'emergent properties'. We probably would not be able to predict what water is like if we only knew its component molecules hydrogen and oxygen. When they combine, an unbelievably creative substance, water, emerges.

Water vapor also protects life, through partly shielding us from certain harmful cosmic rays and enabling temperature balance on earth. Much, and possibly most, of the water on the planet arrived from outer space with meteorites and comets early in earth's history, again emphasizing our connectivity with the cosmos. This flux reminds us that indeed *all* is connected. Even some of the water molecules in our own body passed through other humans living many centuries ago. We all have a little bit of Shakespeare or Caesar.

Then there is something much more telling about water that underpins everything we do in terms of our well-being. It morphs according to our thoughts and feelings. This has been researched by the creative Japanese scientist Masaru Emoto in some remarkable books, including *The Secret Life of Water.* His point is that as we think, let alone behave, so it is reflected in the delicate pattern of ice crystals and snowflakes. Ill-intentioned and ugly thoughts lead to malformed crystals. He then goes on to say that the water flowing within us is part of the water flowing through nature and part of the rhythm of life being played out throughout the universe. Inevitably, as we think, so will those thoughts have an influence on the vibrations in the water in our bodies, with good thoughts giving good vibrations, and bad thoughts leading to those which are not in harmony.

Loving thoughts not only produce loving vibrations in our body, but also radiate those vibrations to others. It is all a wave action flowing in and around our body, enhanced on its way by resonance from our inner being.

These enhanced vibrations associated with loving and harmonious thoughts also have an influence on the billions of other micro-organisms, made up mostly of water, that live inside and on our bodies. These vibrations, or waves of love, will then tip the balance of power against the bad micro-organisms and in favor of the good ones, with the result that diseases are kept in check, and any of our damaged cells healed. This happens at all levels and places on or in our bodies, whether inside our cells, including the brain and heart cells, every one of which in turn houses and bathes our DNA.

We are an extraordinarily successful animal due to two primary features: an upright posture and a large brain. Standing and walking upright go back a few million years into our ancestry. It has been a question of more than just standing upright but also of having developed the ability to run upright. This came about in association with development of large bum muscles, the gluteus maximus, the largest of over 600 muscles in our body, and our physical powerhouse. It is not such a coincidence that our glutes feature so strongly in physical attraction among both sexes. They have had strong survival value.

Yet running, especially in the hot savanna, required an efficient cooling mechanism, and this has come about by development of a skin threadbare in hair and amply dotted with sweat glands. Evaporation of sweat from our bare skin enables us to keep cool. But there is a downside to this cooling system: we must always be close to water. This means that from our earliest beginnings we have had an enormous affinity for water. It has even been argued by feminist writer Elaine Morgan that we were once aquatic or at least semi-aquatic, with features typical of this way of life, such as a fatty layer under the skin, slightly webbed hands (just look at the skin connection between your thumb and forefinger), nostrils that point backwards when we swim, and we cry with salt. When all these are put together, it comes as no surprise that we so often go on holiday where there is water. It cools and washes us, as well as freshwater being our most critical survival resource.

Then there is also the consumption of fish and shellfish, which are rich in omega-3 fatty acids, and are so essential for brain development. With brain development, among other anatomical changes, came language, group living, and group cohesion, so that today we have become a very chatty being, with both men and women each using about 16 000 words per day. It is an urban myth that women are twice as talkative as men. The genders simply use language in different ways.

It is no co-incidence that water and physical love go hand in hand, from kissing to coupling, from crying to laughing, and swimming sperm cells to amniotic fluid. Love, harmony *and* happiness, are all based on water, its life-giving qualities and its vibrations. When drinking a glass of water, hold it for a while, and give thanks for its life-enhancing wonder, and those vibrations will be transferred to your body. Then also give thanks to the joy of a fresh shower or bath, knowing that the water is such a fundamental part of our survival, and its health is responsible for so much of our own well-being.

## Think young

With air being both our friend and foe, and enabling us to live but gradually burning our body chemistry, illustrates just how essential it is to think young. As you think, so shall you be. Youth is also innocence, and love is innocence, and innocence is harmony. By thinking young, in creativity, actionable activities, you will have fun in what you do, and the positive vibrations will flow. Combine this with enjoying water, bathing in it, splashing in it, and swimming in it. Let the sound of water, the feel of it on the skin and the glint of it in the eyes, flow into you, just as you did when you were a child.

The innocence of youthfulness is closely coupled with a sense of wonder. Explore and investigate all around you, and be curious, intensely curious. Discovery, no matter how tiny, is always a joy. In turn, joy creates a sense of love for, and harmony with, the world about you. This then sets up good vibrations in the body, and helps the body repair itself from the ravages of bad thoughts.

"But I can't go jumping in puddles as I did when I was child, people will think I'm crazy!" Then do it in private! The real point is about the thoughts, which come before the doing of something youthful. While at a meeting, commuting to work, doing the washing up, reflect on happy childhood memories, halcyon days as a youngster. These thoughts will caress and link with your inner being. But still jump in a puddle when you can!

There is nothing wrong with daydreaming on special moments, as it is a feature of being human and is fundamental to our well-being. Daydreaming is a forgotten art in our fast moving, target-oriented world. Daydreaming is amazingly harmonizing, and always leads to good, joyous and loving thoughts, all of which are so enhancing for our bodies and mind. Maybe you think that this is not living the present, but in reality it is. It is the harnessing of the very essence of harmonious life that is all around us at this very minute.

While daydreaming, you will often find that suddenly you get some bright ideas about doing something youthful. Perhaps bungy jumping is too hectic on the body, but imaging faeries in the undergrowth will not break the body and it will fire the imagination. Go for a walk along the beach, across expanses of grass, or in the forest, and experience again all those smells, sights and sounds you enjoyed as a child.

This brings us to valuing nature, whether plants, animals or whole ecosystems. This valuing is a circular process. When you treasure a plant or animal, it returns to you an increased sense of well-being. This then increases your compassion, which increases fulfillment and a sense of oneness with nature. Treasuring a pet plant or animal means actually living with another organism, which you can love and cherish, find companionship in, and together feel better about the world around you.

## Laugh and feel good

> *If we look at someone with the eyes of love, we see good qualities not perceptible to others. Just the act of looking at someone lovingly may also bring out these qualities and help them to blossom. If you meet someone with an extremely refined spiritual nature, he or she will probably be happy, smiling, laughing, almost childlike. This is because they look at the whole of humanity with the eye of love.*
> Jonathan Black

The spiritual adept, Da Free John, is said to have been born enlightened, and has taught his disciples to absorb the Buddha Field around him and 'surrender' one's self and undo the knots that prevent the free flow of life energy. The word 'surrender' is the same as lightening up, letting go, releasing the bad thoughts and feelings, so as to reach higher levels of consciousness. This aura around Da Free John includes laughter. It is not laughter *at* anything, just laughter for its own sake. There does seem to be something in this approach, as illustrated by the well-known adage that laughter is the best medicine. Laughter stimulates good vibrations because it is creative thinking and it stimulates the body's biochemistry into the realm of well-being possibly through better tuning into the good resonances of the universe. Indeed, a really good laugh is a resonance from deep within, and comes from the center of our bodies where the life energy is most connected with the cosmos.

Knowing that laughter is a healing activity means that if you are feeling down or unhappy, it is important to be with people who make you laugh, or watch a funny program on television, or a funny movie, so long as the humor is genuinely funny and not black. Slapstick is one thing but fun being made of others' misfortunes is quite another. Hidden camera comedy is usually harmless as it enables us to laugh at ourselves as humans, and does not focus on damaging the reputation of any one person in particular. Indeed, comedy is a highly social activity, a harmonizing factor between people, as it holds a mirror up to the ego, and often shows how ridiculous it is. We need more humor in our world today.

Smiling is not the same as laughter but nevertheless on the way, and may lead into laughter. Smiling is often a personal activity, and while bonding when sincere, is not such a social activity as people laughing together. Also, smiling has often been degraded in our greater social world, where smiling is often portrayed as a way to gain social advantage or acceptance – as with CCTV, "smile you are on camera". If you respond, you are grinning, not smiling.

Nevertheless, smiling that comes from within is a profound activity that is positively reinforcing. To smile at a little happening, like a child standing on tiptoe to reach a higher shelf, is spiritually enhancing, as it involves a transient absorption in something good, an instant awareness at the present moment of something that bears no harm to anyone. Then, one smile leads to another, and is a fundamental connection with inner human nature as well as nature at large.

We can see the converse of this with traffic, as there is little to smile at when it comes to vehicles, capsules of much frustration and rush, and which are not spiritually connecting us with the world around. This does not mean of course that from sitting in a vehicle we cannot smile at something we see as drivers or passengers. We just have to look for it a little harder. If anything, that is the real advantage of travel, there is always something new and interesting to smile at.

A very valuable attribute of smiling is as an antidote to the ego. While it is very unlikely that we will actually laugh at ourselves, unless in a harmless social context, it is very good practice to smile even at some of the silly things we sometimes do, like catching our sleeve on a door handle or spilling the coffee outside the cup. Smile at your small misfortune, rather than grumble, and tellingly, the more you smile at these insignificant misfortunes, the less they happen in the future. The real smile comes from the inner being, and the more you smile both at yourself and *with* another person, the more you will connect, and feel a love of life, a harmony developing and a sense of well-being and happiness flowing.

## Just make it happen

It is an interesting facet of human nature that we expend great energy, hardly without thinking, when we do something we really desire. Yet when it comes to having to undertake small physical actions over something we don't like doing, yet forever prevalent in our everyday lives, it seems to require proportionately much greater effort. Getting a mug out to make coffee is one thing, to wash it up is quite another. These little reluctances come at us a hundred times a day, and the route of least resistance is to languish. The reason that they are an effort is that we make decisions about them, and small as each may seem, they do add up over the day. The point is that it is not the physical effort on its own that is the issue. It is the effort of making the decision because of the energy required in making a decision to overcome reluctance. It is feelings of reluctance, making decisions, and dealing with small dilemmas (wash up now or later?) that can disharmonize us. The key to overcoming this seemingly insignificant, rarely talked about aspect of our lives, is simply to do it while minimizing the time taken over decision. In short, just make it happen, just do it.

In the case of complex situations, this 'just making it happen' also means tuning in to deep lying, very instinctive feelings. Our minds are fantastic at assembling and processing huge amounts of information. As our minds are intrinsically good (as they are the product of a selection process over millions of years), the instinctive thoughts and feelings are often highly intuitive. Take note of these hunches, as often they hold opportunities that are lost when we deliberate too much. This intuition is different from planning strategically. But by all means build your hunches into your strategic planning.

The 'just make it happen' principle runs through much of what we do in life and how we harmonize and feel love. Dealing with the small challenges in life instantly and without a second thought (quickly washing the dishes without fuss) frees up the mind for tackling the more major things, including life decisions. Indeed, it is these that really require the valuable input from hunches.

Dilemmas and frustration are two of the most undermining aspects to finding our path to enlightenment. In dealing with these, firstly there must be a decision on what are your goals, your long term goals and your short term. Then decide which are the steps needed to achieve those goals, then take those steps without hesitation ('He who hesitates is lost'). This does not mean pressing on regardless and without flexibility, but with rational re-alignment as required. You will need to periodically re-assess your goals, and your feelings towards those goals. Everyday positive actions include never being lazy in thought and action ('The lazy man goes to the greatest lengths'), never take short cuts, and follow through. Set small goals during the day ('I will work on this until 12, then go to the shops'), and stick to them.

Having dealt with these small steps by 'just making it happen and just doing it', leaves the mind free to reflect on other challenges, and for re-assessing your path in life. No one said all these small steps are easy, and even less so for the bigger steps ('If it was easy, everyone would be doing it'). The absolute key is to dissolve dilemmas and frustrations, and let them go, cast them into the universe.

When 'just making it happen', there are two parallel paths which you will be following. One will be towards career and/or family goals, with subtending romantic love and harmony, and the other will be towards your inner development and enlightenment. These two paths need to be woven together. In other words, if you set certain career goals, these must be achieved with the giving out of love and compassion, otherwise happiness will never arrive. Reconciling these two parallel paths is not always an easy task, with the key being always to continually recall the importance of the connection between the two paths. Then react positively to keep them in step.

There is one last thought here: 'Don't put off until tomorrow what can be done today'. The old adages have stood the test of time, and they have crafted many people's lives in the past. Deal with the everyday tasks quickly and efficiently without even thinking about them. Set yourself a reward, albeit a small one, for completion of the task. A physical reward is fine (a piece of dark chocolate, which anyway is good for you as it contains antioxidants), but only when the task is actually done, or at least a step towards completion of that task as reasonably set by you. Even better, leave your computer, walk the dog, so that you can feel alive again as you see the clouds and trees, and feel the fresh air on your face.

When you are engaged in dealing with tasks, focus intensely on each task at a time. By all means multitask, but do so over a time span. The reason that focus is so important is that by doing so, your intelligence is effectively increased momentarily while the intense focus is taking place. The importance of this is that you can bring more mind power and more intuition into that instant, making solutions more easy to come by. In short, focus, solve, do, and move on.

Be fascinated too! It seems that taking a wide interest in a variety of topics, from news to history, from art to architecture is good for well-being. Such a wide interest is also rejuvenating. Besides being of intrinsic value, it also has social value in that you will be able to converse on a far wider range of topics, and so interact with a far wider range of people than you would if you were narrow in your outlook.

There is always a little extra magnetism between people with similar interests. Also, with a wide knowledge of topics, there is always the chance to share a chat or two with new acquaintances, who may later become friends. Yet there is a balance here. Never feign knowledge in a field while conversing with an expert. You will soon give the game away. Then, where you are knowledgeable in a particular field, do not speak down to someone who is not, else you become a social bore, with benefit accruing only to your shallow ego.

## Pas de panique!

There is a plaque behind the bar in a small hotel right at the top of a mountain in Helberg, a small village in the center of the volcanic island of La Réunion in the Indian Ocean, which simply reads "Pas de panique!" – Chill! The message here is that in that magnificent expansive landscape, there is no need to fret and disturb any good resonances. If only we could just do that all and every day of our lives!

Dealing with the frustration factor in our lives is often a greater challenge than we think, but only because we make it a frustration. Practicing a task (learning a musical instrument) and overcoming challenges is one thing, but beating yourself up over a frustrating new computer package is another. Dump the frustration, leave the task for now, and return afresh, and don't fret.

One way of dealing with some of the normal everyday frustrations is to enjoy the physical activity as body practice. Strange as it may seem, it does work. When doing a normally onerous daily task, think good and harmonious thoughts. When washing the dishes, practice aligning the glasses, hold your stomach up and in, and stand upright to straighten the spine. Then smile to yourself. While this is literally kitchen philosophy, it is about dealing with the small steps and frustrations that bedevil us in our everyday lives by living in the present moment. So, turn a chore, a frustration, a negative thought into something worthwhile for your well-being, and in turn, to benefit those around you (i.e. your grouchy behavior is reduced), leaving you more time to reflect and harmonize.

## Exercise

Walking in particular is such a basic part of our being that the more we can do it the better it is for us. Our bodies are made in every respect for walking, and when sufficiently lithe, also for running. Walking is good for our mind as much as it is for our bodies. While we need to keep our muscles and skeleton in trim, we also need to keep our psyche in trim too. We need to experience daylight through our eyes for well-being, as well as through our skin for vitamin D enhancement. The experience of regular daylight, say 20 minutes a day, automatically harmonizes us, and it is one reason why a picnic is always so memorable.

The mind tends to throw out ugly experiences and retain the better ones, especially those that give well-being. The point is that walking has been fundamental for our evolution and success. This is why it is exhausting continually walking around a city but invigorating when walking in nature. Our eyes are taking in all the variety of nature, the colors, particularly green and blue, and the inherent variety. The complex shapes in nature, from grasses, flowers and trees to rocks, the sea and the sky, trigger well-being because they are not just complex, but are also dynamic, moving, waving, shimmering and morphing. This inherently resonates with our inner being, and the more you can experience it, the better it is for your well-being. This all happens subliminally and with a huge amount of mental processing and tuning in to resonances of the cosmos. During this process, we are also being tuned to be aware of our surroundings. The subliminal experience becomes a process of increasing awareness.

While walking, the real joy comes from taking in everything around you, all the detailed wonders of nature and its dynamics and interactions. The mind can be trained to almost photograph those images, which you can recall even after the walk. This sense of awareness is a thread running through so much ancient and modern wisdom. To be aware is to be alive, and to feel alive is to feel good, and to grow from feeling good, leads to ever increasing love of, and compassion for, the world around you.

Climbing hills and mountains is also both good for the body (as it really exercises the muscular, skeletal and circulatory systems) and for inner well-being. One of the reasons for this seems, in part, to be that it is inherent in us to climb (as seen in children on jungle gyms). This activity is good for stretching as much as it is for muscular contraction, which enhances all round wellness. It also involves deep breathing, where the bottom of the lungs is cleared out, which is also harmonizing. In addition to the physical advantages of climbing, are the experiences both through the hands (holding on to grass or rocks) and through the eyes, much as for walking. The exercise gained from climbing has the added advantage that small judgments of foothold and handhold are required, which is excellent for scrambling the vertical, chattering thoughts that so occupy us in everyday life. During such activity, you will find that you are exercising more than just your physical body. You will also be feeling the joy of being focused and present, and at one with nature.

Interestingly, gardening can often provide the same sorts of exercise and stimuli as climbing, and is one of the most well-being enhancing exercises that we can engage in. Similar things have also been said about bird watching, which although not always involving great exercise, is thoroughly pre-occupying, and therefore highly therapeutic.

Swimming is also one of the best types of exercise for some of the same reasons as climbing, as it involves both stretching and contraction. As well, it involves the sensation of water around our bodies, the medium in which we feel so secure, so long as it is safe. The splashing sound, being white noise, also dispels those incessant thoughts that dominate so much of our waking life. All this of course is well known to physiotherapists, with water often being so therapeutic for recovery following illness.

## 3 x 8 Rule

A harmonious life is about balance in life. This means finding balance between achieving professional goals (work), recharging the body (sleep) and interacting with life in general (family, friends, pastimes, exercise, reflection, daily activities). These parts of our lives should, on a daily basis, be divided roughly into three, 8 hours each. This also means that the third involving 'interacting with life in general' must also be carefully balanced, with time being set aside each day for spiritual growth. This may be done while simply sitting quietly, or while exercising or even while doing daily chores.

A useful rule of thumb is to scan in your mind as to how you are doing with 7 manifestations: good health, confidence, patience, sincerity, honesty, wisdom and humility. How well did you do today? You have another chance tomorrow, while living for today. Why was 'fearlessness' not included in this list? Because if you are caring for your health, feeling confident, being patient, sincere and honest, and showing wisdom and humility, you will not have any fears anyway. It is a question of living well and mindfully (in the present, with present experience), having carpe diem, and not creating fears over what may never arise.

It is good to remind ourselves of the importance of sufficient sleep, ideally and if it suits you, between 6 and 8 hours average a night. Its restorative features are enormous. Adequate sleep makes your heart healthier. It helps reduce inflammation and assists the body's repair mechanism, as well as contributing to improved weight management. It is believed it also helps reduce ailments such as cancer and diabetes, as well as reducing depression. It is certainly important for maintaining a good memory, keeping you alert and altogether enables you to live a more harmonious life, hence the expression 'beauty sleep'.

It is important to keep an effective sleep rhythm, aiming to maintain your 8 hours per night. This long period of sleep enables expression of the various phases of sleep, during which the restorative activities take place. Adequate sleep enables dreaming, about 2 hours per night. While it is still not clear as to the function or value of dreams, they seem to be an important part of the activity of our subconscious in processing experiences during wakefulness, and presumably for enabling better survival when we are awake and conscious. Indeed, it seems that the subconscious is a powerful harmonizer with all about us, whether close by or into the cosmos. The complexity of all the interactions taking place within and among all the 75 trillion cells in our body suggests that there is indeed much more we need to learn, but meanwhile always recognizing the absolute necessity of a good night's sleep.

Even napping during the day can be highly restorative, even for just a few minutes, especially if in a quiet and warm place. Similarly, daydreaming, while traditionally considered an anti-social and out-of-touch activity, is now known in some highly successful people to be a very important part of creative thinking and visualization. Yet daydreaming does not always have to be about career advancement. It can be an important part of creating harmony by reflecting on pleasurable, interesting and valuable moments, which, in turn, improves wisdom. While this may seem to be not living the moment, it is in fact a time of evaluation and development of the subtle senses, as the body is calm, reflective and expansive.

So, how do you deal with sleeplessness, whether trying to fall asleep or after waking up during the night? Sleeplessness is often because of the continuous thought processes related to everyday stresses, decisions and dilemmas which are interfering with the letting go process. And it is this letting go which is so important for taking you along the path to enlightenment. If you really do find it difficult to sleep, or you wake up during the night, this is because your mind is being crowded by imposing thoughts which are blocking the subconscious from doing its healing work. The key is to scramble those vertical, obsessive thoughts with more creative, even apparently non-eventful, thoughts, or even better, no thoughts at all. The first thing to do is the age-old, but effective method of getting up, writing down what is going through your mind (often it is what things you have to do), make a warm, comforting beverage and going back to bed.

Then, once you are lying down, and are warm and comfortable, breathe deeply three times and consciously relax your muscles all over, starting with your toes. Imagine each of your muscles gradually letting go of all tensions, so that your body feels heavy yet floating. Then begin to focus on something non-significant and mind-occupying, which is where the traditional concept of counting sheep comes from. But it is best to focus on something that you really enjoy, especially something from nature or something natural, no matter how simple. It may be simply a yellow spot, a flower, a cloud. See this image with absolute clarity, increasing the clarity as you continue to focus on it. See the colors, and increase their intensity and then soften the colors in your mind. Then let your image morph and grow without in any way forcing it. Then let the image drift into a new form, and even let it develop into a full picture of interacting forms and colors. All the while, enjoy this morphing of forms, and even relish all the little transformations. It can be an amazing experience. The morphing of pictures in your mind is the subconscious taking you on a journey of harmony, the message of the cosmos. As these forms change, move and recombine, so you will find yourself drifting off to sleep, where the subconscious then takes over its healing process.

If you wake up in the night, jot down those tasks for tomorrow and make that drink, and have a small snack. Then have a good novel on the go which you can pick up where you left off, and where you are engaged in the unfolding story. By being absorbed in a story, particularly when absorbing and interesting, will really help you set the vertical thoughts (the chatter of monkeys) free, and let the subconscious take over. As soon as concentration on the novel starts to wane, put the book down and gently close your eyes.

* * *

***Feeling Beauty and Finding Enjoyment*** As we take our first breath, we take in the essence of life. This is also our age of innocence. Breathing well is essential not just for survival but for our spiritual advancement as well. To breathe well requires practice on a regular basis.

Our bodies are mostly water, that amazing substance that flows through and around our bodies, linking us to all in the cosmos. There is even some evidence that we may have been aquatic in our distant past. We must never take water for granted, as it harmonizes us. Water feels the vibrations of thought and intentions, with ugly thoughts causing snowflakes to distort. On the other hand, good thought creates good vibrations in water, which by extension, means that we must create good vibrations in others (as people are mostly water) when we think of love and compassion.

It is essential to think young, which also means playing with water and enjoying deep breaths. We can reflect harmoniously on past adventures with water, which is always a magnet for us. Water and daydreaming go together, as both flow and morph, scramble vertical thinking, and lead to creativity. Combining these with a joy of all living things, and the feel and scent of fresh air, combined with a smile from our inner being, enables us to feel truly alive and to grow spiritually. Laughter contributes to this too, as it is a creative activity.

While it is important to enjoy all around, sometimes we just have to accept aspects of our everyday life. But this does not mean being unhappy. Where there are everyday small chores to do, duties to perform, we just deal with them. Where there are small obstacles, we just overcome them. With all these small trials in life, we just make awareness happen and move on. We accept these trials with grace and enthusiasm, then move on to something enjoyable.

Chore time can be made positive and even enjoyable by thinking and feeling about love, and more wonderful things at the same time. Procrastination is not even on the agenda. We aim to focus, solve, do, feel, love, and move forward. All the while we are fascinated, as well as enthusiastic. We don't fret, we just chill by doing. At the same time, we are aware of our body posture, and are kind to our spine.

Walking in nature is so refreshing because our eyes are being filled with all the wonders of nature. As well as breathing air and building vitamin D, we are getting sensory stimulation from all the dynamically wonderful shapes, sounds, feels and smells of nature. This physical activity helps bolster our sense of well-being.

When we feel physically good, we are also more able to be in touch and resonate with our inner being, as well as with all around us. Swimming is excellent too, as it is such a comforting medium for us. The sound of splashing and, by the sea, the smell of ozone in the air, help scramble the chatter in our minds, and propel us into awareness of the beautiful world around us.

Our lives are essentially a balance between work, rest and taking time out. Have a 3x8 rule where you divide your day equally between these. Having adequate sleep is essential for restoring the body physically, which includes mentally and emotionally, and gives us strength to make better decisions, as well as to resonate better with our inner being. Dreams are as much a reality as what we see in our waking life. As we think love and kindness, we dream love and harmony, which resonates with all about us.

* * *

# 9

# Senses, passion and motivation

## Seeing, hearing, smelling, touching and tasting

Our physical senses are our window on the world around us. While we have the primary senses relating to what we see, hear, smell, feel touch (and give touch) and taste, we also have a sense of subtle awareness. This subtle awareness, often coupled with intuitive thinking, can be highly significant in the case of some people. It can also be honed with practice.

It is not clear how this subtle awareness works, but it does, as shown by psychic assistance at crime scenes, many cases of which have been successful. Subtle awareness can also suggest who is on the other end of a ringing telephone, and knowing who is standing behind us. Women are generally more honed than men in their subtle awareness, and interestingly the words 'seer' and 'seeress' derive from the expression 'to see', but are said to have extra insight.

This subtle awareness is a complex of insights from purporting to see into the future, which stems from the subconscious, to sensing the aura of someone close by. This perception of an aura seems to be related to chi, the life force, which we know exists but as yet is not scientifically explained. However, some psychic phenomena, such as fortune telling, can be explained by more conventional, albeit still subtle, means. Some of these so-called 'psychics' are simply highly perceptive of various subtle facial expressions and body language in the person they are addressing, and with a well-versed set of questions to elicit reactions in the listener.

Sight is our dominant sense by far. Yet seeing color is a rarity in the animal world. This ability seems to be linked in part to seeing the color of fruit as food, and therefore whether it is harvestable, palatable or even poisonous. We have an amazing sense of color perception and are able to tell apart several thousand different hues. Such sensitivity must have had strong survival value in the past, not just for gathering the right food with its necessary nutrients but also for reading other people's feelings through subtle changes in not just facial expressions but also through minute changes in facial color as the circulation reacts to various emotions.

Colors not only play a role in the type of food that we select, but also in its quality. Besides brighter colors being associated with fresh food, the color itself relates in part to the nutritional quality of the food. Our selection can be subliminal, with choice of a certain color of food being a way of selecting certain required nutrients. Carotenoids, for example, which give many fruits and vegetables their rich red, orange or yellow color, are antioxidants, reducing risk of some cancers and can help slow muscular degeneration, and when converted by the body into vitamin A, help keep eyesight keen, skin healthy and the immune system strong. At the same time, essential trace elements, so important for healthy metabolism, are also taken in.

Seeing is a joy, whether the seeing of form or the seeing of color. Seeing of form is extremely well developed in humans, and an appreciation of art goes back many thousands of years in our ancestry, and is closely linked with bonding and self-expression, especially in caves of the last Ice Age, 20 000 years ago. Many classical paintings that have endured respect over the centuries are fundamentally based on The Divine Proportion (also known as The Golden Section), a set of proportions with a mathematical underpinning that stir within us a sense of esthetic comfort.

Seeing is much more than looking. When we see something or someone, we are absorbing the form, color and motion. This all happens within a fraction of a second, and a remarkable tribute to the complex functioning of our brains. Yet seeing, while well developed, can be developed much more through practice, coupled with enjoyment. This development can be accelerated by putting a sense of love into the process of seeing.

As our brains are so remarkably complex and adaptable, the development of seeing can also be developed into providing greater insight. This is done by noticing all around you, no matter how small. You can practice this by seeing the colors, especially those of nature, the blends of those colors and how they relate to each other. Then notice the form of the things around you, the shapes, the sizes and the relationship of the forms, how they come together or separate, or how they change. You can even do this with your peripheral vision while you are engaged on looking at something else.

All this seeing must be done without judgment. Just see and absorb. See and feel love. See and feel positive. An important additional component is to reflect on what you have seen. You will find that it is the most pleasant things that you saw that will remain in the memory most. These memories then become reflections. Then, by reflecting, you are transferring visual images from the short term to the long term memory, which can be reinforced by reflecting again on what you saw earlier at a later time in the day. Then, by continued affirmation of those pleasant images, the feeling of warmth is lodged in the subconscious as present-moment messages with healing power.

This seeing is at its best after having eaten modestly and when you are feeling relaxed. Exercise of course will help you relax, and walking will enable you to see at the same time, as it is fundamental to how we have been honed in evolution to look around as we walk. Yet this process of practicing seeing and relaxing works both ways. The more you see, the more you relax, as this is a harmonizing process that enters into us and calms us through the solar plexus region.

Hearing is also an important sense, and like seeing, orientates us within the physical context of the world in which we live. Hearing, like seeing, can be honed, but with the additional feature that in our mechanical, cacophonous world, we also need to *not* hear some things. There is too much noisy onslaught on our sense of hearing, particularly from vehicles, mall clatter and from television. Notice how ugly an operational television set sounds when you hear it while passing by and just see the flickering reflection of the screen on the wall. The reason for this acoustic infringement is that each program, each advertisement is vying for our immediate attention. Indeed, it is clamoring for our attention, and in doing so it is dulling our sense of awareness through sensory oversaturation. In addition, it is so often aiming at us with highly negative and competitive messages, from the news, which is rarely positive, to advertisements suggesting you need to be slimmer, have a new car, and go on vacation to lounge around grinning.

That is why subtle music can be so enlivening, because, by and large, it provides a sense of well-being. This is why, besides being a universal currency, many songs are melodiously about love. Then, combining that good sound with a visually soothing atmosphere, such as candlelight instead of electric light, provides a double enhancement. The dancing flame and its flickering on the wall are soothing. This is because it gives us a deep sense of security, going back to the time when a fire under an overhang or in a cave was a gathering point with calmness and social cohesion. Fire was also repellent to large predators to which we were so susceptible in past millennia. This is also why simply staring into the flame of a fire and hearing the crackling of wood burning is so comforting, as it is re-assuring us of immediate security. Visual art adds a further layer of comfort.

> *According to Confucius, great music is in harmony with the universe, restoring order to the physical world through its harmony. Music, as a true mirror of character, makes pretense or deception impossible.*
> Priya Hemenway

Other sounds are also therapeutic, especially rain. This of course is not surprising as rain is a life giver, and is so fundamental to our daily survival. Then the combination of the sound of rain drops falling with the wonderful smell of freshly soaked earth gives a strong sense of well-being. This stems from the time when we inhabited the savanna and were strongly dependent on the coming of life-giving rains, both for our drinking and also for the animals on which we depended through hunting.

Smells also have other connotations. Fine cooking smells and the delicate aromas of flowers give us a keen sense of well-being, with meals being among the most bonding of all activities. This does not always mean that the woman has to cook! The man should do so too, and while it is said that the way to a man's heart is through his stomach, it is also the case for a woman, especially when combined with other security messages, such as flowers, music and candlelight. A small effort, done with love, has enormous returns, and assures harmony. When a man is prepared to go some way in this direction, while also bringing out his feminine, yin, nurturing side, it is a great gesture of affection, and secures a relationship.

Giving of love brings loving thoughts. This stimulates other aromas that we receive through our noses, that of pheromones, airborne hormone messengers. These are the secretions of the skin from both sexes that stimulate a feeling of warmth and arousal in a partner, and are crucial for ongoing pair bonding.

The bonding is then completed through touch, which does not have to be much, and sometimes just a brushing of the hand against the skin of another. This is so because our skin, especially that of a woman, is rich in sensory receptors which play an enormous role in pair bonding. It is a positive feedback system, with touch then stimulating secretion of more pheromones, which in turn stimulates the brain to produce serotonin and endorphins, the inner compounds of love and sensual arousal, and ultimately well-being and bonding.

Touch of course is so important in the development of the bond between mother and baby, and this is combined with the emission of pheromones from both. Yet we seem to lose this ability to touch, or rather, forget it, yet it is lodged as a deep necessity inside us. Touch is both gentle, as with the fingertips, and it is firm, as with the arms. We need both gentle touch and firm holds, with both being expressions of love.

While traditionally, it was for a man to hold a woman firmly, as with dancing, it is also important for a woman to hold a man firmly. This would not of course be the case with a man with whom she is not familiar, as it is too suggestive too quickly, but it is important for maintaining the pair bond in a long term relationship. Indeed, to stop touching is a rifting factor for a romantic partnership. Touching can be especially important when for re-assurance rather than sexual advance. It is a complete fallacy that a man has always to be the one holding a woman, with any pair bond remaining strong when *both* partners are being nurtured and sensually nourished.

Another aspect of touch deserves a mention. We evolved in an environment where we were touching and feeling natural items so vital for our survival, whether stone tools or foodstuffs. This is reflected in the great sensitivity in our fingertips which are so rich in sensory nerve endings. This is manifested in our modern world by blind persons being able to read Braille textured script with their fingertips.

This physical feeling of the world around us is a major component for tuning our bodies and harmonizing ourselves. Touching is also a two-way giving and feeling of love. We even have a special word for it 'caressing' which is about feeling with appreciation. As well as caressing a loved one, we can also caress the physical world around us, and which sustains us. Feel things with your hands (and toes too) just as you did as a child, squelching mud in the hands, and enjoy the textures, rough and smooth, with your fingertips and with your palms. It is a loving experience.

The sense of taste is also well developed in humans. It has important survival value in that it enables us to be selective in what food we take in. Taste, and its apparent change in moods, enables us to target a foodstuff that contains nutrients that we require. This goes hand in hand with our selecting food of a particular color and aroma. This selection process is remarkably subtle and much of the time we hardly even notice that we are making the selections that we are. One of the reasons that we take so long deciding over a menu, apart from its social significance, is that we are being deprived of much of the information. The color, smell and initial taste are all not available, so we are really just making a wild guess when we finally make our selection, or we glance at the neighboring table to assist us in the decision.

Taste has another important function, and that is bonding through lip to skin contact. Even a light kiss still takes in taste. And an important feature of romantic love is the taste of a partner's skin. That taste factor has a major bonding function, and it is a major part of 'the chemistry' between two people. This is why it is so important to kiss a partner's skin. Besides feeling wonderful, it is a strong declaration of intimate togetherness.

## Colors to enhance your life

Colors surround us, yet so often we do not notice them. Why is that? It is mostly because we are so absorbed in our vertical, everyday thinking. This 'mind chatter' screens out the literally wonderful world of color. Yet when we do focus, as when we are choosing clothes and furnishings, they mean a great deal to us. Sometimes color is so powerful that it can almost replace form and create strong moods.

Your feelings and mood can be changed by the colors around you. There are both the colors in your surroundings and those on you. Choice of colors in the home is of vital importance, and sets the general tenor of the mood in your home. Unless you wish to make a statement of some kind, such as a fashion mode, colors of the walls need to be harmonious and relatively neutral. Usually the same goes for furnishings. It is against this background that you can add more dramatic color through seat covers, cushions, pictures, and of course, flowers and a bowl of fruit. Lighting also plays a vital role, as we spend most of our time at home at night. Colored downlighters are particularly effective for this, as are appropriate lightshades. While pictures are fairly permanent, they can be moved around. Large, abstract prints can be particularly effective.

It is not just the colors per se but also a combination of colors that can be enhancing, and these you may want to change from time to time, or even seasonally. These additional splashes of color can be extraordinarily enlivening, as they resonate with us as equivalent of splashes of colored flowers among the expanse of green foliage. It gives us a sense of well-being through fertility, as this is associated with rain after a dry spell deep in our savanna-oriented psyche.

The colors you wear are important for setting and sustaining your mood for the day. Of course, the social context is important, but within reason this pertains more to the type of clothing, formal versus casual, rather than the color. Enjoy choosing your colors, and combine that choice with texture too, such as the feel of silk or smooth equivalent, or perhaps the feel of cotton. Colors are not just about the primaries, red or blue for instance, but also the subtleties of color combinations both within a garment as well as between different garments. The relative boldness of pattern, and whether linear or floral, all conspire towards an appropriate mood.

While it is important to choose clothing on any particular day to suit the morning mood, you may like to consider choosing clothes that will help swing your mood into a particular direction, such as calmness or sexiness. You can steer your mood a little by the clothes that you wear. While obviously recognizing personality and your likes and dislikes of certain overall colors, there is also the consideration of hues. An intense pink is distinctly different in mood from ash pink, and depending on your personality, you may wish to swing your mood towards lightness by adding a coordinated yellow, or go a more moderating route and add a grey.

Yet there is a fascinating irony with colors of clothing. What may seem exciting in nature, may not work for clothes. Mid-blue, which can be so eye-catching in flowers such as cornflowers, can be lacking that something in clothing, unless employing a particular enhancing technology. This is partly because of the dyes used and partly to do with the complex nature of flower light reflectance as opposed to the flat nature of clothing, but this is where choice of shine for example can make a difference.

Only you know your inner moods and what you really enjoy and love. When it comes to color, there are of course many books on how to choose colors, matching with season, enhancing your looks, but in the end you must choose your path, and if you are looking for love, harmony *and* happiness, you need, in your color, to give out that feeling, in all its glory.

Radiate yourself onto the world, radiate warmth and loveliness, and at the same time feel radiant. This cannot be every day and all day, but then it is a case of choosing your moments. Choose strategic moments to use color to show how much love you have to give. Life is often about showing panache and then consolidating, which means selecting your color according to your mood and all the while moving along your path to enlightenment where the color is an enhancing step in that direction.

There is also the color of you, your natural color, and color to enhance your radiating of love. Know first of all that you as a woman are beautiful, the most beautiful being on the planet.

> *The human female has undergone dramatic changes during the course of her evolution – far more than the human male. She has left behind many of the feminine qualities of other primates and, in the shape of modern woman, has become a unique being of an extraordinary kind.*
> Desmond Morris

It does not matter whether your skin is fair or dark. From a man's perspective, it glows with a beauty that is rare and wonderful. Your skin, with its glow and its emission of pheromones, is the passport to every feeling of love you ever wished for. The skin of a woman is the organ of the most consummate wonder that has ever graced the world. Every part of it, with its glow and its moisture, radiates love, beckoning love in return. The skin is a magnet and such a magnet deserves being graced with color, as that is what our eyes see, that is what initially draws sensual love in its most powerful form.

This means choosing skin colorant and decoration carefully, with every man, perhaps in a primeval sense, attracted to beauty coloring, especially eye- and lip-enhancing effects. Colored lips for example enhance attraction. Lip gloss, which represents moisture, invites passion. The paler the lipstick, the more the message is one of requesting tenderness. Strong messages are also conveyed by other types of makeup. Mascara highlights the eyes, asking them to be looked at and admired. This is the same as asking for affectionate love, as it is a behavior drawing on neotony. This is further emphasized by eyelash extensions, which soften the eyes and create a dreamlike look. The signal is a strong request for affection, with some passion. These adornments are essentially highly yin, and an appeal to be appreciated by yang.

The old ideas that you should deny passion and be coy have now been cast aside with the discovery that we are an intensely sexual and loving primate. We crave warmth and togetherness, and part of that expression is the use of color. That is how a man perceives and reacts to it. Of course, there is much more to any relationship, at whatever stage in its development, than simply color, but it is an extraordinarily powerful message bearer that is fundamental. While these messages may seem like superficial meanderings relative to loftier ideals of spiritual development, they nevertheless serve to remind us of our fundamental biology and the red chakra. There is absolutely nothing wrong with feeling physically and esthetically resonant as well as continuing along the spiritual path as if following the chakras along your spine.

So what has this seemingly base approach got to do with finding a higher path? Well, unless you are an ascetic, and feel that denial is your path, the reality is that as early primates, we were small in stature and therefore vulnerable to predation. We were scarce and therefore in need to streamline reproductive strategies. In response, we became a highly sexual species, where almost every facet of our being has been directed towards sex and procreation based on intense and supportive pair bonding, which is as strong today as it was in pre-historical times.

Love and harmony are part of that sexual and pro-creational package, and maintaining a bond involves spicing life with color. This is not to deviate from your path to enlightenment but to consolidate the lower chakra in the lower part of the body so that you can move upwards in the body to other parts where love is expanded to embrace spiritual levels as well as physical, as outlined in the *Kama Sutra.*

## Resonating with your inner beauty

With more perceptive seeing, hearing, touching, smelling and tasting, we become more aware and we resonate more meaningfully with the cosmos. In other words, as we truly experience the world around us, so we become more attuned to our inner being. This is based on knowing that our inner being is the gateway to the greater cosmos. Sensations are not just about us keeping in touch with the physical world, they are also converted to resonances within us.

An important part of this outside/inside experience and growth is to simply let this experience happen, with no resistance, and as a wonderful experience without judgment. This is known as mindfulness, where we are highly aware of the sensory input both from the outside world as well as from our own body posture and activities, especially breathing. We are acutely aware of all. We then move around from one sensation to another so as to avoid habituation. As we cannot focus on one set of sensory input for prolonged periods, because our bodies literally switch off, we rotate our focus of awareness from seeing to hearing, to sensing the straightness of our spine, to listening, to breathing deeply, and so on.

The inside/outside experience is actually a two-way process. It involves letting the positive sensations come in, and after integration from within, it is then about giving out of love. In this process, the sensations and thoughts are translated by our emotions. This also involves letting go of vertical intrusive thoughts that detract from this two-way experience. The well-being from this two-way process comes about from living the experience inside of ourselves. It is literally the 'ah' and 'mmm' of a beautiful sight, of a lovely sound, of fine music, of a wonderful scent, of a fine touch, and of a delectable taste, among many other sensations.

As these sensations resonate with the calming influence of your inner being, you will feel a smile, an inner one, coming about automatically. This then reflects in your aura. In turn, this then leads to more meaningful bonding with those around you, and to the interchange of good feelings, which is the precursor to the interchange of loving feelings. These lovely sensations, by their nature, then combine with warm and giving thoughts. This then automatically leads to a mutualistic interaction taking you along your path to higher consciousness, carried by fine sensations and love.

## Passion

Passion is so often thought to be the opposite of peace and calm. We need peace and calm to gather positive thoughts and evaluate recent events. Peace and calm also enable us to move along our path of spiritual growth through letting go of negative thoughts and actions that detract from giving out love. We can practice finding peace and calm through having exercised, through meditation, yoga or tai chi for example, or simply sitting quietly and letting all the noise and rush of the day pass over us. Yet we as humans did not evolve just to be peaceful and calm. We are a strongly motivated species, with passion intrinsic to us. This enables us to make new discoveries, to experience anew and to 'seize the day'. These are profoundly important issues in our lives, and we will not grow spiritually unless we do experience passion in all its magnificence.

But what is 'passion'? It is simply intense feeling for someone or something, and usually sustained over some time because intense interest is there. As it has a time element, it is crucial that you direct your passion along positive, spiritually-elevating lines. Yet interestingly, there is physical time and experiential time, and during moments of passion, our sense of real time virtually fades away. The point is that passion is often strong motivation where the physical and spiritual are intertwined. It is the doing of something enthusiastically, coupled with an intense feeling of well-being. This well-being comes both at the time of heightened passion and after a period of passion where something has been achieved or something wonderful has been felt. The key here is to sustain that passion without it being misdirected into channels of negativity.

In the case of romantic love, the first reaction is attraction to a partner. This comes firstly through the sex drive, with our senses responding to a sexually appealing person based on our sex hormones, estrogen or testosterone. Romance and being in love, along with that concurrent sense of attractiveness, beauty and passion, then arises from sensory input from sight and bodily pheromones, as well as the sound of the voice and other aspects, even the taste of the skin, of a particular partner. This input triggers the internal chemistry, with production of phenylethylamine or PEA, known as the 'trigger hormone', as it is a releasing agent for dopamine ('bliss hormone'), which is associated with good feelings from rewards, and the release of norepinephrine or NE ('excitement hormone'), which gives the sparkle in the relationship. There is also release of the neurotransmitter oxytocin ('love hormone'), which is released after sexual arousal especially of the nipples and genital tract, and evokes feelings of contentment, calmness and reduced feelings of fear. It is also associated with pair bonding, and an increased feeling of trust following close contact, and so is also known as the 'cuddling hormone'.

These are the passion or motivation chemicals of the body. To sustain that relationship, there has to be a move from 'being in love', the PEA/dopamine/NE/oxytocin modality, towards including 'loving and feeling connected', which comes about from release of endorphins ('feel good hormones') and serotonin ('well-being hormone'), as well as vasopressin, believed to be important for long term pair bonding, hence its name 'bonding hormone'. Interestingly, vasopressin is also associated with homeostasis of the body, regulation of water, glucose and salts in the blood, suggesting that bonding is also good for overall health.

It is through this change in body chemistry from lust, to being in love, to truly loving, that long term beautiful love and harmony are maintained over time. This becomes especially strong when this loving of a partner is aligned with a wider love for all around. This general love can stem from the romantic relationship, as security and comfort are now well grounded chemically. This wider love may include a community love, religious love or a deep love for all nature, as well as for family and close friends.

The point is here, that your feelings of passion are not to be denied but channeled into goodness, which includes compassion as a strong element. In other words, you need to keep up the chemical momentum of sustainable goodness by entering into a beautiful feedback cycle of giving and receiving.

## Comfort and security

Passion is delicious. It is beautiful, wonderful and gives us a zest for life. Yet there are times when we also need comfort and security. This is why it is so crucial for you to direct your passion, whether romantic, religious or for some activity, into the realm of light and spiritual development, rather than into dark arenas of envy, jealousy, competitiveness, and other ego-driven negative feelings and reactions.

Many a love affair has unraveled through venturing into these self-destructive areas instead of developing into something good and lasting. 'But he ignored me!' you may well say. Then, don't react! In such a case, know firstly that if you react, you are not in the driving seat, and secondly, that it is your chemistry, fueled by your ego, that is letting you down. It is as if you have become addicted to the feel good compounds of your body and in effect, it is like going through withdrawal symptoms. Rather *respond* by working through the non-loving experience. Take the initiative and resolve any miscommunication through transparent, honest discussion.

Should a relationship, after all your efforts, not work out, it is critical during such periods of loss for you to enjoy comforts and have security. It seems almost as if passion makes us oblivious sometimes to these fundamental necessities of life. Indeed, when that passion is thwarted, the loss is a feeling of loss of comfort and security, even when the relationship has been stormy. For comfort, and to regain a sense of security, sleep is a fundamental necessity. It is also important to be around those that give us unconditional love, especially our family and a close friend.

Your feeling of being distraught should not be shared with others in general, unless they are someone close and compassionate, or a well-being professional. Rather spend time in as much fresh air and among nature as possible, as these natural surroundings have healing power. Then also cuddle up in a warm, comforting blanket and enjoy the quiet. Feel the healing powers of the universe, knowing that all is connected. Enjoy too, the unconditional love of your pets. Eat well, but really resist the temptation to overindulge. If you must keep eating, make sure it is a variety of natural foods of fiber and vitamins, which you rotate. Breathe deeply and regularly, stretch, and really try to exercise. Take your mind off your disappointment by engaging in other activities, especially the quiet of a good novel. Whenever you can, keep your senses tuned, and absorb as much of the natural world around you as you can. Also, hard as it may seem, do some good deeds for others. Although you may be in need of compassion, it is a fact of life that the more you sincerely give out, the more love will come back to you. As you give, so shall you receive, with the universe being as compassionate in accordance with the level of compassion that you give.

## Proactivity, love and happiness

It is so easy to get hooked on the chemistry of being in love. So much so, that reasoning often goes out of the window. Totally unromantic as it may seem, remember that it is your internal chemistry that is making you feel so good. Think proactively, and think of where the chemistry is taking you. Critically appraise the path that you are now going along. Does it have long term survival value for you? Will the being in love develop into mutual loving? Will it be equal on both sides of the relationship? Most of all, and the most neglected aspect of our life planning: will the relationship uplift you spiritually?

There is so much unhappiness in the world, simply because we do not do this self-appraisal. Use your subtle senses too, and listen to them. Does this relationship really have a long term future in terms of mutual security through mutual giving of genuine love? If the relationship does not look as if it is going to pan out in the long term, best if it is terminated early, as the longer it is left and the greater the commitment, the greater will be the fall. Also, the harder will be the letting go of the accumulated passion.

When you are in the driving seat (which does not mean dominating the relationship), and when both of you are sharing yin and yang, and when the glow of higher giving and spirituality, communication and companionship are blossoming, then what a wonderful path to eventual happiness. Nevertheless, there are still some ground rules for this growing relationship. These include honesty, transparency, trust and caring, which must be an intrinsic part of the relationship unreservedly.

## Motivation

*Happiness is achieved more by one's state of mind than by external events.*

HH Dalai Lama and Howard C. Cutler

Sustaining passion over time can be translated into motivation, where goals are set. This may be a career goal, but it may also be a goal towards greater love and harmony. This returns us to the importance of you taking small steps, one at a time, towards a goal. This takes discipline, and making the effort to actually make those small steps. This may include individual philanthropic deeds, such as not cutting in on someone's conversation by interjecting your own egotistical viewpoint, making a beverage for others, giving compassion even in small positive doses, and simply giving someone else a bit of quality time. It is this discipline of surmounting the small steps that puts you in that driving seat as you are directing and continually re-correcting your path into the realm of love and harmony. All these steps also accumulate wisdom, even if everyday wisdom, about what works and what does not.

Yet going up the small steps also means experiencing feeling as well as exercising the mind. Turn your feelings into positive ones and do not judge or query ('why should I make the coffee?'). As we have said before, just do it, just make it happen. And do it with a strong sense of goodness and determination, and enjoy the steps, not just reaching the goal.

If you choose to be only motivated by achieving the final goal, there will be a letdown at the end after the goal has been reached. This will be because the ego has taken control of your motivation, instead of your motivation being directed towards a higher cause. Getting an award, medal or a promotion only gives short lived satisfaction as the goal attainment was driven by the ego. There is of course nothing wrong with receiving an award, winning a medal or getting a promotion, but this is still feeding the ego, and the way to deal with this is to impart your sporting, financial or other skills to others, so that helping the common good puts you into a higher level of consciousness. In other words, don't brag about your success but use it to help others, with humility, which in our modern, highly competitive world equals bravery.

Sustaining your motivation really means savoring the steps that you take. This involves making choices, your own choices, and then you are free, as you are doing the driving. Keep steering your motivation along a path to your higher and long term goal. Be aware of distractions that can overwhelm you, and deal with them without fuss, or simply ignore them if they really are of no importance. Make sure too, you have breaks, refreshing breaks, from your motivational tasks. Do something different for a while, whether it is cooking a meal, daydreaming or going for a walk.

Freshness is critically important for maintaining motivation, and having a complete break, or even better 'sleeping on it', often leads to new creative ideas that you would not see when you are in a state of frustration, saturation or ennui. See your tasks from above, from a distance, and return to them with joy and enthusiasm.

When you are hitting a wall of non-progress, then leave it, and let go for a while. This is not a dropping of discipline, but it is seeing discipline as a chance always to seize on the most creative moments for moving up the next step. By doing this, you are loving yourself, because you are being compassionate to yourself, and the more you take this positive approach, while at the same time giving compassion and love to others, the more you will feel the inner wisdom develop along the path to higher consciousness and awareness, and into the realms of universal love.

## Feel, no matter how busy you are

Discipline is an interesting concept, which is not metaphorical self-flagellation. It is about setting a long term goal, and knowing that there are also short term goals to achieve along the way. These short-term goals can be considered as continually correcting your course. We can liken this to climbing a mountain, where the goal is to reach the peak, but making decisions along the way to gain new footholds on the path upwards. While the overall goal of climbing to a peak may involve the ego to a lesser or greater degree (hence the phrase 'to conquer' a mountain, where the mountain does not care a hoot), there are choices that need to be made that are safe, sensible and enjoyable, and there are those unwise ones that put both yourself and your fellow climbers at risk. Then of course a climb may also put your rescuers at risk should things go wrong. So, you can press on and upwards and lose your sense of well-being both with regards to yourself and to others. This means you making sure what you are doing is compassionate and considers everyone's best welfare.

The same principles apply to life in general, and the 'peaks' you aim to 'climb' should not be conquests to make your own ego shine. By all means busy yourself, through strong motivation, but feel as you go. In other words, be sensitive to others, and be aware that they have needs and feelings too. Give time to your loved ones, and give them your full attention when they need it most. This is the feedback cycle of love, the giving and the receiving.

Always handle what you can with the wisdom of knowing that time is finite. Also know that your in-tray at work will never be empty, and that there will always be those people in the greater world that are clamoring for your attention, either by broadcasting through advertising or contacting you personally. This is where your ability to sometimes just say 'no' is so important.

It is important for you to have the ability, agility and determination to quickly shut out much of the redundant information vying for your attention. Your 'Power of No' is to deflect this clamoring and all, what is in effect, redundant information, so that you can rapidly prioritize in your mind. This prioritization is about deciding what is really meaningful for your growth, your love, and for the cherishing of your loved ones. This is also part of your personal focus as part of your personal journey.

While on this motivational journey, you will find that intense focus is one of the most valuable attributes you can develop. The art of real, intense concentration not only makes going up each step that much easier, through increased awareness and concentration, but it is also greatly fulfilling.

Focus does of course depend on having your short and long term goals *visualized* clearly, and then acting decisively on them. Yet focus does not stand in isolation. It must be counterbalanced with reflection, and making new choices. It also means you staying there at the steering wheel, while feeling fully aware of the consequences of your new choices.

Where your discipline is tested to its greatest is when developing the ability to switch focus, sometimes instantly. Focus also has to be balanced against all the other activities in your life. You may say you can multitask, and of course women are much better at this than men. The reason for this multitasking ability lies in our evolutionary background, where early female humans maintained social cohesion, prepared food and cared for the children all at the same time.

Men on the other hand became more adept at focusing on quarry and finding land where resources might prove better, and this was often a trade-off between knowing where the best water resources lay as opposed to the best place to hunt game, yet have safety and shelter. Nevertheless, whether woman or man, it is extremely valuable to have the ability or discipline to be able to switch intense focus from one task to another. Switching of intense focus enables you to maximize on all the options in life for a balanced interaction between you and others. For example, leaving off your computer for a while, and immediately giving your full attention to another task, especially if it involves giving love to someone else, is a great asset.

Before leaving motivation and focus, it is worth mentioning the pitfalls of excessive perfectionism. While without doubt, it is essential to have perfectionism in the case of engineering, especially where vehicles, craft and structures depend for safety on perfect products, qualities or services, it is not healthy to have obsessive perfectionism in our everyday lives.

It really doesn't matter in the bigger scheme of things whether there is a speck of dust on the sofa, or a hair scratch on the car. These are not going to have an effect on the more important things in your life, especially your spiritual development. Probably you are the only one that wants this absolute perfection regarding things that are largely irrelevant, along with the ego's excessive pride. While we need some form of order and hygiene in our lives, we do not need excessive obsession and perfectionism. We should not have a mentally unhealthy focus on extreme perfection, which in all likelihood, is more of an irritation to others, often especially to those you love most. Feel the joy of being free of obsessive perfectionism!

* * *

***Senses, Passion and Motivation*** It is through our senses that we view and interpret the world around us. We have strong senses, and we have subtle senses. Often what we call 'insight' is actually great sensitivity to certain happenings. Our dominant sense, sight, has sensitivity to physical form, proportions, and color. All of us can practice seeing much better, to enjoy and be enthusiastic about all the pleasant combinations of images around us. We can absorb and process an enormous amount of visual imaging as we are biologically honed to understand the many and varied subtleties of nature.

Know too, however, that there are many intrusive sights and sounds in our modern world that overwhelm our subtle tuning in to nature. It is essential to recharge ourselves by seeing and listening to nature: plant, animal, and even the inanimate nature, like the whoosh of water, the flicker of a candle and the crackling of a home fire. Rain is an extra therapeutic bonus, as it is life-giving.

A man needs to relate to his yin if he is to truly relate to a woman deeply romantically. In our biological roots are activities like dining together, giving flowers, and chatting by candlelight. When the atmosphere is right, it inevitably triggers the release of skin hormones, or pheromones, which are also perceived by our senses, and are the secretions of sensual arousal and love.

Touch is also a vitally important sense. To touch, and to hold, is to love. Fingertips, which are so richly endowed with sensitivity, can say so much. A firm hold can also do the same. This physical touching is essential for nurturing and being nurtured, loving and being loved. Caressing is an essential feature for maintaining the pair bond, and the woman should take the initiative as much as the man.

Taste, which is allied to touch, is finely honed for selecting foods that are good for our health and well-being. Taste is also immensely powerful for pair bonding, as tasting a romantic partner's skin has strong arousal and commitment energies.

Color perception is part of our natural survival strategy, as it has enabled us to select nutritious food. Our visual perception is so acute that colors have become pivotal for setting our mood, especially when combined with particular textures. We can select colors to direct our mood, as well as to define it. Colors also combine with the giving out of love, with the tenor of that love being partly defined by the color of the item in the gesture.

This glow surrounding the warmth of color is particularly strong when it comes to a woman's skin. The glow given by the skin is an immensely strong indicator of how the woman feels, and how she relates to those around her, especially her potential or actual partner. A man senses this, along with the style and extent of the makeup used for enhancement of the message of love. This is also combined with the powerful aromas given out by the skin. All this is associated with our particularly strong drive for procreation, coupled with strong pair bonding.

There is mutual reinforcement between the flow of energy, chi, and our physical senses. Our experience of the world, which is modified by our thoughts, determines how we will resonate with our inner being. The final outcome is how we experience love, and how we feel and enjoy the beauty within. That beauty is indeed the resonance within us, which in turn, resonates with those and all around us. All this wonderful interaction helps us along our path to higher consciousness.

While peace and calm enable us to let go of negative thoughts and move closer to illumination, we still need to feel and have passion. It is deep within our biology to feel strongly, as this is what motivates us and gives us enthusiasm.

Passion can be viewed as the intertwining of strong motivation and spiritual awareness, so galvanizing us towards a higher plane. When we feel well, we feel passion, and we can also feel spiritual growth. This is based on a whole set of biochemical compounds. These give us the feelings, but we also determine the extent to which they are released by what we do and how we think and feel. The key here is to keep it all in balance, as determined by our inner being and its alchemical sense. This means that we can channel our passion into goodness, which feeds back into our receiving of love.

While passion swirls deliciously inside us, there are also times when we need comfort and security. This means bypassing the dark realms of envy, jealousy, competitiveness, and other thoughts and actions being driven by the ego. We need to steer our thoughts and feelings, and therefore our biochemistry, into alignment with the resonances of our inner being by letting go of darkness and embracing positive thoughts of love and compassion.

We need to know that peace and comfort are the natural and healthy counter balance of passion. Then, the key is to maintain that see-sawing balance over the fulcrum of the integrity of our inner being. All the while, we are not letting any ego-driven force rock us out of balance.

The chemistry of romantic love and passion is a powerful and addictive brew. When it matures, it must be converted into true, compassionate love. This also means being proactive, and growing that relationship spiritually for both partners. Ground rules for doing this are based on honesty, transparency, trust, and caring.

Motivation for making a relationship work is the surmounting of the small steps. This is the consolidation of true love. The aim is to seize every moment to undertake them, to make them happen. This occurs through resonating with our inner being through loving those around us. When we feel full of *enthusiasm* for love, and feel it all the while, we are sure then that we are on a path to harmony and greater enlightenment.

This all requires discipline, but enjoyable discipline, and joy of discipline. The joy comes from bypassing the ego and focusing on our path onwards and upwards. Of course there will be times when we slip, are set back, or are deflected, but no matter, we get back on track again soonest. We invite light back into our life, so that love shines and harmony once again prevails.

All the while, we are enjoying this getting back on track. This will always require having focus. Along with its close ally enthusiasm, focus is a tool to help us to be at one with our inner being. This focus does not mean being an obsessive perfectionist, but a resilient and resourceful lover of life.

* * *

# 10

# Tuning into your subtle senses

## Mysticism

For a feeling of well-being, it is essential to lead a physically balanced life. This means eating well, exercising, and finding quiet times, as well as having fun meanwhile. It also means enjoying interaction with others, and communicating your feelings of well-being to others. Yet the world in reality is much more complex than we realize, with all sorts of interactions taking place, sending resonances of various sorts through the cosmos.

Mysticism is simply recognizing that there is more to life than just the physical plane as we normally perceive it through our basic senses. There are interactions of time and space that we do not yet fully understand, but we *feel* that they are there. This is that gut feeling (tellingly described as coming from within our trunk and not from the head) about things. Some people feel that something ominous may be about to happen. This might for example be associated with driving a vehicle, in which case we drive with extra alertness and care.

Such ominous things may not actually happen, but you may sense that they *could* happen. On the one hand this may be due in part to the tuning of your body's inner rhythms and you are sensing that your judgment relative to your safety may not be 100 percent that day. On the other hand, you may also be sensing a warning from the greater world around you.

At other times, you may sense something good is about to happen. This is not about winning at dice or cards, which is outside your control and is determined by physical activities of the thrower or dealer and of the game elements themselves. In such cases, this is your wishful ego hoping that you will win. Yet where something genuinely good is about to happen, something that is life-improving for you and for others, the reward is often one of being able to send out good thoughts and feelings. This may not sound like much of a reward, but the reality is that it enables you to connect and grow spiritually, and so the reward in the future is you being on the road to greater consciousness.

Mysticism is about connecting literally with the mysteries of the world, which are those things we do not yet fully understand. While science may not at present be able to fully explain these mysteries, mystery schools of sages through the ages purport that they exist in terms of manifestations, and it is likely that the human mind and body may well in the future be able to tune into these to an ever greater extent as part of humankind's journey to higher consciousness.

What all this means is to experience the deep inner joy of being alive, where the heart and all the rest of the body resonate with the cosmos, and where eventually there is only one thing, and that is the wonderful white light of love. This comes to us occasionally as sudden illumination of joy where there is the deep feeling and understanding that all is connected and that all is love.

These flashes of intense awareness, insight and apparent understanding are known as satoris, or epiphanies. They cannot be described in words as they are, according to ancient mystics, knowing without knowing, and seeing without seeing. They are peeks through the misty curtain of everyday life into another world where there is a joyous celebration of life and ecstasy, and of total giving of love, like a deliciously warm blanket of insight connecting us with all around us, and where dreaming and reality become one. As Yatri says of the ancient Chinese philosopher: *Chuang Tzu doesn't know whether he is a butterfly dreaming he is Chuang Tzu or Chuang Tzu dreaming he is a butterfly.*

## Sacredness

Something sacred is that which is venerated and respected. This is especially the case of life itself, the organisms making up the biosphere, us, and all our interactions. We so often are oblivious to all these amazing interactions in this fast-moving and competitive world. Yet today it is ever more important in view of the earth's diminishing resources. Indeed, our planet is sacred, and besides, it is the only one we have got. Veneration and respect, which goes hand in hand with humility, is more than just about us and other organisms. It is about our relationships with nature and with each other.

Whether you are a person dreaming that you are a butterfly or a butterfly dreaming does not matter, because the essence of higher consciousness is to revere, respect and love all around you. It is the iterative process of giving out reverence, respect and love, which then wraps itself around and within you in a wonderful white light of being. This is not at all a serious activity, but one of joy, often described in a religious context as Earthly and Heavenly joy. It is also chuckling inside, like the freshness of a child having a new adventure.

> *The magnificent here and now of life in the flesh is ours, and ours alone and only ours for a time. We ought to dance with rapture that we should be alive and in the flesh, and part of the living incarnate cosmos. I am part of the sun as my eye is part of me.*
> D.H. Lawrence

What all this tells us is that our materialistic-driven world is not giving us our freedom to evolve spiritually. This common spiritual path is arguably the future for humans on this planet. It is as if we were born in innocence and our minds and hearts become corrupted as we grow older. This does not mean of course that we must throw out all our possessions (nevertheless, the fewer the better) but it does mean throwing out our mental, egotistical baggage that holds on to the concept of materialism where recognition is the only way to have a fulfilled life. Our course in life is to seek fulfillment through the joy of experiencing life rather than the joy of accumulating physical things and social recognition. This is the process of being at one and harmonizing with the universe through feeling and experiencing love.

## Chakras and color therapy

As we saw in the last chapter, color plays an enormous role in our lives, in our consciousness and in our subconscious. Let us now consider color from a more subtle, mystical point of view. Color interacts with both the yin (the receptive) and yang (the forceful) aspects of our being, leading to a balance in our lives, and giving rise to the triad of yin, yang and balance. This triad runs alongside another triad: enthusiasm, activity, love. In turn, these triads interact with the chakras in our body, with these chakras being the interceptors of resonances in the universe. For a balanced, healthy and enlightened life, all the chakras must be in harmony. Each chakra is represented by a color in the spectrum, red, orange, yellow, green, blue, indigo (navy blue) and violet. All these colors in harmony give white light, which is equivalent to full consciousness. To have a spiritually fulfilled life involves harnessing enthusiasm, resulting in activity, leading to love. This must always be done with balanced yin and yang, and illuminating the body with red through to violet.

Where your body feels out of balance, it can be stimulated to realignment by associating with certain colors. These may be in the clothes that you wear, the colors surrounding you, the lights in your home, and you associating with particular colors in nature. The effect of these colors can be counterbalanced with harmonizing colors which can enhance the effectiveness of the prime color. Red, associated with the base chakra at the bottom of the spine, enhances feelings of physical activity and vitality, with associated motivation (will), stability and spontaneity. When you need to be energized, seek association with red. Red is well counterbalanced with green, hence the popularity of plants like geraniums and red hibiscus. Red is strong on yang. It is also counterbalanced by yellow, giving the wonderful glow at the start of a sunset.

Orange is exuberant. It stimulates creativity, enthusiasm, optimism, pleasure and productivity. It is associated with the sacral chakra in the lower back. It is often awakened in a wooden sauna where you can even feel the energy being absorbed by the body. It is counterbalanced by deep blue and green, and even violet, as seen by the pleasure of African violets.

Yellow is light and bright, and associated with great joy and fun, as well as creativity and the lateral power of humor and intellectual crispness. It has illuminating value and so is associated with logic too. It relates to the solar plexus chakra, and with confidence and openness with others. Yellow is counterbalanced with violet and to some extent by red and blue. The sun on blue tropical waters is particularly enjoyable, and enhanced by the white of the waves.

Green, which via plants, is the foundation of life on our planet through capturing sunlight and turning it into energy and growth. Not surprisingly, it is representative of balance and harmony, true love, acceptance and sociability. It is so important for balancing. The sight of beautiful green trees, with their subtleties of various greens, and their cool, shade-giving foliage, make us feel so good when we walk among them. Being associated with the heart chakra, it is associated with universal harmony and goodness. Green is counterbalanced with red and orange, although in furnishings and clothes this may also be with violet.

Blue, moves into the realms of yin, receptiveness and shallow depths, as with the sky and calm, clear water. It represents freshness, peace, calm, kindness and humility. It is a giver of life.

Blue is associated with the throat chakra, and is counterbalanced by orange, and also yellow.

Indigo or navy blue, is distinctly yin, and is seen in the cool, still realms of night skies and ocean depths. It represents deep peace, trust, loyalty and honesty. Like the greatest depths of the sky and the oceans, it also holds Sirens calling you to take risks. This is seen in navy blue clothes, which represent corporate power, giving out a message of authority. Indigo is represented by the brow chakra, and is counterbalanced by the lightness of orange and yellow, but when combined with red usually represents power.

Violet and purple are the colors of intuition, imagination, great creativity, meditation and insight into cosmic consciousness. It is represented by the crown chakra at the top of the head, and integrates physical and spiritual energies. It has great purifying power. It is counterbalanced by yellow, but also orange and green.

## Colors, tones and hues

Appreciating the counterbalancing colors is important for choosing the colors with which we surround ourselves. If we feel that our sense of joy and intellect need to be increased, then wearing yellow clothes would be a good choice, whereas green would enhance gentle love, communication and balance.

With clothes, these colors are generally communicating those feelings to others, as they are seeing us in those colors. Choice of color is then also influenced by our body coloring, especially the hair, with makeup usually being harmonized with both the skin color and that of the clothes. The point is that the choice is not just about the way we feel, but also the message we wish to convey.

The tones white and black also have significance, with their base being respectively to lighten or darken the prime colors. White is pure light and represents openness and transparency, as well as freshness and good hygiene. It also represents strong harmonizing with the cosmos. White is enhancing of other colors, but is at its most forceful when on its own. Although in traditional Chinese culture white represents death, interestingly, the connection always remains between those who have died, the ancestors, and the living.

Black, of its nature, is the tone of darkness, and represents the wish to blend in, virtually to disappear. This is why it is a slimming tone. True black is rare on earth, except in caves and the ocean depths, and is represented by the vastness of outer space with no light.

Black though, can be enhanced by white, making a strong statement of balanced contrast. Black is yin and white is yang, and together they suggest strength, solidity and reliability coupled with sensitivity, the message conveyed by black tuxedos and white shirts.

Gray is a blend of a small amount of black with a large amount of white, and by its nature is neutral, and so a major toner of other colors. By itself, it represents uniformity, conservatism, impartiality and detachment, as are clouds and fog. It represents a fundamental platform for other colors and hues, each of which has its own story to tell. Yet when the white dimension of gray is lit up, alive and glowing, it conveys oneness with the cosmos.

Gold may be considered as a hue and a higher octave of orange. It balances the physical force of red and the joyousness and intellectual power of yellow. Yet gold also adds a further dimension, that of cosmic awareness and ultimate wisdom. It represents arrival at a higher level of reliability, compassion, respect and understanding. It is a highly expansive hue that communicates immutability and radiates warmth and love to all humankind. Gold is above the base aspects of life and is in the realms of grace, spirituality and a joy of life of itself.

There is also a dark side to gold. When it is personalized too much, it can lead to self-gratification and greed, which is why it must rest on a well-balanced base of deep understanding of the world and indeed of the resonances in the cosmos. Gold is a major color of Buddhist temples, and many statues of Buddha himself are painted gold to represent his enlightened linkage with the cosmos. Yet gold has also seen greed over the millennia, and is responsible for more theft of artifacts than any other hue or color. Interestingly, a combination of gold, purple and white is particularly striking in confidence.

Let us consider some of the other hues. Rose or pink has special significance. It is a highly harmonizing hue, blending with many other colors in its various shades. Being a blend of red with much white, it represents physical energy yet with a strong ethereal and spiritual component. As it blends physical strength with spiritual awareness, it has a strong tendency to aim for harmony and a wide perspective for the good of all. It is a strongly supportive color that radiates well-being towards others, and the harmonizing of disparate viewpoints. Rose radiates a sense of deep compassion, and it suggests determination to realize the dreams and aspirations of others, and it does not quit at this.

There is also a downside to rose. Its expectations of others are determined and high. Yet this strong sense of determination can become converted into coercion and control, leading to frustration and loneliness, especially when poor time management is involved. Yet rose, when sitting on a sound foundation of confidence and a feeling of oneness with the cosmos, can lead to loving kindness and the wishing well of others.

One other hue deserves some focus, and that is the group of tan, khaki, fawn and beige. Being a mixture of other colors while strongly influenced by white, this group of hues is a highly balanced one. We can relate to beige as it is the color of savanna grasses in the dry season, the evolutionary stage for our beginnings as developing humans. Beige has freshness and warmth, especially when combined with pure white, as in a beige skirt and a white top. Yet, as with gold and rose, it has a dark side in that it is the color of camouflage and surprise attack, as well as of authoritarianism, hence these colors for army uniforms. Authoritarianism is especially so when the tan is dark and combined with splashes of blood red, as with Adolf Hitler's usual uniform.

By and large, hues of various colors, whether pale blue or peach, are a subtle mixture of component colors strongly blended with the illumination and openness of white. They are a toned down version, as well as a blend of the primary colors, enabling us to tolerate them for long periods of time, whether the wearing of clothes all day or the color of walls at home. Yet what we initially perceive in a swatch is always lighter than it is when in a full piece of clothing or on a wall. This is why when choosing a hue for the walls, it is usually necessary to choose the one that you think is right and then actually purchase and apply one or two shades lighter.

## Rapid appraisal

Our minds perform amazing operations, processing up to 100 000 conscious thoughts a day, and sifting through enormous amounts of information. Much of this general information is either not converted into everyday use or is synthesized into discrete information that we either heed or not. Often a large amount of information is distilled into impressions, even feelings.

This incoming information is also reconciled with what we already know, or think we know, and enables us to make judgments. We only have to scan a new room to pick up a lot about the person living in that room. This may include information on color, arrangement of furniture, age of furniture, neatness or not of the movable furnishings, presence of books and their state, and so on. It gives us an impression, which gets integrated by our past experiences and assessments. All this takes place in an instant, and at most in just a few seconds, the time it takes to scan a room. It is these visual and other sensory experiences that enable us to formulate our relationship with the scene before us. These instantaneous assessments underlie hunches, insight and intuition, which are also reinforced by resonances beyond space and time.

These assessments tend to become fairly fixed in our minds, enabling us to make sense of the complex world around us without becoming too overwhelmed with the detail. The more relaxed we are, and the more in tune we are with our inner being, and the more we are in tune with the cosmos, the more aware we become of our surroundings and what it means in physical and spiritual terms. In contrast, when we are in a state of stress, the less aware we are, and the less reliable are our hunches, increasing the chances of making wrong decisions.

What this means is that in your everyday life there is a need to practice awareness. You can practice this by simply observing as much as you can all around you, and by being absorbed in the very activity of seeing. This applies to the other senses as well, hearing and smelling in particular. These sensations should be processed through rewinding a scene or an experience, without any judgment. With continual practice, you will find that awareness begins to develop more fully, with the mind synthesizing these sensations into meaningful patterns, with a joy for living beginning to emerge.

These various sensations often resurface in our dreams, enabling us to steer our lives into a more meaningful direction. They fine tune us, so that hunches and feelings of what is right and good in terms of the universe and our spiritual evolution, become more and more regular in our lives, steering us towards higher consciousness. Physical awareness becomes spiritual awareness, so harmonizing our being with all around us.

## Realizing your intuition

Life coaches James Redfield and Carol Adrienne in their interesting book *The Celestine Prophecy: An Experiential Guide* point out that coincidences in our lives have deep philosophical and spiritual meaning, and that it is important in our spiritual evolution to be able to read them. Coincidences and subtle messages come to us as we cultivate awareness through discipline and activity.

Through continual practice, you can grow awareness of coincidences and subtle messages where they can help you make decisions in your life which otherwise would be difficult to formulate. With development of awareness, you will be able to make snap decisions, even in the case of major life events, and know inside yourself that they are the right ones.

You may have found that you have agonized for hours, sometimes even months, over making a major decision, usually in connection with a physical move or a change in a relationship with another person. Yet after practicing the art of awareness, and feeling the messages in your dreams, you will find that rapid decisions become easy. This may involve a period of gestation where you gather many little blips of awareness and all perspectives, ideally flavored with a little humor now and again. These inner feelings then become synthesized. After some dreaming, even some daydreaming, letting go of trauma and any negative thoughts with sustained discipline, an answer will often just appear.

This process is about absorbing all significant hints, turning negative thoughts and feelings into positive ones. When you let go of blockages causing indecision and you cast indecision and negativism aside, you will then find that the universe in turn will show you the way forward, and will give you the right decision. This casting out is really just a releasing without concern, truly letting go, almost as if you are letting the agony of decision fall off you. It cannot be forced, with forcing leading to internal conflict and frustration, often leading to a panic decision. When the decision is based on intuition combined with a feeling of universal love, it will inevitably be the right one.

During this process of the resonances of the universe providing you with the answers to your dilemmas, it is important that you practice reading the expressions on the faces of others, understand their viewpoint and develop a sense of intuition in your relationships with them. Doing this involves being passive and receptive, not forcing any issues, but subtly reading all events, and as Redfield and Adrienne say, appreciating all coincidences.

This finding a solution is a question of tuning in to the messages and happenings emerging from the physical world and from intuitions coming from the resonances beyond space and time. Read them instinctively, without thinking, feel them, and interpretations will then present themselves. At the same time, simply be in tune with your inner being, leaving behind all aggravations, hurt and anger of the past, and observe and feel with a sense of absolute openness. Notice all feelings or hints of messages that seem intuitive. The interpretations then automatically take place from within you. When your responses are done with a sense of giving universal love, which is through the heart as well as the mind, it will give you extraordinary clarity.

This tuning in to subtle messages, from outside, from within, and from beyond space and time, is best done with a sense of profound beauty. This beauty is a 'small excitement' that you can feel in your fingertips, in your heart, and it shimmers around your body, and seems to flow in and out of you. You can tune this sense by thinking and *feeling* divinely beautiful things, by embracing the exuberance of life and love. Practice developing a sense of warm joy within. This then glows and morphs as colors form, which literally wash out the grays with warm yellows and oranges, which then swirl with light blues and greens, turning into violets and purples as you begin to attune with the resonances of the universe. These color-swirls are beauty in action, linking all your chakras, your yin and yang, with all around you, and all in the universe. This is the growth to higher consciousness, where the universe effectively makes the right decisions for you because you have prepared the spiritual soil to receive the seeds from divine sparks.

As you see these colors, feel yourself floating up and away, beyond earthly realms to a cosmos of universal love. Feel yourself giving love, and in this process, you will feel a sense of 'knowing', that is, a sense of sublime acceptance. That knowing is the universe giving you the answers that you are looking for. These answers, which will allow you to make decisions in your life, may be seen as resonances vibrating in accord with your own positive and lovely thoughts and feelings. These rewarding resonances cannot be requested. They can only be received automatically after you have given out love and felt beauty.

What you receive back may be a wonderful sense of divine nothingness, as the ancient Chinese would say. This nothingness is totally expansive, and is of no-space and no-time. It is a tickling essence that fills you from within, yet flows back out again as pure love. It has an almost strange all-knowing but not-knowing, and just 'is'. Your inner being feels and breathes it all in and out.

On this journey of divine beauty and love, everyone and everything has a message, often coming in subtle forms of intuition. You need to focus on these so as to perceive. Some of these intuitions will be negative, and in being so, are guiding you on how not to be. When someone is being grumpy or unfair, do not react or retort, just deflect those incoming dark actions away from you and out into the universe, and spiritually move on. Nevertheless, seek to understand the underlying causes of those egotistical outbursts, and return compassion. Do it in just an instant, knowing it for what it is: someone out of harmony and who needs help.

With the glow of higher consciousness, you will feel the

heavy, base interactions of everyday life become mere events, each with a lesson. Simply give, give out love and beautiful thoughts based on the insight from the universe and your intuition. Let no ego impose bad energy on you or draw on your energy. Remain at peace, remain at one, and remain connected with the universe, where the dance of colors and ultimate love and compassion prevail.

## Giving thanks

Prayer is often misunderstood. Prayer is meditation and the giving out of love and beauty. It is not the asking for something. Prayer is an essence, not a thing. It is the tuning of the heart and mind, all the chakras, the balancing of the yin and the yang, so as to find God. It is to feel the universal life force permeating all plants, animals and humans. It is the feeling of the dance of the cosmos, its higher vibrations and its bathing light and joy. It is you giving thanks. Thanks for this wonderful and joyous life. Indeed, praying even extends human life expectancy.

Prayer is a time of quiet, of peace, of loveliness. It is time to attune with the universe. The universe, in all its expansiveness, will then receive your prayers. Prayer is a time for you to give out your thanks for all life. Yes, that is all very well, you may say, but I am so distraught, I need comfort! Then, first all recognize the trauma, define what it is, and define its dimensions. Then imagine packaging it up and releasing it into the universe. Use your imagination to do so, this, your wildest and most vivid imagination. Use all your inner strength and discipline to define the setback or trauma. Try, and try again, to do this. Then let the universe receive it as a defined package. Empty your being of all that has been heaped on you. With every bit of release, the vacuum will be filled with healing and love. This is 'as it is', simply because that release is actually a giving out, and the universe will receive. The release is the giving out of what has traumatized you, and not because you feel any ill will. It is your inner beauty connecting with the heart of God, and resonating with the no-space, no-time. Only the universe connected to your inner being and beauty can really sort out your lack of balance and harmony. This is helped by those people close to you giving you comfort, which is gratefully received. But your healing will only come about from within you, from connecting with your own inner being and beauty when it resonates with the cosmos.

Make a great effort to learn from any setback or trauma you are currently facing, and treat it as a new challenge to overcome. Do this, knowing all the while that you will be stronger from overcoming it. With your inner being connected to, and resonating with, the universe, the sharing of your bad times with the universe will lead to a healing and development process, where you will grow in vibrational energy. This will not come about when you just bemoan your fate, as this is your egotistical 'I' sharing your misfortunes with others, and causing negative resonances. This approach then leads to a circle of discontent, as the ego will not let go of the misfortunes, and dark memes (the inherited and coercive pieces of information) will then swirl and dominate, leaving you ensnared. Overcome this entrapment by thinking positively, with humility, having compassion, giving out love, having discipline, seeing beauty, no matter what the odds may seem.

## The discipline of staying tuned

Staying tuned is about continuously giving out love and compassion, with trust and humility being cornerstones. While this staying tuned is best done in moments of quiet reflection, with practice, it can be done anywhere at any time, even while undertaking daily chores. Staying tuned is about cultivating that feeling of love and harmony with all about you. Turn any bad thought into a good one, instantly. Tempting as it is, do not dwell on issues. This is of course different from planning for the future, or reflecting on events in a dispassionate way.

Doing this all the time takes an immense amount of discipline, yet the rewards are enormous. Daily practice is essential, and the more often you practice, the greater will be the rewards. The key is to make a habit of staying tuned, and using every opportunity to intuit over all the interactions that take place in your everyday life. Some of the subtle messages will be very brief, and may involve simply a glance from someone towards you, or giving out a brief glance of positivity to someone else. All the time, feel the strength and radiance of your balanced self.

In practice, do this by always making small gestures of goodwill, such as sincere praise, a warm smile, and a brief touch. Enquire always as to the well-being of others, and do not gripe about your own ills and setbacks. It helps also to reflect. This does not mean dwelling on problems or issues in the past but building on lovely memories and all the fine cameos of life. Picture yourself when you were, say, with your partner or friends, and recall the moment when you were laughing together.

Reflection emanates from inner stillness and completion. Yet the ego will try to turn contemplative reflection into dwelling on how 'I' did/am doing, by letting the mind chatter. These vertical thoughts must be recognized as such, and then released without even the slightest thought or feeling. This bundling up and casting out will refresh, and prepare you for the next social interaction, where you once again give others your focused attention, especially your loved ones.

## Seeing behind you

As you develop your attuning with the resonances of no-space, no-time, and develop your higher consciousness, you will start to see auras around people you interact with. It is seen as a light bluish, almost electric, glow. Depending on how you feel, and how the other person is feeling, as well as how you are resonating, there will be other colors as well. Yellows and oranges can be particularly clear. You may also see violet and purple in some highly attuned people, and even some white. This aura is an envelope around the person, and tends to come and go, depending how in tune you are with universal resonance, and how you drift into an awareness phase and drift out again. It is most clear when you are absolutely relaxed, not preoccupied with social vying and not intellectualizing, and when you are almost just daydreaming. You can also enhance another person's aura, especially when you give out genuinely good thoughts, especially of deep compassionate love.

When you sit quietly, and especially when you lie in bed in the morning relaxing before getting up, with your eyes closed, you can actually see your own colors. After making love, there will be a red glow, but this morphs and blends into other colors as you relax and contemplate universal love. You can feel and even see yourself on your path to higher consciousness, as a purplish flooding of your mind. This usually starts with being fairly light in color, almost bluish, but becoming a flood of purple as you become more and more attuned with universal resonances. When this happens, just let the various shapes and images morph and find their own path, and sometimes, when you are very relaxed, you will see some wonderful pictures that give immense delight.

When you practice letting the universe fill you with goodness in the two-way process of giving out love and harmony, and receiving it, you will begin to almost physically feel people around you, and you can even detect who it is behind you, and how they feel. You will sometimes be able to feel who it is on the telephone when it rings, and occasionally even the mood of the person who is calling you. This normally applies to people you know well, and you will find that you can become particularly attuned to loved ones trying to contact you.

This tuning into the universe can be important for survival in some cases. You will find that sometimes when you travel that you have a feeling of something ominous. This is a premonition, and does not mean that you will have an accident, but it is a warning sign that you should be careful. At other times you actually feel the feelings of others or that there is a message suggesting that you should do something in particular. This is presentiment, and again it is strongest with those who are dearest to you. This attunement also applies to many other aspects of life. People with 'psychic' powers helping to solve crimes are simply following the universe's way of redressing ill will.

## Fine tuning intuition

Throughout our lives when there is not the effort to tune into the good of the universe, the egotistical 'I' can play havoc. This is because of, as well-known psychiatrist Eric Berne has titled his book, *Games People Play*. These games which go under the names of life games, marital games, party games, sexual games, underworld games, consulting room games and good games, are all about pandering to our egos. Our disposition to play them usually develops in our formative years in the home environment. These games, which we play subconsciously, are designed to garner attention in one way or another. This may be by 'playing the part of a child' to get sympathy, to dominate or to gain control, to lead another person on, or to gain advantage, among others. Berne then goes on to discuss what he calls 'autonomy', the attainment of which is manifested by the release or recovery of three capacities: awareness, spontaneity and intimacy.

Awareness means to be fully attuned to all that is going on around you, with vivid imagery, and to enjoy the experience in its own right. It is the living in the here and now without dwelling on the past or the future. This is an intrinsic part of the growth process towards higher consciousness.

Spontaneity is about having the option, the freedom to choose and to express your feelings from the variety of options available. Importantly, it is the liberation from a compulsion to play games.

Intimacy means being spontaneous and free from egotistical game playing. It is about being totally candid and open, and living in the here and now, as a child does when free to enjoy his or her life to the full. Being intimate in this sense, along with having vivid imagery, evokes affection and positive feelings.

This autonomy is the riding in a higher plane above the mundane grayness of unfruitful game playing. It is the enjoying of life for its own sake, without being derailed by all the game playing that takes place in the everyday world of social interactions. To stay in this higher plane of experience requires your attention and discipline to recognize that games are being played. Then you should deflect them away from you so that they do not sap your energy. This requires constant alertness, tempered with an inner smile. It also requires knowing when you are being drawn into a game where someone else's ego, through game playing, is seeking to be fed by your reactiveness. Maintaining yourself in that stratosphere of alertness does have enormous rewards though, as you will to an ever greater extent be connecting with the higher vibrations of the cosmos. In the words of Berne:

> *For certain fortunate people there is something which transcends all classifications of behavior, and that is awareness; something which rises above the programming of the past, and that is spontaneity; and something that is more rewarding than games, and that is intimacy. But all three of these may be frightening and even perilous to the unprepared. Perhaps they are better off as they are, seeking their solutions in popular techniques of social interaction, such as 'togetherness'. This may mean that there is no hope for the human race, but there is hope for individual members of it.*

## Releasing fear

*Strange and terrible were the adventures they undertook with a merry heart...*
John Matthews

Fear arises out of our programming from the past, particularly arising from family scenarios where parents have also been programmed by their parents. Often this programming involves the playing of games by parents, usually without recognizing games are even being played. This often goes hand in hand with the pulling of strings. What is sad is that the growing child is then not perceptively equipped to deal with these games, but assimilates them and develops a behavioral repertoire that accepts them as the norm.

Some of these games have become the butt of humor, such as 'it were tough when I were young'. Yet many are insidious, and it requires an enormous amount of disciplined perception to recognize that these games are being played, and even more discipline to ride above them. A first step is to recognize a fear, and clearly articulate this fear to your own being. Even write it down with absolutely honesty to yourself. Then trace back to when and where the fear first developed. This recognition of a fear is an essential first step to dispelling it. A hypnotherapist can also help here.

The next step is to imagine parceling up the fear and casting it out into the cosmos for it to be dealt with. See it on its way with replacement options such as optimism and honesty, and drowning out the fear with a flood of universal love which you have been developing through awareness, spontaneity and intimacy. Enjoy being optimistic, enjoy the idea that game playing, the past, and the baseness of many social interactions can be overcome with insight and intuition. This may all sound over optimistic. If so, then start in small steps, and make a habit of flooding out fear on a regular basis. The point is that you do not think about fear, and do not even try hard to ignore it, you simply let it go, you let it drift off as 'irrelevant' and a wasting of your inner resources when you could be thinking and feeling so much more enjoyable things!

Fear, being a gray color, can be washed out with bright colors, which you can call upon to lift you up and over the base plane of game playing. Being absorbed in all the complexities and beauty of the world around helps you overcome this grayness. Being absorbed in observing pleasant and beautiful things, especially of and from nature, and feeling enthusiasm and compassion, all help overcome fears and make you alert to game playing which is often the root cause of fear. Be alert to social interactions and media influences that promote game playing, and in effect, promote fear. News media are one of the worst offenders. Although these media say that they are telling a situation as it is, the personal reality is something different. The media moguls want to stir up emotions, make us feel addicted to adverse news so that we part with our money in the future as we buy more newspapers and watch more television.

It is the complex fractal dimensions of nature and the way it is imbued with color that scrambles fear. The same goes for the white noise of crashing waves, and the melodious beauty of bird song. This is the theme of the famous book *To Kill a Mockingbird*, where the symbolism is that to destroy the beauty of nature is to lose one's integrity.

Optimism is not a naïve hope, but a willingness to fly above the realm of game playing and the ego. It is a search, a search for wonder, beauty, and glory of the cosmos. To use the analogy of a half-filled bottle, optimism is also the active intention to fill the bottle, fill it with awareness, spontaneity and intimacy. It is the holding of hands with goodness, to dispel fear, and the traveling together towards higher consciousness.

## Feeling what is right and good

Intrinsically, we have a strong sense of what is right and good. This is deep within us as uncorrupted children. There is actually a hard physical base to understanding what is right and good. As the geneticists point out, survival is about looking after those who are closely related to us, a process known as kin selection. Biologically, we will look after our children first, cousins second, and strangers last. In order to maintain those family bonds, it means that we must do what is right and good, as it leads to survival, procreation and the passing on of our genes to the next generation. This also goes hand in hand with morphic resonance, and is what biologist and creative investigator Rupert Sheldrake has described as resonances beyond space and time where 'attractors' draw the process of inheritance forward along paths called 'chreodes'.

During the process of evolution, we have been so immensely successful at procuring resources that we have virtually overrun the planet. Yet at the same time, we have been blessed with great awareness and sentience, meaning that, at least theoretically, we can understand what we are doing to the physical world on which we depend. From a sound ethical foundation, this translates into using those capabilities to ensure future survival of all on our planet.

The world has become so large and interactive that what we do in one part of the world reverberates in another, with global climate change now of major significance. We are all in it together, and the way forward is to find solutions together, to instigate policies and actions that enable survival for our descendants. While much of this is in the realms of science and policy, there must nevertheless be a sound foundation of good ethical behavior. We cannot blindly go on coercing nature at our whim without carefully working out the consequences of our actions.

The foundation for this survival into the future is the collective development of a higher consciousness, which will come about through more and more individuals finding their individual paths of enlightenment. This is a tough call, which requires great effort from many of us across the planet. Survival will come about through our continued wonder at all life, and the partaking of the joy and ecstasy of it and its connectedness.

As well as being a personal path forward, survival will be a collective one too. It will involve behavior that is right and good, which is built into us genetically and through resonance. This collective consciousness, based on our amazing sentience, will enable us to face the environmental and social challenges ahead of us, so that we are able to leave a better world for our children.

While current science has still little to say on how that conscious foundation works in practice or will play out, we know inside ourselves that solutions will be found. This will be through higher awareness, as well as good science and technology, on a sound ethical foundation and a tuning into the right morphic resonances. Yet time is short, and so it is essential that we all start on this path of love, harmony and compassion. Of course we are not so naïve as to think that all will be a utopia of cosmic pink roses, but the point is that more now than at any other time in history, it has become imperative to get on this good path. Those societies most able to do so will have the greatest chance of survival into the future.

> *And what of us, the last* unenlightened *emperors of the old guard? Do we wander gracefully down that lonely road to extinction raging against the dying of the light? Can we help the new child on his way? Can we help ourselves? And for us, what can we do? Perhaps we all too easily forget that life is a gift. The miracle is to* be alive at all. *And now we have the special privilege to be witness to the birth of a new era.*
>
> Yatri

* * *

***Tuning into your Subtle Senses*** Mysticism is about understanding more than what comes from only our basic senses. It is about tuning in to our subtle sensitivities, and unveiling some of the beautiful mysteries of the world. Mysticism is part of the appreciation of our journey to higher consciousness. Mysteries unfold when we see the white light of love after having gone through satoris where we have started to become more aware of all around us through much greater sensitivity and much greater insight. It is the joy of a dreamlike state.

To reach these higher levels is to revere, to respect, to be compassionate and to love. It is about a deep appreciation, and a welling up of beauty, where joy and enthusiasm make us smile and chuckle inside. It is all about the joy of experiencing, of overcoming the shallow feelings of just having the material. It is the tiptoeing of illumination along our spine.

Color is a fundamental part of this upwelling of beauty, as it is associated with the various chakras. These chakras are associated with having balance in our lives through two triads: yin, yang and balance, and enthusiasm, activity and love. The chakras are the interceptors of cosmic resonance, and each is associated with a particular color.

Our body can be re-aligned with the help of color therapy. Red is yang and associated with the base chakra. It resides at the bottom of the spine and enhances physical activity, vitality, motivation, stability and spontaneity. Orange is associated with the lower back and is represented by orange associated with exuberance, creativity, enthusiasm, optimism, pleasure and productivity. Yellow is around the solar plexus and is associated with joy and fun, creativity, humor and intellectual crispness. Green is associated with the heart chakra and represents balance, harmony, unequivocal love, acceptance and sociability.

Blue moves into the realms of receptive yin in the throat chakra, and indicates freshness, peace, calmness, humility and kindness. It is the giver of life. Indigo or navy blue is associated with the brow chakra of the forehead and represents peacefulness, trust, loyalty and honesty. Violet and purple are associated with the crown chakra at the top of the head and are associated with great creativity, intuition, imagination, meditation and insight into cosmic consciousness.

All these colors have counterbalancing colors, and choosing the right balance of colors is important for our well-being. The colors we wear and interact with are not just about the way we feel but also the message we wish to convey. This also applies to the two tones black and white, with black being yin, conveying the message of blending in whether physically or with the social corporate. White is yang, strong, fresh and illuminating.

In turn, gold represents arrival at a very high level of reliability, compassion, respect and understanding. As with other colors when used to excess it can have a downside, and in the case of gold, this is greed. Other colors, especially rose, beige and gray also have significance, and these as with other colors can be used to enhance our lives.

Our mind processes an enormous amount of information every second, much of which is redundant to our well-being. Often what we think is a 'sixth sense' is actually our mind making sense of more of the information than normal. This is, in effect, becoming more aware. The more relaxed we are, and in tune with our inner being and beauty, the more we are able to cue in on subtle cues in the world around us.

We can practice tuning this awareness, which is seeing without judgment. In turn, this honing of our physical awareness assists us with our development of higher consciousness. It is awareness to create awareness.

As we become more attuned to the subtle message all around

us, we come to be aware of happenings such as coincidences, and their significance. Tuning the subtle sense also helps us make better informed and rapid decisions. Usually this tuning cannot be forced. It must be left to develop through daydreaming, switching off from the chatter of monkeys in our minds, and simply tuning in to all sounds, sights, and aromas, whilst enjoying doing so.

We can clothe this developing awareness with thoughts of beauty and of love, and there will be enhancement of our becoming aware. This is being aware of nothingness, which is the being aware of everything. Remaining at peace with this awareness is our path to delicious warmth and enlightenment. For this we give thanks in prayer. We give thanks for this lovely feeling of our inner beauty which is connected with the heart of God, the resonances of no-space, no-time.

Being at one with the good resonances of the cosmos takes discipline. It means the continual dissolving of thoughts and actions arising from the ego. Our vibrational energy also increases as our inner being connects with the universe. We stay attuned by keeping our body well, our spirit uplifted and our passion and enthusiasm unwavering. During this process, we truly appreciate the colors that ebb, flow and swirl as we tune in to the red through to the purple. We feel the colors filling us with harmony and goodness.

This tuning and development of conscious awareness enables us to develop a finely honed sense of intuition, not just in terms of physical happenings, but emotional and psychological ones as well. We become able to immediately pick up and assess the games that egos play. We become able to see straight through the ego in others and what its intentions are. In response, we seek to understand, not react, and give compassion.

All the while that we are spiritually reaching out, we have no fears. This is because fear is reaction by the ego. It is darkness. Yet this darkness can be outshone through integrity and love. We can flood it with color and dreams. All the while we are feeling optimistic, which is just another word for wonder, and seeking the glory of the cosmos through increasing awareness and consciousness.

We have a good sense of what is right and good when we are children, yet seem to lose it as our ego grows in power. As we become aware again, we begin to realize the destructive and selfish behavior of the ego. We then need spiritually to grow again and to know what is lovely and beautiful.

Connecting with each other has a positive biological base in terms of co-operation for obtaining resources. In other words, when we work together sensibly, we increase our chances of survival. When engaging in this co-operative effort we also grow spiritually. It is a path for our own survival through finding love and harmony. This path is then magnified by interaction with other loving beings, leading to a more compassionate and harmonious planet.

* * *

# 11

# Finding your partner

*Stories of adventure, of magic and romance are the stuff of the Arthurian tradition.... From the complex ethic of Courtly Love, defined like a religious code, came a new attitude to women, who were no longer seen as Chattels to be bought and sold in the matrimonial market place of feudal Europe, but as potential goddesses all. This gave rise to unforgettable women such as Guinevere, Isolde, Elaine of Astolat and Dindraine, and to the legion of ladies wooed and won, rescued and Championed, by the knights who loved them.*
John Matthews

*Talking about relationships is just another way of talking about love – either love lost or love fulfilled. We can't be human alone.*
Dan Baker and Cameron Stauth

### You and your special zone

From the unromantic perspective of physics, our bodies are open systems where physical energy flows into us and out. Our body maintains its shape through agency of the genes and some other forces which are not yet understood and termed morphic resonance, which knows neither space nor time. Interestingly, our body maintains its structure and function while maintaining this through flow of energy. Yet at the same time our body is continually renewing itself with new cells and so new tissues.

In the greater scheme of things, our body and inner being are, in a way, a focal point of great complexity in the vastness of universal order. The order in and around our own structure and existence depends not only on breathing well, having a healthy diet, being compassionate, and having positive thoughts, but also maintaining a sense of harmony with all around us. We are, in effect, a marvelous center point of an enormous amount of connectedness with other people and all of nature.

Just as our body will always seek optimal conditions of warmth and comfort, our mind and feelings will find their optimal operating conditions, as long as we let them do so. What this means is that we must create the best conditions for them to thrive in a healthy way. This can be done, and will happen automatically, when we let positive energy flow, so that connectivity with all around is always maintained. This connectivity resonance is brought into being by attractors in the cosmos which are guiding life and consciousness onto a higher path. It is the nature of the universe as we know it. In fact, making a decision on making and maintaining our connectivity with resonances around us is an essential first step in finding love and harmony. In practical terms, this means maintaining a healthy physical lifestyle and freely letting love ebb and flow from us and into us.

Looking at this another way round, greed is not just about food and possessions, which inevitably leads to disharmony, it is also about feelings and thoughts. Disharmony in an existing relationship or failure to attract a partner is about being too greedy for attention and affection, and too unwilling to give out as much as you want to receive. This is because the egotistical 'I' is discordant with your inner being and its resonating beauty. So it is essential when seeking a partner, to put aside the greedy 'I' and let the natural resonance of your inner being do its natural goodness of letting love ebb and flow. When you let this happen, you will attract according to how you give in terms of thoughts, feelings and compassion. So as you attune to the resonance of cherishing, so you will be cherished. This is the intrinsic yin and yang of being, the wellspring of goodness and love, leading to a romantic relationship.

You can view this as letting natural energy flow, knowing that goodness will be there so long as you let it. Blocking that flow – and the ego is very good at it – will leave you out of harmony with the universe. So do not think "I want this or that", but rather just bypass the ego, and know that you are a special focus of good energy that will automatically resonate and connect with other sources of good energy. You can imagine this as setting up a vibration so that as you vibrate, so will a potential partner. If you are looking for a special partner, then set up a special vibration. Just let it happen, and it will.

"But what if my emanating vibrations attract the wrong person?" you may well say! You are not then thinking and feeling in the right way to attract the right person. Meanwhile, just enjoy the company of another person. Then, if after more contact, no real companionship is developing, gradually let it go, and see it as just another thread in your tapestry of life. It is about the journey as much as it is about the destination. Everyone has something to offer, and so enjoy the company according to your own time budget. If the company does not suit you, gracefully bow out, knowing that sometimes saying 'no' is inner power, and that your special zone is remaining intact.

## Going about the search

Any search must have a goal. What sort of relationship are you looking for? Is it a friendship, a companionship, or a lasting, romantic relationship? While there is the strategic search, there is also serendipity, a happy chance find. This means stepping back and deciding on what type of lifestyle you are looking for. While most rewarding experiences are based on living in the present, it is sometimes necessary to view life retrospectively. Imagine for a moment that you are 80 years old and you reflect on your life, what sort of life would have been fulfilling for you? In other words, what do you want to achieve? This is a multidimensional exercise, because there are professional goals, personal goals, physical goals (visiting another country, writing a novel, climbing a mountain) and there are family goals (enjoying a partner, having children). Then of course there is also your spiritual journey.

These goals need not be forever fixed, and happy chance occurrences may alter your course. Be attuned and ready for serendipitous events, as they can be life-changing, even though they may have occurred over just a few seconds. You may for instance accidentally bump into someone while shopping. As you are already attuned in preparation for a happy chance encounter, you respond with a lovely smile. Now your life may be taking a new direction, simply because you were all the time living in joy and constant vigilance.

These are goals about happenings, while there are also goals about feelings. There is really only one ultimate goal, and that is to be kind, and give love and compassion. There are many books devoted to influencing people, winning friends, and improving sales. There is nothing wrong with this approach but as is the case with everything in life, there is a trade-off.

Life is beset with choices, and choosing one option means compromising on another. So, if you do use contemporary techniques to achieve goals that influence how people react to, or feel about you, there will indeed be a trade-off. Unless your techniques are filled with love and compassion, and thoroughly genuine, there will always be the effect that the influenced people and the newly won friends are simply an accumulation of acquaintances. The final result may well be a happy ego but without any lasting fulfillment, nor any lasting love. This then will not lead to any real happiness, simply because this cajoling of other people is an act of taking and not one of giving. True fulfillment and finding true happiness is all about being genuine and sincere.

If your search is simply to meet people for a common interest, from yoga to tennis, and the interaction level is mutual, then the goal may be an ephemeral relationship. This may grow into one that is long lasting, which is wonderful. Nevertheless, sincerity is still the foundation on which to build the relationship. In yoga, it just feels good to share a common experience, and with tennis, a good fair challenge will inevitably lead to more good games in the future. It is great exercise too.

We are highly social beings, and in the end, we all like to have genuine friends, a warm family and a sense of wonder, as well as fulfillment in all that we do. It is just the way we are made. This then means giving out love, acting with enthusiasm, and really trying our best. Your search for a partner is firstly about having the right frame of mind, and then being in the right places, and taking the right, positive and sincere actions.

The place where you actually meet a potential partner has an enormous bearing on how the relationship will grow. Meeting at your sports club, local church, on a hike, or at a convention, immediately means that there is common ground, which may not work so well should you meet in a more arbitrary location. In short, circulate in the arenas where you are likely to meet a like-minded person, from a pilgrimage to a party.

While there are places where you are likely to meet a potential partner, but it is not really quite your comfort zone, then the spin-off may not be successful in the long term. You could take up golf, and easily meet a man at the golf club, and one who is very willing to show you the way to becoming a top player, but then, down the road, would you want to be a golf widow? This is a harsh statement, perhaps too harsh, but the point is clear. Likewise, as a man, by all means go to cooking classes, but be prepared to do the cooking in the future! The point is here that the search must be sincere.

You have now decided on your aspirations and dimensions, and you are determined to move forward with a positive frame of mind and with sincerity. You really do want to find a partner.

There are many ways of finding such a partner, the internet having become the most popular. But let's be honest, there are disadvantages with this approach. Firstly, it is all too easy to search and scroll and basically to move into the virtual world that can have little basis in reality. While some long-term romances do come from internet dating, there have been many disasters. You simply do not know who you are dealing with, and there is also little privacy.

An additional concern with the internet is that many yarns are spun in cyberspace. Fun as electronic exchange of risqué messages may be, it is not possible to sense all the subtleties that would normally occur with face-to-face interaction, such as pheromone essence, eye movement, facial expressions and body language. Reading these subtleties in a real encounter is important, as they help forge a meaningful relationship. Also, sifting through all the written messages and semi-distorted, often years-old visual images on the internet takes much perseverance and circumspection to uncover the safe and secure from the unsafe and insincere.

While there are many genuine people on internet dating, there are also many charlatans, who seem hardly to know that they are. The trouble is that the imagination does tend to go a little wild on the internet, with egos often larger than life. Yes, it is exciting to play around on dating sites, but even more than a masked party, you cannot see and sense all the subtleties that make for a lovely relationship. So inevitably, much crucial information on which you need to make a sound decision is missing. You will only find that out once you actually meet the person, literally in the flesh with their chemistry.

Another downside of internet dating is that it is often not sufficiently spatially explicit for making sound decisions. Hopes are raised that you meet someone that seems to be perfect for you in many ways, only to find that he or she lives several towns away, or even farther. This can be overcome should the motivation be there to meet, and even so when the relationship is underway. But often, the practical realities of physical distance become tormenting. Hopes are raised, and hopes are dashed. This is not a problem for a relationship that needs space, but then you would have needed to have decided that beforehand, not after.

Nevertheless, in the end, the relationship may have a future through one of you relocating, but that carries risks, which were not apparent in the earlier, long-distance phase of the romance. These seemingly important challenges with internet dating are not a reason to not use it, but just do so with circumspection and not too much optimism, at least at first. Also bear in mind that the electronic communications move much faster than good sense.

Now, being a loving person, a giving person, sincere and warm does not mean that you are also a pushover. Shrewd judgment and fair assessment of another person are essential tools in your dating kit. Bearing in mind that we process something in the order of 10 000 bits of information a second, means that you can instantly sum up another person by many telltale signs in their facial expressions and body language, as well as intonations of the spoken word. While you are giving out your love and warmth, continually process the stimuli you are receiving. Treat it as a fun exercise, with humor and a sense of adventure. Only then, with adequate information and insight, make a firm decision on whether to develop a true relationship or not.

## Striking up a conversation

> *...if you wish to overcome that feeling of isolation and loneliness... our underlying attitude makes a tremendous difference. And approaching others with the thought of compassion in your mind is the best way to do this.*
>
> HH Dalai Lama and Howard C. Cutler

Now you are about to meet someone for the first time, and this may be at a function, a party, or on a first date. First of all, consider your own image, knowing that the 5 Cs: confidence, conversation, communication, charisma, and chemistry are all vital ingredients. Be bold, alive and astute. Confidence comes from being at ease with yourself, and knowing that you are thoroughly loved – by you! This is not about being arrogant but about harnessing all your loving thoughts around the kernel of your being and radiating beauty out into the world around.

Grooming also matters, and being contemporary in dress is an essential. How fashionable you want to be is your personal choice, but do not wear anything that even hints at being old-fashioned, as this definitely puts dampers on the meeting. This does not exclude wearing clothes that you are comfortable with. Choose whatever makes you feel fresh, contemporary and confident. As you dress is as you will attract, and it matters. And always dress as if today really matters. Feel that inner glow beaming out around you. Then smile, without grinning, and hold your body high. Posture and poise: you have arrived!

Opening a conversation may seem daunting sometimes. The key here is to know that you are interesting because you keep in touch with the news, you have a wide interest in many things, you have had a shot at many activities, and of course you are a lovely person! Then just breeze into the conversation, with charisma. At this point, you switch from any thoughts of yourself to thoughts of what that other person is really interested in and what makes them tick. By all means, with a smile, just say "I'm, (your name), pleased to meet you" shaking hands in the same motion. The other person will automatically respond. If the name is an unusual one, that you do not recognize, say instantly, "That's interesting" followed by "How do you spell that?" After the details, then ask, "What is the origin of your interesting name?"

No need to ask the person 'what they do', as this often comes over as being pointed and is almost equivalent to asking how much they earn. Rather throw out conversation hooks, on which the other person can respond. Ask what their interests are, whether they have visited any interesting places recently and have they ever visited a particular place which you particularly like. Never start with a grumble, platitude or gossip about someone else, or be facetious.

Conversation is like a gentle volley, where you are passing the ball in a way that it can be passed back. And always answer with more than one sentence, all the while maintaining eye contact and nodding and making small gestures of appreciation at what the other person is saying. Even better, make the occasional empathetic remark, like: "You are making a good point there", "That's interesting!" Have intense interest in them, and do not go warbling on about yourself. Imagine the spotlight and focus is on them.

Your most valuable word during this exchange will be 'you'. Everyone loves the word, such is the power of the ego in all of us. If the other person asks about you, keep it light and fairly short, with ample opportunity for the other person to respond.

Listen carefully to what they are saying, picking up inflections and words of significance which display the person's interests. If there is a hint of a particular topic that interests you too, you are well on the way for a great interchange of thoughts and perceptions. Conversational communication automatically starts with a wide, shallow, exploratory thrust, and only after a while does it focus more on the particular, the penetrating and the personal.

You can stimulate thoughts on safe ground, such as cuisine, as we all like good food. Then let the conversation move into cooking or places of interest that have interesting cuisine. Art and artists, good books, doing yoga, going to the gym or exercising, and interesting gardens, are also easy-chat topics to get the conversational ball rolling.

This exchange chat approach is not being shallow but finding an area of comfort for both of you. It is about communicating.

Avoid bringing up a highly technical subject unless it is clear from the start that you both have an interest in, say, computer technology. Enjoy the exchange of thoughts, with a smile, and with humor to give sparkle. No heavy ideas, and no dark comments, cutting remarks or platitudes.

Just a suggestion at this point: the language we use in conversation is a remarkable give away as to our personality and inner thoughts, and how we perceive life. A listener to your conversation is absorbing and processing all those nuances of your speech, its rhythm, intonation, context, mood and indeed your whole outlook on life. Of course, you will be doing the same as a listener, and you will be combining your assessment of speech with those of expressions and body language, all with remarkable speed.

Then, positive action leads to pleasant reaction. Good language creates a good impression, positive thoughts lead to a positive reaction, and kind thoughts mean that kind thoughts will be returned. That's all well and fine, you may say, but the other person is not responding or is not being scintillating in your eyes. Then simply move on politely and gracefully, with a smile.

All interactions lead along a path of discovery, but if that path is not the one you want to be going along, and knowing your time is always precious, move on. Other interactions will then start to unfold with a sense of adventure for both, putting you on a roll. This is connecting, and this is where the 'Chemistry' part of the 5Cs starts to function. Now you are on your way, with an interaction that is bubbling along, and it is more than just an exchange of words, it is becoming an exchange of glances and subliminal messages.

## Body harmony and touch

The eye movements that you make, and those that you receive, say a lot. They communicate to a large extent what you are thinking, as well as what you are saying. The eyes are also a medium of communicating emotion. Lingering eye contact between the sexes is a very powerful message indeed, and is communicating a wish for intimacy. Being looked at in a gentle way and looking deep into the eyes of another actually does stimulate the well-being chemistry of the body. A man will directly watch a woman more than a woman will watch a man, and generally most men really enjoy any theatrical eye movements of a woman, traditionally known as coquetry. This does not mean a woman is not observing, but she is doing so in a much more passive way, using her advanced peripheral vision, and integrating a huge amount of incoming information using her subtle senses.

A woman can glance away and show her neck and ears, enhanced by earrings, and this also displays the lips in profile and a man will watch this movement instinctively. All a woman need then do is turn her gaze back to the man and smile widely looking straight into his eyes. A man will be mesmerized by this movement. Then do the same with the eyes cast down, which a man will interpret as a flirtatious move coupled with modesty. Most decent men will fall for the attractive, modest woman who engages his attention.

With eye movements, coupled with head glances, you can easily pace the development of the relationship. Furtive eye movements will continually draw a man's attention. This eye and head movement can be enhanced by hand movements as well.

Moving of the fingertips is also highly attractive to a man, as is the showing of the inside of the wrist, which, surprising as it may seem, is a very personal part of the body. It is well known as a perfume application area, and touching the inside of the wrist by another is a very personal gesture indeed, yet one of comfort and caring.

All these movements are interactive with how the man is reacting to you, and there is always a one-quarter of a second gap to change your thoughts and change your body movements.

This also means your whole body movement, including your shoulders and breasts, which are strong messengers of level of confidence and therefore of willingness to interact more closely. Never pull a cardigan (or other open-front garment) in front of the breasts on a continual basis, as this is a sign of lack of breast confidence. Either do up the cardigan or change into a top that is more enhancing of your figure.

Growing a relationship also means 'being present', where you are cultivating the here and now, as if there was no other person you would like to be with or place you would rather be. This is not being insincere or theatrical for the sake of it, but being attentively courteous. If you do not want the relationship to develop further, then enjoy the moment on its own merit. You always have the option of refusing a future date if you have decided that this is not the person for you. At least remain friends. Yet if you do want to cultivate the relationship into something more meaningful, then being present is still an important feature of the interaction, and sadly neglected in many communications. Being present is to show interest and to put aside your ego for a while, and being attentive to your potential partner.

This being present is also about interactive orbits of the physical, emotional and mental. Being present also involves, as we have seen, physical interaction such as eye interaction and confident body language. This physical orbit interplays with an emotional orbit, where you are showing some of your feelings about the world around you. This is not the same as judgment, but about saying how certain sights, sounds or actions appeal to you or excite you.

In turn, the mental orbit is about showing some acuity, humor and wit, as well as an interested knowledge of the world in general. These interacting orbits are like floating, connected bubbles of beauty and aliveness. This positive aliveness dances with your chakras and balances you inside.

Any personal interaction that is developing towards

something more meaningful and deep, involves continual engagement of the emotions. The golden rule is to stimulate *feeling*. By all means chat, but never too much, and do not undertake a marathon monologue. In your chatting, engage your partner with the occasional 'what do you *feel* about it' and 'what are your thoughts and *feelings* on it'.

Add excitement into your conversation by including some provocative remarks. All the while maintain a little mystery about yourself, but this does not mean being secretive! Nevertheless, always think in terms of making a link, developing communication and above all, creating excitement. You are metaphorically always putting out your hand, and encouraging another hand to meet yours. All the while you are also listening with an open mind, and not judging the relationship, but appreciating how well the relationship is developing, which may be just a friendship at first.

We also need to bear in mind the nuances of gender tongues. All of us, particularly in our personal interactions, load our conversations with nuances of feelings and perceptions. These are often different between men and women, and sometimes quite remarkably so. Generally, a woman's comments are more loaded than a man's. She will say "what a lovely day!" meaning "perhaps we should go out somewhere: where do you suggest?" He will hear and interpret "what a lovely day!" as a statement of fact.

So you as a woman need to be more explicit when talking to a man than you would if you were talking to another woman. A woman friend might well reply "yes it is, shall we go for a jog on the beach?" whereas a man is likely to reply simply "yes it is". This means that when you are talking to a man you must not expect him to pick up on all the nuances of your speech. You need to be more direct. Rather not say "perhaps we should just stay in this evening" when you really mean "I'd love to go out for a meal". Say instead "it's a lovely evening, why don't we go out for a meal tonight – where would you suggest we go?"

The right assessment of a relationship is about knowing where you are relative to an understanding of the layers of intimacy within relationships. Firstly, be aware that there is a superficial layer, which is one of being acquainted. This is about exchanging of pleasantries and general information, with little or no intimate communication. Then there are various more intimate layers, and it is for you to decide how deep you want to go. This is actually a decision tree with one major initial branch. Is your relationship a romantic-sexual relationship or is it about developing a good friendship, with or without good sex? We rarely seem to plan these depth levels, yet they are significant.

Most of the time, we go into a relationship blindly and without any steering. We confuse the layers and the branches of the decision tree. We often develop a romantic relationship without growing the friendship, which means that the relationship can never really grow to its full potential of exciting yet comfortable levels of joy and real happiness. In tow with a confused relationship is the continual issue of expecting too much from the relationship. The reality is that you should *not expect anything* from a relationship. A relationship with meaning and potential for growth will only take place after first you love yourself and then you *give* love to the relationship as well as to your partner. Indeed, a meaningful relationship is best viewed as life-enhancing for *both* partners, and the simple filling of a need or a gap for either.

## Growing a relationship

Growing a relationship is cultivating a relationship. This means caring all the time, not just some of the time. It is the same principle as cultivating a plant. You can cherish a plant with the right light, water and nutrients for months on end, but you cannot go on holiday and let it fend for itself: it will shrivel and die. The same goes for a good relationship, which needs continual caring for, and enlivening now and again.

This cultivation of a relationship is based on the decision you made earlier on how deep and intimate you want the relationship to go, and which decision branches you have taken. Is it just going to be a romantic, physically intimate relationship, or are you going to grow it into a friendship with passion and with long-term potential.

When it is a long-term relationship that you are looking for, then developing trust, openness and honesty is crucial. This is a two-way process where you share your inner thoughts, desires, dreams, and even anguishes. It is about togetherness where there is genuine sharing of honest thoughts, without any defensiveness, and without any manipulation or game playing. It is about continual exchange of thoughts, feelings, smiles and touches that continually build up the relationship. Seemingly little things, like holding your partner's hand or arm while walking along, even early in the relationship, is to engage, to show companionship and to show togetherness. Such initiative, to use our plant analogy, means bringing the relationship into flower.

A great deal of growing the relationship is about loving by action. Random touches, occasional and unexpected little thoughts (a small gift, a surprise night out, a surprise dinner at home by candlelight) and just spending a little time to put the spotlight of attention on your partner all count to growing a relationship. During this time, you continue to retain your integrity, applying occasional firmness and saying 'no' when appropriate.

Throughout growth of the relationship you appeal to fairness and reciprocation. You encourage connection by loving action, by making things happen. This may involve some flexibility, with occasional change of plans to suit the mood. This may mean going to see a movie rather than going out to dinner, and even doing something different that neither of you have done before, such as going ten-pin bowling, taking out a canoe or going for a picnic on top of a hill. It is about ebb and flow. Returning to our plant, if you think that you are giving your plant too much water, then let it dry out a bit, and perhaps move it to another spot in the home and see how it responds.

During the development of the relationship, you need to stay in touch, which means the occasional message with an occasional thought. And despite common misconceptions, a woman *can* take the initiative!

Yet communication is about space as well, just as a glass is about the space inside as well as its walls. No relationship grows when there is too much smothering, like overwatering your plant. And if you have not had a message back, don't nag and find fault, which has one effect: to antagonize and set back the relationship. Rather show appreciation and give thanks for what you share. Be in the driving seat and in charge of your reactions, or better, your non-reactions. Then, always maintain your integrity, and be alert to any game playing, and unfairness. Assess whether these may be stunting the relationship. If so, recognize them for what they are (the ego interfering), stay firm on your integrity, and realize perhaps, that it is as deep as the relationship can go.

We all now and again like quiet and reflection time, both women and men. For a man at least, reflection time is indeed crucial. Women need to understand this, and not to think that a man is being uncommunicative and is distancing himself from her. This is not usually the case, and a man generally does not have the same motivation as a woman to carefully chat about feelings and use personal speech. He often simply likes his space and his quiet. So rather sometimes just let that quiet reign, and rather than speak, just touch his hand or stroke his head without saying anything. When you are apart, rather send a text message than give a call. Let him do the calling. But do not expect too much as men do not call simply to stay in touch as readily as women do.

During the development of your romantic friendship, which is effectively the first step towards developing a new family, start to generate your own intimate language with your partner, which has enormous bonding power. Intimate and familiar sayings and exchanges, private only to your growing relationship, are in effect a declaration of trust and openness. This goes hand in hand with developing future dreams based on using the word 'we'. Where 'my' dreams become 'our' dreams, is a definite consolidation of the relationship towards one that lives the present moment while at the same time, is growing into one of enduring companionship and happiness.

## Physical passion

A long-term, lasting and companionable relationship has intimate, physical passion as one of its foundations. This is embracing the base chakra, and all its physical manifestation. There is though, one important feature that we so often overlook. This base chakra enlivens our minds in fact more than it does our bodies. In short, sex is at least 90 percent fantasy and just 10 percent reality. And the time we actually devote to physically having sex is less than 1 percent of our time. So why do we place so much importance on it? Sex, safe sex at least, besides being excellent for our physical well-being, is also an important trigger for right brain, creative activity. Daydreaming about sex is a highly creative and healthy pastime. It counterbalances the left brain reductionist thinking we engage in when we are being analytical and involved in our everyday activities.

A good physical relationship also triggers the whole series of biochemical activities that create an immediate sense of well-being, as well as opening up our mind and allowing cherished memories to remain with us and enliven us. Viewed this way, physical intimacy is one of the foundations of a long-lasting companionship. The biological root of this is that such a companionship is the platform for a family. This then, is the cohesion in our lives that makes life seem worthwhile, and why loneliness is so difficult to bear. We are sociable, warm, cuddly, sexy and committed beings. When we have all those things, the rest of our life largely comes together.

Yes, true, men do think a lot about sex, and do often put it in front of emotional well-being. Yet the promiscuity of men is more in their minds than an actual reality, despite what so much popular literature says. Even some social scientific studies cannot always be believed because the results are based on surveys and not on actual recording of sexual behavior. In short, men do fantasize a lot, but then so do women. The difference comes in the fundamentally different approaches to romantic love by men and women. For men, good sex comes first, and when the right partner is found, then there is emotional attachment. For women, this is generally the other way round. Good sex follows the development of emotional attachment.

Women are often dismayed and disappointed after a man has made love to them that he promptly falls asleep. This is commonplace in men, and is the result of physiological recharging, contentment and closeness to a woman, and not because he is uncaring. So, when your man falls asleep, let him be, and have a good chat with him over a meal the following day.

One last thing. Women often find it strange that men should like exotic underwear and erotic features. Many women think it is just plain silly to dress up. But that is missing the point. A man is sexually programmed for change and variety. This is what, quite simply, turns him on. Sameness dulls a man's sexual urge, which is why some men are aroused by their partner just changing hairstyle or wearing a wig. To keep your man really interested, embrace change in how you look, particularly in the bedroom. This is not all one way, as we discuss what men should do in the next chapter.

## When it does not go as well as you thought it would

Not that we wish to entertain negative thoughts, but break-up of a relationship has happened to us all at some time. This is the bittersweet of life itself.

The most important starting point now is to bear in mind that you are the most important person in the world. This 'you' is not your ego, but your inner being. This means that the first thing to do is to really make the effort to harness your thoughts and feelings and at least try to send out loving thoughts, no matter how hard this may seem. This is not to treat yourself as if you were something separate in the world, but having connectedness with all around you.

Now, the next thing to do is to summon all your three Resourceful Cs: courage, courage, courage. There is a whole world out there, and several million other potential partners which is a constructive starting point for moving on. For now, keep that as a vague dream on the horizon. First of all, you need to let go, and let go of all angst and anger, all thought obsessions and all thoughts of feeling sorry for yourself. Such negativisms only beget more negativisms, and all it does is chew up your own physiology and well-being. Of course it is not easy just to let go. But you must. Be brave, have courage!

This is the time to put aside reactivity and bring in proactivity. This means doing things you enjoy, and strange as it may seem, doing things for other people. Give some thoughts and little attentions to those in your family, and to your closest friends. Feel love and kindness, and let it automatically dispel any feeling of fear for the future or of bleakness.

There is always hope for the future. Review your strengths and values, and enjoy the various cameos of the present moment. Be aware, simply aware. Then put these strengths and values side by side with your courage, and determine to move on and upwards with growth and with an increasing zest for life. You have heaps of choices before you, and you have optimism, because you have decided that you are a very special person that *will* find love, which is inevitable because you are giving out love.

In your mind, you create possibilities for new options, even if this means spending some time healing yourself first. It is the moment to have positive, sincere thoughts, to seek solutions and to develop a strategy. On your foundation of love emanating from your inner being, and with courage and determination, you make a point of really appreciating all around you. You practice loving the world and all its possibilities. The more you appreciate, the more your fears and sense of loneliness will disappear. You are growing and gaining in inner strength. Beauty and wisdom is growing within you, and one loss is now becoming an important gain in spiritual growth where you feel your heart is glowing again.

These are not abstract thoughts, because unhappiness is a question of wrong perceptions and misguided reactions. Unhappiness is not a 'thing' in its own right, but a disposition. So now is your opportunity for growth. This will come through a change in perception and reaction, from one of unhappiness to one of happiness. During this process there has to be not one iota of regret or indecision. You are now going to make your life happen!

* * *

***Finding your Partner*** Physical energy flows freely through our bodies, which meanwhile maintain their form through morphic resonance despite continual renewal of cells. Maintaining that form in top condition is helped by having a healthy diet, exercising, being compassionate, having positive thoughts, and having harmony with all around us.

Our bodies will always seek optimal conditions of warmth and comfort, and our minds and feelings seek balance and love.

This spiritual balance is enhanced by the resonance from our inner being, and to which we need to practice becoming attuned, through thoughts and acts of giving and of compassion.

When we let positive energy flow, and we let go of any disharmonious thoughts and feelings, we begin to radiate love. We also automatically vibrate with those around us, attracting a partner that resonates with those vibrations. We then need to assess whether there is a romantic future with this partner. If not, that is fine, and we call upon our power of 'no', release the potential relationship, and seek another. All the while, we never create any bad feelings, thoughts or vibrations. One can always remain friends.

We have professional goals and family goals, and being attuned to our inner being means being aware of new happenings that enables us to grow spiritually. All the time, we continue to maintain our integrity of giving out love, compassion and kindness. We always think positively, but do so with sincerity and humility.

On a practical level, a potential partner often flows to us when there are common interests and when circulating in similar circles. This is simply an alignment of how we perceive and respond to the world around us. This can become important in the long term as there is much in common. If we really like the outdoors, it makes sense to seek a partner who likes that too. Where there are differences, these must be openly discussed early in the relationship so as to forestall any misunderstandings later on.

Internet dating is exciting because the ego is boosted. This is partly because it appears as if many potential partners are interested in us. In reality, it is highly filtered communication because we cannot assess subtleties of personality, body language, facial expressions and skin aromas. Internet dating is often not spatially explicit, with a message theoretically able to come from anywhere, and from anyone. Of course it sometimes works out, but often the reality is different. Nevertheless, if you are motivated, you may be fortunate and resonate in ways to attract the right partner.

Being a loving, warm and sincere person does not mean being a pushover. It is essential that we process all the subtleties of a potential partner, all their facial expressions, their thought processes, their aromas, and assess the extent to which it is their ego speaking.

Now we are about to meet someone on a first date, knowing that the 5 Cs, confidence, conversation, communication, charisma and chemistry are what we are radiating and also looking for. We also aim to feel exciting too, to emphasize our good health and disposition. We combine these Cs with the two Ps, posture and poise, the right body language for initiating a relationship.

Starting a conversation means turning off the ego, literally your 'I', as no one is particularly interested in it anyway. We are contemporary with the news, and we have some ideas about the world. We throw out conversation hooks, on subjects which are likely to be of general and mutual interest, such as food choices, lifestyle, travel destinations and perceptions on the natural world, as these are topics that most people can relate to.

We then stimulate a volley of conversation, always acknowledging the other person's remarks. Conversational communication starts with a wide exploratory thrust, only focusing down to the particular, the penetrating and the personal once the conversational exchanges are beginning to make both potential partners glow. Genuine smiles, warm facial expressions and eye contact are essential.

We aim to treat the whole exercise as simply enjoyable, with no expectations. We are living for that instant and enjoying the presence of someone new in our life. We also aim to be sincere and honest, in control, and aware that our inner being is our spiritual guide.

Eye contact in all its various nuances is such a meaningful way to communicate. A man derives enormous pleasure from watching a woman's eye movements and her expressions. All the while he is also taking in the head movements and the smile. While a man thinks he is in control with a conversational exchange, actually it is usually the woman who is.

A woman's body movements from neck, to wrists, to fingertips, are immensely engaging for a man. A woman will also have a man's attention when she is attentively courteous, with sincerity. Combining these displays with acuity, humor and wit, means being alive, and being immensely attractive.

Developing a romantic relationship with a good base involves stimulating feeling and not just thoughts. This is particularly so for a man when relating to a woman. It is essential to know how your potential partner is *feeling*. This exploration of feeling is also a way of bringing into alignment the vibrations of both partner's inner beings. If this new association only leads to a friendship that is fine, but of course if it leads to a beautiful romance then that is wonderful!

Men and women need to understand that conversation is more direct for a man than for a woman. Also, a woman needs to be understood in terms of how she *feels*. As this is often difficult for men to grasp, a woman needs to be much more explicit in her conversation with a man than she would be with a woman. The different ways of expressing thoughts and feelings by the two sexes is known as gender tongues, and as a consequence, there must be gender ears, which means being able to listen and interpret a potential or actual partner's thoughts and feelings.

Only with this good communication, which is about touch as well as voice and expressions, can a strong romantic relationship really grow. To ensure this growth requires cherishing. Cherishing moments, cherishing even the smallest of exchanges, and reassuring your partner that all is well. It is about sharing thoughts, desires, dreams and even anguishes. All this requires openness and honesty. The growing of a relationship is about reciprocal stroking, without letting the egos interfere. It is enjoying the ebb and flow of thoughts, feelings and touches, coming from your inner beings.

A woman can take the initiative as much as a man with little gestures and ideas. All the while we are in control because we are thinking about true love and giving thanks for what we are sharing. Finding love and harmony is about cultivating the relationship, and just letting it unfold without adverse nibbles from the ego.

As a glass is about the space as much as the form, so it is for a relationship. To grow there must be space. We all need this as by nature we are reflective beings. As part of letting your mutual dreams unfold, you begin to use language that uses the words 'we' and 'our', as well as special and personal expressions, so as to affirm solidarity.

Sex is essentially 90 percent fantasy and 10 percent reality, but nevertheless fundamental to enlivening our base chakra. Sex is a creative and healthy activity that triggers a whole host of biochemical activities that open the mind and lay the foundation for long-lasting companionship, and eventually family. It is the gateway to social cohesion, as we are essentially sociable, warm, cuddly, sexy and committed beings.

The way through this gateway is often different for men than women. Most men see sex as a step to emotional commitment, while women see emotional commitment as a step to sex. Understanding these subtle differences is important for both genders, with a man needing to reinforce the commitment by ongoing gestures and attentions, and a woman providing variety in the way she looks. This is not shallow. Rather it is recognizing our basic biology which is the physical platform for growth in spirituality.

Should a romantic relationship not work out, then all we need to know is that we are special. We summon our three Resourceful Cs: courage, courage, courage. No need at all to beat ourselves up over a break-up, as that would be the ego in full sail. It is time to reflect, not dwell, and to know that there will always be new possibilities. This is because we are well connected with our inner being, its beauty and its resonance. We also are aware of and appreciate all around us. We seek a solution, we give out love, we let go, and we move on. New adventures await us.

* * *

# 12

# For men only

## It is ok: we *are* biologically different!

Men have evolved as the hunting, protecting, territory-gaining sex. This is complementary to the food-gathering, nurturing and child-bearing woman. For millennia upon millennia, both sexes have had their well-defined roles, based on a fundamental biology that is very much with us today, despite issues of political correctness and equality. In the past, men scanned the horizon, planned the hunt and relied on understanding the landscape so as to be successful in procuring protein. They also watched out for competitive bands of hunters, and wife-snatchers. This all required a high level of testosterone for visual and mental focus, aligned with a good sense of spatial orientation.

In contrast, women, with low levels of testosterone but high levels of estrogen, evolved to engage in intimate communication and create harmony within and surrounding the family group. The emphasis here is on family, because it is with family members that we share the greatest genetic connection, and are therefore most motivated to protect.

The high testosterone in men means that they are also driven by sex, with many men thinking of sex on a regular basis, in some cases, every few seconds. Yet sex is not highest on their list of priorities in life, with less than 1 percent saying that it is. Translating this into the sex/love relationship, means that men find romantic love arising out of sex, while for a woman, sex comes mostly after some emotional bond has been formed. Men generally do not understand this; simply because they are not biologically programmed to do so. For a man to find long-lasting happiness in a romantic relationship in today's world, he must make the effort to develop sensitivity as to how a woman deeply functions biologically.

We are missing so much of the biological plot today by pretending that the sexes are the same, when they are not, and this difference is hard-wired in our bodies. Women have much more cross-over of the right and left hemispheres of the brain, which provides much more flexibility in behavior. This is why women can multitask so much better than men. Women can listen and talk at the same time, and do it so much better than men.

Men prefer to focus on one thing at a time and provide solutions to challenges and problems. Men like to think things through on their own and come to conclusions for their own and their family's benefit. During this mental processing, a man generally needs either peace and quiet or a distraction like watching or doing a sport, tinkering with something mechanical, or watching television.

In contrast, a woman likes to talk things through, to verbalize, without necessarily being given the interruptive solutions from a man. She likes to share these thoughts with other women, as shown by over four-fifths of women saying that their best friend is another woman. Women easily form bonds of friendship with other women, often through chatting and listening to each other all at the same time, on a whole variety of sometimes disparate subjects.

Men, in contrast, usually only connect with another man when undertaking a task. Often this bonding is without any verbal communication, as in golf or fishing. Bonding for men is about engaging in an activity, and sharing the experience rather than talking through issues. What this means is that for a man to bond with a woman, he must put aside his intrinsic verbal solitariness and spend time listening to a woman.

Men must constantly bear in mind that women are free-thinking, sensitive and highly intuitive beings, whose brains are processing a huge amount of relationship information. A woman will be chatting yet at the same time taking in a whole range of details in the immediate environment, from noticing a man's fingernails, his sense of color coordination, and all the subtleties of his facial expressions and body language. In addition, women will be absorbing and processing all the changes in voice intonation, body reflexes and emotional feelings within an interpersonal interaction. While sitting in a restaurant, a woman will know who else is in the room, and what their relationships are with each other. This is all possible because a woman's peripheral vision and creative thought processing is so much better than that of a man. Men just don't see all these subtleties of interaction because they are hard-wired to focus on the task at hand, which is usually seduction.

Men need to know that women are not actually objects just to be grabbed and hauled into the cave at the whim of testosterone. A man often thinks that he is making so much progress with his seduction, and that the woman is being charmed by his advances. The reality is very different, with the woman's creative thoughts, acute sensitivity to sounds, body scents and body language meaning that actually she is far ahead of him in the game! Even a kiss, which to a man is largely a step in the process of seduction, for a woman has much meaning, and she can assess a man's health and level of commitment in it.

## What women really want

So why then do women spend time with a man, knowing that he is mostly wanting sex and he is oblivious to the fact that she is ahead of him at every move? Firstly, she is being given undivided attention, and secondly, she is assessing him to see whether he is trustworthy and whether he might take her into a meaningful and long-term relationship.

There are three things that women want above all else: to be noticed, to be cherished, and made to feel special. Women are, by definition, the decorative gender, and by far the softer one, the fairer one. The female psyche is built on being seen and admired, recognized for worth, and to be cherished accordingly. For some women, this is about being cared for, but not smothered. For others, it is about being respected, but with warmth.

A woman's ego is closer to herself than that of a man's. A woman will think of her looks, her bearing, her interactions, and her immediate environment. Her name is vitally important: forget a woman's name and a man is doomed. A man, in contrast, will think of his position (career), possessions, his territories, his dominance. Yet both genders, in the end, want to leave a genetic legacy of children. Despite what women often think – that a man's penis is on his forehead – most reasonably balanced men do want to settle down and have a family. Yet this is intimately tied in with most men also wanting a career. This is because a career also means security for his family. The career represents the ongoing successful hunt, the bringing in of complementary nutrients alongside those harvested in fruit by women.

Seeing that both men and women want to procreate, have security, well-being and happiness, makes it seem remarkable that men and women come together in the first place, given their substantially different agendas. Nature has devised a powerful plan to deal with this. This is the cocktail of chemicals that we call falling in love. A man initially reacts to a woman through his visual senses. He is drawn to her shape, her looks, her grooming.

Yes, men do notice how a woman presents herself, and how she is perfumed (which includes her natural aromas), and much more than a woman thinks he does! He instantly notices the sparkle in her eyes, shininess of her hair, and whiteness of her teeth, simply because these are a sign of state of health, of vigor, and of strength of her immune system. This all adds up to the subconscious assessment of the value of a woman as a potential mother of his children.

Many women tend to think that all men want is sex from a

skinny woman. This simply is not true, as it goes against all the fundamental survival issues surrounding the having of children and surviving lean times, something we have forgotten about in this modern prosperous era. Men see, albeit without realizing it, the circumference ratio of waist to hip, with 70 percent being highly attractive, as it indicates good health and fertility. Women instinctively know this and emphasize it with clothes tight around the waist and hips. For most men, it is not an issue of an extra pound or two but of the ratio.

It is during this initial phase of a relationship that a man instinctively puts all his focus on seduction and re-seduction. Also during this time, a woman has assessed whether this is a worthy partner to make love to in the first place. In recent times this has all changed, and there is often much more freedom of choice than in the past. It is during this time too, that a woman will sense a man's degree of commitment, and if it is not there on his part, she may well end the relationship. More than three-quarters of all break-ups are initiated by the woman.

After the initial phase of attraction and physical intimacy, there is then the 'in love' or infatuation stage, with health, immune system and alertness all functioning optimally. This is all due to a change in the body's biochemistry, promoting conception and, at least before contraception, healthy growth of the fetus. This is such a powerful phase, that societies have in place many conventions, the modern form of which is marriage, to ensure that this enormously powerful magnetism leads to long-term security for the woman and potential child.

Nature has made this 'in love' phase last up to a year, during which time, more attachment and commitment develops. If the woman feels she is not getting that commitment, there is a high chance that she will end the relationship. This is natural, because biologically, the woman selects the man, despite men generally thinking to the contrary! A man must realize that a woman must be cherished, adored, complimented, spoiled, looked after, stimulated to laugh, listened to, attended to, excited, treated with respect and care, indulged, and given passion.

## Wooing a woman

In this age of so much self-conscious anti-sexism, there has been a tendency in some quarters to portray men not just as sex-driven automats, but also as virtual morons at the same time. While indeed this may be true of some men, it is not at all true of most. Strange as it may seem to some women, there are some decent men out there!

Courting a woman now seems to be out of fashion. This has probably come about through a combination of factors, from women having greater liberalness, ready availability of contraception, and a faster pace of life. There is pressure on men too. With this new, fast lifestyle, a man may well feel he is considered odd or slow if he does not make sexual advances within the first few dates. Yet a lot of the real joy in life is about savoring the journey as much as seeing the arrival. What men really do not understand today is that women love to be wooed… cherished, adored, complimented… Wooing is style, and it can lead to a wonderful relationship. But first, a man needs to be able to understand the needs of a woman, knowing that underneath, her biology is as traditional as it has ever been.

Commitment to a relationship by a man is something that requires a great deal of working through. This is because that once there is romantic commitment, there is also substantial financial commitment, especially of course where the man is the sole provider. This may not be the case, but a man has to build this into his contingency plan, because, as a matter of self-esteem, he would want the best for his long-term partner or wife.

Yet there can be a disconnection between a man's basic biology and the inherent risks of a commitment. As a man is driven on by testosterone, it is simply natural to him to seek sex whenever he can with a willing and, to him, attractive potential partner. This may happen even though he is emotionally involved with a steady partner. The reason for this is that a man often separates sex from love and will readily chase a woman at the first opportunity. This is a totally foreign concept to a woman who sees sex as a result of emotional bonding, not as something completely separate. Indeed, many relationships break up, on the woman's part, simply because a man is flirting with another woman. Yet this is what a man is hormonally programmed to do.

So a man has to be really sure, as much as a woman does, that the woman he is getting involved with is as sincere as she appears. The problem is that men are not very good at picking up subtle cues and the telltale signs. One of the most revealing of all signals given out by a woman is how she wears the rings on her fingers. The point is that a woman views her hands as very special, as indeed they are, as they indicate dexterity, health, and wealth. This is not pure material wealth as a man sees it, but as a sign of how much she is, or made to feel, special.

## Reading the rings

The type, array, or even absence, of rings on a woman's hands in public is a strong message about how she feels about herself and her romantic relationships. This is because her fingers are a highly sensitive part of her body, and highly visible, and therefore a major connection between a woman's inner feelings and her outer world. The fingers also reflect the various chakras in the body, which are associated with harmonizing the body.

We first need to standardize, and for this we will make the ring finger (second finger in from the outside) on the left hand the commitment finger to a long-term relationship, which today we call marriage, and signified by a traditional wedding band or engagement ring. A single ring on this finger is an emotional and physical commitment to a long-term relationship. This does not necessarily mean that there will always be a total commitment to fidelity though, with an affair possible in the future. Yet maintaining a ring on this finger indicates an emotional relationship with her husband. A double ring on this finger means a commitment in the strongest sense, and a woman with such a ring array is totally committed to her husband, so long as both rings stay on in public.

A single simple ring, which is not a wedding band, on the ring finger of the left hand is usually indicative of a woman that is not in the first instance encouraging a relationship, but should the right man come along, may well do so. Such a woman needs careful courting if there is a strong attraction. Yet contrary as it may seem, this ring array may not mean that she wishes to marry.

Sometimes there is a single large ring (often with a large stone) on this ring finger which is not a simple wedding band. Usually this signifies commitment to another cause, especially a religious one, with for example, a commitment to Jesus, in addition, perhaps or perhaps not, also to a commitment to a husband.

When there is a single ring on the ring finger of the opposite hand for our purposes i.e. on the *right* hand, the message here is that a woman would dearly love to have a committed romantic relationship.

Where there is a ring on each of the ring fingers of both the left and right hands, then the message is one of commitment to a partner or husband, but also seeking romance. Husbands and lovers should be attentive to such a woman, as an affair is likely if she is not given special and relatively continuous romantic attention. This is not a certainty, but this is the *message* being conveyed.

A ring on the middle finger of either hand indicates sensuality, especially when the ring is eye-catching. Such women often enjoy physical sensuality and may have a passionate or high sex drive. A ring on both middle fingers (i.e. both hands) without any on the left or right ring fingers indicates great sensuality combined with independence. Such a woman often also has sensuous lips. When there is a ring on the middle finger and another on the ring finger, the message is one of a highly sensuous, yet committed relationship.

A ring on the middle finger of either hand and adjacent to a ring on the ring finger of the right (non-marriage in our case here) hand suggests a willingness to commit to a highly sensuous, long-term relationship. For a testosterone-rich man seeking a long-term partner, this is a woman to court.

The index finger is for pointing. A ring on this finger signifies authority, strength, precision, and non-negotiation. The indication here, especially when just on this finger of either hand, is that there is likely to be little warm soft tenderness in the relationship, with the woman not likely to be ultra-feminine. This does not mean that the woman is without sensuality, but that the priorities are different. Such a woman may well be a good companion for many men who like precision and social activities such as shooting, golf or tennis.

Traditionally, a ring on the little finger is an expression of established power and authority. This is especially so when the ring is mounted with a large stone. A ring on this finger usually means that she likes to be in charge, maybe not of a large corporation, but certainly perceived power in one form or another.

When a ring on the little finger is combined with a wedding band on the left hand, the message given out is one of power over others, especially other women, through her link to her husband.

The message conveyed by ring on the thumb is one of extroversion, and of being little phased by the opinions of others. As the thumb is the main digit of grip, the message is also one of physical strength and a touch of higher than normal testosterone, with a strong sex drive which may or may not involve emotion.

No rings at all on a woman's hands, as seen in public, conveys a strong message of independence and self-sufficiency. Such a woman is likely to carry on her life regardless of a man's overtures, although this does not necessarily exclude commitment should the perceived right man come along. Women with no ring adornment usually feel comfortable about their selves, and are often sincere and intelligent. Lack of ring adornment is becoming increasingly common as more and more women enter the professional market place.

There are various other combinations of rings, although the message generally is a mix of those given out by the individual placements on the fingers. Then there are some women who wear rings on every finger, which at first sight seems like plain extroversion, but in reality often indicates insecurity. Overly bold wedding rings, beyond the traditional simple wedding band, usually indicates emotional insecurity, with security coming from the marriage.

Toe rings are also strong messengers, particularly of sensuality and a love of physical romance. In a way, they are in lieu of high heels as the two often cannot be worn at the same time for practical reasons.

One note of warning to you men! If you quiz a woman on why she is wearing a particular ring on a particular finger (aside from a wedding band), you will likely be told it originally belonged to a deceased relative or it was a gift from a friend, and there has not been time to have it re-fitted to preferred finger. Hmmm!

## Messages from other jewelry

A woman's skin is remarkably more sensitive than that of a man's. Jewelry touches the skin and is, by definition, highly personal. Yet jewelry is not necessarily comfortable, with many cultures engaging in extreme beautification activities from neck extension rings among Karo women of Asia to the lip enlargements of the Makonde women of East Africa.

The first and most powerful message-giver, aside from finger and toe rings, is earrings. Men hardly notice them, yet the messages being conveyed by a woman are enormously strong yet sensitive. The reason for this is that the ear lobes are very personal and highly erogenous. Besides being highly sensitive as a local area, they are close to the neck, with a woman's neck also conveying a strong sensual message, which in turn draws the eyes to the breasts. Earrings and, in turn, necklaces, complete the portrait of a woman's being and her sensuality. This is why perfume is applied to the neck and cleavage, both of which are warm and eye-catching. The aroma adds another dimension to the visual attractiveness.

Large earrings denote bearing. This is because it is not easy to engage in physical activities with earrings dangling and swaying, and so such earrings convey the message of being comfortable in a still position. This does not mean that such a woman is never active, and, on the contrary, it often implies a person with a good balance between activities such as gym or tennis (without the earrings) and comfortable confidence in a physically passive role.

Large, round earrings, often as a ring for lightness, imply sensuality in accordance with their curviness. They take the eye on a tour of the cheeks, eyes, neck and breasts. Large, pendulous earrings imply power and dominance because they are taking the movement of the eye away from the neck and breasts and point straight down. Formal, royal jewelry is usually of the large, dangling type.

Small, point-type earrings, whether pearl, precious metal or colored stone imply some sensuality. Yet such earrings are not bold and do not take the eye to the neck or on a tour of the upper body. They imply more modesty and generally less overt body awareness than large earrings. In a way, they imply simply being fully dressed. Large, point-type earrings usually indicate enjoyment of a power position. Interestingly, such women often also drive powerful cars.

Necklaces also convey strong messages, with a tendency for status to be attached to the type and financial worth of the necklace. Yet that aside, there are still messages being given out by the type of necklace, especially in relation to other jewelry and the extent to which the skin is bared.

A necklace with décolletage draws the eye to the breasts, but this is not by any means an overly sexual message. The necklace is drawing the eye to the center of a woman's being, her heart. A necklace is about her person, her being. It is representative of balance and harmony, deep feelings of love, acceptance, sociability and goodness. This is why a necklace is often worn over a turtle neck jersey, and why necklaces often bear a religious symbol such as a cross. Unless ostentatious to convey power, they are usually relatively simple with a repeat pattern of a chain or a string of pearls signifying yin.

Short necklaces on the breastbone and close to the fonticulus (the scoop at the base of the throat between the collar bones) send out the message of peace and calm, freshness and warmth, with a hint of liking strong passion at times.

An ankle chain is something different altogether, and as a woman's foot is very sensitive and loves to be kissed, it implies a highly physical woman, and one who has no wish to be dominant. With pretty shoes and elegantly treated toenails, an ankle chain is one of the most eye-catching and sexually attractive adornments a woman can wear.

## Fallacy of the fantasy of being single

There are so many misconceptions of the success or not of relationships in the wider world that one sometimes wonders how all the complexity of romantic relationships work out. First of all, let's be clear: a woman is primarily thinking about looking good, feeling special, being truly loved and having security. This is the case for all ages, and has been the case for all time. For men, there are changes that take place with age. Yes, true, young men are driven by their testosterone, and the physical look of a woman, with her pheromones then driving him to distraction. But as a man matures, while the sex drive may still be strong, there is much more of a need to have a family base.

Despite what many women think, most well-balanced heterosexual men do like to have a female companion, and a sense of family. Yet many men who are in this position think that the ideal is to be free, have a sports car and a flock of women. The evidence however, points to this being a fantasy rather than reality. Unless a man is a confirmed bachelor, gay, or really is a playboy, most men when they are single, whether a widower or divorcee, will soon settle down with a new woman companion that he finds attractive and who engages his attention.

While a man in the workplace or sports club may enjoy the company of other males, when at home, he generally really needs a woman at his side. This means that a slightly more mature, well-adjusted single man will not be on the market for a partner for very long, as the drive to find a partner is so strong. This is the time for a woman to take the initiative over a man that appeals to her, because if she doesn't, another will. It is the nature of things.

## Understanding a woman

"Impossible" you may say! Maybe – simply because the gender tongues are so different, stemming from the way that brains of men and women are hard-wired. Although women talk a lot about feelings, they are also summing up relationships a great deal more than is a man. This means that to understand a woman is to listen, acknowledge and not immediately offer too much in the way of solid recommendations as you would to a man.

A woman must be appreciated, which means being patient, courteous, attentive and empathetic. By all means intersperse a conversation with a woman inclusive of wit, humor, reliability and firmness. But it is critical to read the gender tongue with perspicacity so that you can interpret what is really being said, or at least implied. When a woman says she likes a man who can be trusted, this means not so much trust with the family jewels, but a warning not to flirt with another woman.

All suggestions must be made with that added sensitivity that is not usually necessary to employ when speaking to another man. You need to temper suggestions with a genuine sense of communication, which means linking with all facets of woman's personality. However, this changes a little throughout the month with the changing hormone levels.

In a conversation with a woman, there must be that little extra giving of yourself and this is best done with some physical touch at the same time: an arm around the waist, touching her hand with your fingertip and even caressing her cheeks and hair. All the while you must engage her eyes as well. If you make her feel special, a woman will naturally respond and make you feel fulfilled too.

Remember too, women like pretty things, and you are not pretty. Yet women also like the security and solidness of a man. So, by all means be a real solid man, but for the special woman in your life, you also need to be highly sensitive to her needs. This also means giving little things as well as attentions, some flowers, some perfume, a surprise. There is nothing devious in this, as it stems from our fundamental courtship biology, and known as sexual appeasement. The man enjoys the giving, and the woman the receiving.

Kissing is a highly personal activity, and extremely important to a woman. Done well, it is a vitally important part of any budding relationship. Men so rarely realize this. The lips and tongue are richly endowed with sensitive nerve endings, meaning that the activity of kissing leads to powerful sensations, and triggers the imagination.

Kissing also boosts the pulse rate, increases blood pressure, deepens breathing and dilates the pupils. These are powerful responses in both partners, and they are also powerful releasers in your partner, so there is a positive feedback cycle. A woman kisses not just because it feels good, but also because it supplies her with much information, contained in the saliva. The way a man kisses also coveys crucial indicators about aspects of personality, genetic vitality and level of health. A man can also sense a woman's well-being, as well as the time during her menstrual cycle by her kiss.

A first kiss is an important romantic activity. It must be done well. As sexologist Helen Fisher puts it, a good kiss must be tender, passionate and considerate to assess whether a partner is a potential partner and eventually co-parent. Two-thirds of women ended a relationship after the first kiss, which as Fisher says, turned out to be the kiss of death. So, if there is a woman that really appeals to you, kiss her beautifully, first time and every time.

## A bit of the beast

So, you have been a thorough gentleman and your woman feels secure and loved, but you can sense that a little something is being required of you. This may be a bit of the beast, and it is more likely to occur at ovulation, half way through the monthly cycle, when her testosterone levels are slightly higher than their normal low levels. Some women, some of the time, do like to be loved a little more fiercely at times.

This is not a sexist view, but one based on fundamental biology in a social context. Before the industrialized society overwhelmed many cultures, there were often tribal rivalries. The indications are that this is likely to have been taking place over many thousands of years. During these times, it was not unusual for women to be captured from rival clans and taken back as prizes. This would also have genetic advantage, as it would increase genetic vigor through outbreeding.

During these times, there would also have been strong natural selection pressure for neoteny, for physical features that have childlike and non-manlike manifestations, such as proportionately small shoulders, large eyes, soft and smooth skin, and importantly, a relatively weak physical power compared to the man. In such situations, for survival, a woman would have to be remarkably resilient to such activities if she were to survive, especially with a child in her new tribe. This would suggest that deep down some women at least have a deep resilience that translates into excitement at being so desired. Base as this may seem, it was probably a reality for a long period of time prior to our modern, more genteel ways.

What this means is that there are times, within a secure and loving relationship, and at the right time of the month, that a woman really does like to be treated with strong muscular action and passion. It is a desire for true manliness, of muscle and chin. This does not at all mean that there must be any unkindness or cruelty. Quite the opposite, it means firm demonstrativeness, followed by attentiveness. Strong love followed by quiescence.

* * *

***For Men only*** Men are the hunting, protecting, territory-gaining sex, and strong on yang. This is complementary to the food-gathering, nurturing, children-bearing woman, who is warm on yin. These differences are nothing to do with political correctness and equality, but our biology honed by millennia of natural selection. Men essentially scan the horizon, hunt together and procure protein, while all the time watching for competitive hunters and potential wife-snatchers. This goes hand in hand with high levels of testosterone and straight-forward focus. Women also have testosterone, but low levels, and high levels of estrogen, associated with intimate communication, family cohesion and harmony.

While men think a lot about sex, in reality issues of territoriality such as career, are top of their priority list. Sex is a means of forming a stable emotional relationship. To find such a relationship means understanding how a woman ticks. This implies appreciating a woman's ability to think of several things at the same time and to be able to multitask.

While a man likes to quietly plan, a woman likes to chat and plan. For a romantic relationship to come together, this means letting a woman talk with the man listening. This is how the sexes bond, with the woman alert to so many subtleties of personal behavior, using remarkable peripheral vision and compassionate thinking.

A man meanwhile, when not focusing on his hunting career, is hard-wired to thinking of seduction. Yet the woman is usually far ahead of him in all the nuances of the gender interaction, and generally knows the man's next move. Nevertheless, a man needs to know that a woman needs to know that she is being given undivided attention and respect. In short, women above all, want to be noticed, cherished and made to feel special. This is why a woman is so beautiful.

A man also needs to recognize that a woman's ego is closer to her than is his to him. A woman is all the time fully aware of her body and looks, while a man is thinking more distantly, at his position, territories, and possessions, especially his toys. Yet a well-balanced man usually does want to settle down, have a career and have a family, because that is how he is programmed.

The remarkable way nature has enabled women and men to come together for a meaningful relationship is due to the cocktail of chemicals associated with what we call falling in love. A man is drawn to a woman because of her shape, her appearance, her grooming, and not because, as a lot of women think, she is easy prey. Nor, as most women seem to think, that a man is only interested in a skinny woman. The real attractor is the waist to hips ratio which ideally should be 70 percent, with no worries about the extra pound or two.

Men need to understand that a woman is weighing up a relationship all the time, while he is often only thinking about the enjoyable side. If a man does not shape up in terms of commitment, trustworthiness and honor, his chances are slim, with three-quarters of all relationships being ended by the woman. Not that a woman does not like fun, and she does like a man with a good sense of humor, but also a low sense of vanity, and who is strong on commitment.

A man needs to know that a woman likes to be courted, which means being wooed in style, even if it does sound old-fashioned. That is the way it is. While a woman is seeing the romance, a man is weighing up the financial commitment, his ability to bring in sufficient mammoth for the future whole family.

His testosterone is often to blame for misunderstandings, because in time, he is looking for variety and a flirt. While seemingly innocuous to him, a flirt is a serious violation of the relationship in the eyes of a woman. A woman needs to be sure of her security, and she can assure this in part by keeping the sensual side of the relationship alive with variety.

A woman's hands are enormously special to her. It is really strange that men generally do not know how to read a woman's hands despite the fact that she is giving out messages loud and clear. Positioning of the rings on a woman's hands is a powerful message as to who she is and the nature of her aspirations.

A man needs to practice reading the rings beyond the simple seeing whether she is wearing a wedding band and whether she is sexually available or not. Similar messages come from other jewelry as well, especially earrings and necklaces. A man must learn to read these as well as the rings. Notice too how the nails are groomed, both on the fingers and on the toes.

It is a fallacy that men really like to be single, free and play the field. Strange as it may seem for many women, and even for some men, this is not really what most men are seeking. True, a man likes to have a high disposable income to buy big toys. Nevertheless, most decent and well-balanced men will not be on the open market for long. This means that it is essential for a woman also to take the initiative, knowing all the while that she is whole inside and on a spiritual as well as a romantic path.

A woman must be understood, which means being appreciated. A man must listen to what she has to say, as a woman's words are extremely important to her. A man must also be courteous, patient, attentive and empathetic.

He must also understand the difference in gender tongues. A man must interpret what a woman says. When a woman asks a man whether a newly purchased skirt looks nice on her, what she really means is whether it is slimming. A man must be able to read this instantly and must simply agree. His honest answer is not required.

Attentiveness to a woman is about touch as much as it is about words, especially bearing in mind that a woman's skin is much more sensitive than that of a man. Also, a lovely kiss to a woman means a great deal, which men must realize.

Attentiveness also means giving little gifts and surprises. If a man is genuinely really attracted to a woman, he must pay these little attentions. If not, his future in the relationship will be bleak, despite the fact that he thinks he looks great, is cool, is professional. Without really understanding a woman, he is playing outside his league.

* * *

# 13

# Loving family and friends

*Hurt not others in ways that you yourself would find hurtful.*
Buddhism: Udanavarga 5:18

*Is there one maxim which ought to be acted upon throughout one's life? Surely it is the maxim of loving kindness. Do not unto others what you not have them do to you.*
Confucianism: Analects 15:23

*All things whatever ye would that men should do to you, do ye even so to them; for this is the law of the prophets.*
The Holy Bible, Matthew 7:12

*You can relate to [other fellow human beings] because you are still a human being, within the human community. You share that bond. And that human bond is enough to give rise to a sense of worth, and dignity. That bond can become a source of consolation in the event that you lose everything else.*
HH Dalai Lama and Howard C. Cutler

## Simply saying hello

Whomever you meet, greet with a smile. This also means your own family members, which we sometimes forget, as we take them for granted. Besides, an outward smile with eyes shining is an inward smile of the heart.

If you greet a stranger across the shop counter and the response is sour, no need to react. Carry on because you are not letting your ego take a little insignificant knock simply because someone is out of sorts that day. It is their problem, not yours. You opened the way for communication with a greeting and a smile, which is the best you can do to encourage an exchange. The next person you greet may respond more positively, and then you have renewed warmth in your day.

When folks out there are being unpleasant to you, there is no need to respond. There is absolutely no point in stirring up your inside by reacting to adverse comments and attitudes. No need to let your ego grasp the hook that has been thrown out with the intention of snagging you. Let it all go and move on. These barbs may even come from a friend or a relative in game-playing mode. No worries – seek to understand that there is a game being played, smile from your inner being, and think something positive instead.

## Empathy

Being able to put yourself in another individual's metaphorical shoes is a distinct manifestation of higher consciousness. As psychologist Rebecca Cutter points out, intuition, combined with a rich imagination, makes it possible for you to commune and connect through empathy. It is the ultimate means of communication, as it is the ultimate measure of connectedness.

Empathy involves an appeal process (the asking for empathy) and a giving process (being empathetic). Exactly when someone is asking for empathy may not always be clear. This is because it is a personal issue, and also because we have largely grown up to be self-reliant. Yet we all have feelings, and empathy is about understanding the feelings of another person.

The necessity for empathy may arise in a work situation as well as a personal one. Indeed, empathy is an important part of developing emotional intelligence, which, according to psychologist Daniel Goleman, architect of the concept of emotional intelligence, is firstly about developing the capacity for recognizing our *own* feelings. Then the next step is to recognize the feelings of others. This then motivates us for a meaningful communication and mutual understanding. This actually helps manage our own emotions as well as those within our relationships.

Empathy in the personal environment is not just about talking and listening, it also has important tactile and visual components. We listen, we express concern, and we also use our eyes and our touch to underscore our sentiments. These complementary actions are an important part of literally being with and emotionally within your partner, family member or dear friend.

When another person needs empathy, it takes much courage and harnessing of honest, deep emotion and understanding to reach inside another person's feelings. This is where the strength and immutability of your inner being must come to the fore, putting aside the egotistical 'I', with humility now being an important feature of your empathy.

## Support and caring

While we like the idea of exciting relationships, deep down we all need intimate and caring ones. It is how we function as a thoroughly social being. Relationships deepen as reciprocal caring develops. It comes about when there is a reinforcing of mutual respect, understanding, inspiration, honesty, and acceptance of the other person.

Trust is also important, and it is closely related to transparency and honesty. It is a powerful concept that depends on a deep mutual understanding between two people. That understanding can only come about through absolute communication. This may involve, for example, a situation where various hypothetical scenarios are discussed and truly understood by each, without any confusion arising from differences in gender tongues or historical issues arising from past relationships.

Even more fundamentally, it also means understanding that the two sexes function in different ways. Let us take an example. Imagine a male partner at a party filling his eyes with an attractive and sexy woman. Firstly, it is important to understand that this is simply a man reacting in a way that he is genetically programmed to do. It does not mean that he is planning on falling in love with her. Nevertheless, the female partner may say "That woman in the blue dress was very attractive, wasn't she", when she really means "I saw you ogling that woman and you think she is more attractive than me, don't you". But because of differences in gender tongues, the man hears and interprets the question, which is actually a rhetorical one, at face value. So inevitably he puts his foot in it by saying quite openly "Yes, she was", which instantly infuriates his companion, leading to the brewing of a conflict. The man needs to read the original 'question' in female gender tongue, and say "Yes, but so are you!" And then by way of reinforcement also to say "I love *you*."

There may be a reverse situation, where the male partner might say to the female partner something like "You really did enjoy chatting to him" and the female partner might well respond with something like "Yes, he is an interesting man" which will cause male competitive ire to rise. So she would be better to add a rider such as "but I admire you because you are even more interesting!"

During the early stage of a friendship or a romantic relationship, it is essential that both partners are able to listen. Regularly let your companion have center stage with all the focus. Give undivided attention. This means responding with acceptance and without any judgment. Just accept, with sincerity.

When adverse comments are made, seek to understand why your friend or partner has said such a thing. The words may well belie what is really being meant. Let all breeze around you, without letting the 'I' pique the situation. Know that your inner being has the ability to absorb what another person has to say, and what they really and truly mean. In other words, this means that you can acknowledge what is being said, and even if a pointed comment is made, you have no need to defend, because you are confident from within.

Mutual respect is so important for a relationship to continue to develop. This does not mean that you have to agree on all issues. Indeed, it is important to agree to disagree on some points. That is fine, because that is the spice and variety of individual relationships.

Respect seems to have lost ground in recent times, yet we all love and arguably even need it. As that is the case, then why not give respect. Sometimes, it seems as if we respect unfamiliar faces and acquaintances more than we do our dear friends and loved ones. This apparent paradox arises out of familiarity, which as the maxim says, breeds contempt. The important point here is to always be considerate to your friend or partner, and ask questions as to their thoughts, feelings and securities. Make suggestions at the appropriate time, usually a quiet time, such as over a meal. This is not just about life-changing events, but about little thoughts and caring: "shall we go to the mall and see if we can find those shoes you liked so much" or, "you just stay there, I'll make the coffee". Small and simple as these gestures may seem, such thoughts are important glue for a long-term relationship.

On this theme, sometimes you may need *not* to ask a question. Simply just do something, undertake an inspired act of kindness. This is generally easier for the man (so long as he remembers to do it!), by giving a small bouquet of flowers, a perfume, or if he is prepared to take a high risk on size and style, an item of clothing.

Understanding another person is closely allied to caring and accepting, because it means taking the time to sketch all the possible responses, aspirations and dreams of a partner. This requires imagination and contemplation.

In the case of the person you love, can you really say how you think that loved one will respond across a whole range of situations, good and bad? Can you really say that you know what your partner deep down really likes and does not? Do you know what your partner would like to achieve in their personal and professional life? Above all, are you treading only very softly on your partner's dreams? To know these answers is to chat, to spend dedicated time together, with openness and honesty, so that trust, and hence love, harmony *and* happiness, prevail.

Encouragement follows closely on the heels of understanding. It is an important dimension of love. To be able to encourage is to truly care. Sometimes simply listening is encouragement. At other times, encouragement may need to be more affirmative and active. The physical setting is the stage for resolution, so a suggestion like "come, let's go for a walk, and chat about it" may be the most loving gesture. Indeed, changing environments is important for all aspects of a long-term relationship, as it creates variety, new inspirations and novel perspectives.

Where your partner has a major issue to deal with, such as consideration of change of career, encouragement and understanding can best come about from a distinct break, like going away for the weekend. Encouragement often leads to actual growth in lifestyle and outlook, which inevitably strengthens the mutual love.

## Honor

An important first step towards developing your relationships is to know yourself, know your dimensions. Do you know for sure your own responses, aspirations and dreams? These will not be fixed but will evolve over time. You also need to have some sense of knowing to what extent they are changing. You need to know too that they are changing for your spiritual growth.

Real love, harmony *and* happiness only come about when you instinctively know that the immutable beauty of your inner being is your foundation, and also knowing that it is central to your spiritual growth. This involves, among other things, the realization that we are all connected, and that the stepping stone to this great connection is through your personal relationships. Your inner circle of intimacy with a partner, friend and family, and a strong connectedness with your inner being will open up your love to a wider universe. This is your honorable course in life, which only starts to become clear as your spiritual growth develops, and as your chakras begin to open up to the great sense of beauty in all around you.

While traveling this path, there are other, everyday guidelines that need to be adhered to. Among them is being able to stand by your promises. Your word must be your truth. As you say, so will you do. What you promise is what you must do. Besides being reinforcement of your own self-reliance, so keeping your promise will strengthen the connectedness in your intimate relationships. It then also strengthens your interrelatedness with the greater world. Your promise is the yardstick of the extent to which you can be relied upon, and, by extension, how much you will be loved.

When you do waver, make a mistake, or let your emotional intelligence slip, that is alright, so long as you redress and apologize with sincerity. We are all fallible, and we can all do with a little more humility, and there is no better time than this, right now. Breathe in, hold your breath a short while, and be totally honest in your apology. You will feel much better for it, simply because this is correcting your spiritual path upwards.

Coupled with the development of your emotional intelligence as part of your spiritual path, is maintenance of your dignity. Originally, dignity meant worthiness, elevation of the mind and character, but has since been corrupted into the realms of egotism to mean exaltation and grandeur. In a way, we could say that your dignity is the maintenance of your path to becoming a higher being, where you actually rise above exaltation and grandeur. Whatever words we use, the message is clear: to maintain honor, we must change in our worthiness in accordance with our spiritual development. In other words, honor is about not just keeping promises but also sticking by your moral worthiness, doing what is right and good. This does not at all mean not having creativity, spontaneity, passion, excitement and even daring in your life. The key is to have honor with inspiration. This is an enriching path, as your connectedness with your friends, partner and family continues to grow. Honor too, enables you to feel the right dimensions for goodness and love to continue to manifest from you and towards you.

So, how do you know that you are on the right path? One way of doing this is to imagine writing your own tombstone. Would the words say 'this was someone who found love, harmony *and* happiness.' As there are no practice runs for life, it is a rather sobering thought that perhaps we need to get moving and actively pursue the path of greater enlightenment right now.

## Home harmony

As life is tough enough, we don't need to fight battles at home. Turmoil inside of you or between you and your loved ones must be resolved. The point here is not to let any miscommunication, misunderstanding or angry issues simmer. Occasional mild and controlled anger may well be inevitable in some situations. Severe and prolonged anger, in contrast, serves no constructive purpose, and takes you backwards on the path of personal development.

One way to view anger is the big 'I' bursting out because it has been thwarted. Anger's terrible twin, blame, is then the ego satisfying itself. These two, anger and blame, must be deflected or tamed. There are some well-known physical methods for doing this, like breathing deeply and counting slowly to ten. Nevertheless, it is valuable to reflect on the fact that patience, caring, humility and humor, which are cornerstones of inner beauty, have in effect all been foolishly cast aside when anger and blame flare. And many other good things, like joy, warmth, connectedness, love, harmony and happiness, so important in our short lives, have also wantonly been let go. It is almost strange, isn't it, that we actually become angry: especially as it is good time wasted.

## Better communication, better relationships

Anger, disappointment, deceit and other negative behaviors often arise from poor or inappropriate communication. It is a constant challenge to continue to improve communication, even within the home. In a way, good communication is about employing empathy all the time. Communication means discussing, chatting, touching, expressing, relating and doing caring things for each other. Good communication leads to feelings of sharing, companionship, cohesion, kindness, excitement, healthiness, intimacy and sexiness.

Effective communication is also about asking your partner how they would like to be loved, not about imposing how you think that they should be loved. If good communication leads to such good things why don't we do it all the time? Psychologist Rebecca Cutter lists several reasons or barriers: lack of trust (we must feel trust if we are really to communicate), failure to include your partner (talking about a subject without sensitivity to the listener), one-way communication (talking at instead of to your partner), sending mixed signals (ambiguous or incomplete messages), lack of self-awareness (the talker has not thought things through clearly themselves before trying to communicate them), aggressive or abusive language (which underscores the talker's inability to use communicative language and creates alienation), abstract language/indirect communication (failure to really address the topic clearly and the real meaning has to be decoded from the words being used), topic avoidance (keeping to emotionally safe ground and not really getting to the heart of the issue), withholding (keeping back some information of feelings, and doing so can lead to mistrust), timing and pacing of the message (long-windedness and marathon monologues lead to disinterest), monopolizing (not letting your partner respond), stress (communication becomes poor when the topic is uncomfortable or painful), alcohol and drugs (these tend to cause distortion of the true message), competition/power struggle (when talking is aimed at dominance over the partner), inability to remain in the present (dwelling negatively on the past, and speculating negatively on the future), personalization (misconstruing an objective message as a personal slight or attack), and finally, blaming (which achieves nothing).

The length of this list serves to illustrate how easy it is to fall short of good communication, especially where emotional issues are concerned. There are also interpretations of feelings to consider as well as the technical text of the message. What this all means is that we must work especially hard to make sure that we communicate meaningfully and lovingly.

Communication is not only verbal. Along with the spoken word, there is a whole host of other messages arising from eye movements to facial expressions, body language and gestures, as well as good deeds. There may well be subtle pheromone changes too. It all adds up to a message being conveyed, which may or may not be the one intended. In turn, the message may or may not be received as intended. As a conversation is a back and forth activity, and as there may also be conflicts between the verbal message and the non-verbal communication, there is huge room for misunderstandings. It is almost bewildering to think that we communicate at all, and often we don't, leaving in its wake many stressful relationships.

For a relationship to develop positively, the message being communicated must be clear, from both partners, and the replies from both partners must also be clear. This means communicating feelings as well as facts. To do this, bring in as much non-verbal communication as possible, and with a loved one, that means a lot of touch. This affirms the verbal terms of endearment.

Loving is also more than just chatting, important as it is. Loving is also doing. It is showing affection by making things happen so that your partner feels loved. This is more than the man fixing the car and the woman buying curtains. It is about doing those little special things that are specifically, unequivocally for the loved one. This may be the giving of a well-thought out personal gift. Or it may be an enabling activity, such as going for a drive to your partner's favorite viewing spot. It also works in a home maintenance sense, such as putting the grubby socks in the washing basket, or polishing your partner's shoes. A little, caring gesture creates big pumps of the heart. And, by the way, don't forget to say "I love you".

## Kindly criticism

Try as we may, the home front is not always smooth. When a drama boils, tame it. So many domestic mini-crises arise simply through bad communication. So hold on there, take it easy, relax, and start all over again. It is really not so difficult when you bury that 'I' and just think in terms of the good of your partner, family or friend. Give calmness, round off a row, parcel it up and dump it. Now you can get on with doing something so much more pleasurable and know that you have taken another small step towards well-being, and one away from angst. And *enjoy* taking these right steps.

Maybe your partner is doing something that is not right, or perhaps he or she is oblivious to harm being done by a certain type of behavior. With tact, using the right verbal and non-verbal communication, broach the subject with ease and open-mindedness, and suggest a new way forward. Most partners take positive, kindly criticism well, especially when a solution is proffered at the right time. Timing is critical. Do not suggest parking the car differently when your partner is unwinding after a long day, or is carrying the hot casserole from the oven to table and closing a cupboard door with her foot and yelling at the little one to turn down the television. Few things are that urgent that they cannot wait for the appropriate time. Then, do make sure you phrase your suggestion well. Rather "it really is a nuisance that the birds are always bombarding the car" and hopefully the reply will be "you are right, maybe we should park it in a different place". This is a much better approach than "I have asked you a hundred times not to park the car under the tree where the birds are forever shitting on it" and the reply is "here are the keys, you go and move it". The right gestures and body language help too, as with humor: "have you seen the avian abstract painting on the car?"

Your inner being and its beauty have no need to be right. It is what it is, an immutable shining, golden light that is a beacon of spiritual growth. In contrast, it is the egotistical 'I' that is the problem, because it really must always be right. It is the nature of it. When there is a difference of opinion, does it really matter who is right and who is wrong? Surely, the most important thing is that the issue is resolved and that everyone feels content, enjoys a smile, and moves on to the next wonderful topic or experience.

This moving forward highlights an important point with regard to the free flow of information and feeling. It is like a journey, where the real fun is to explore, to share experiences and move on to the next mini-adventure, without getting stuck on ego thorns, as if they are real thorns in the tire. Enjoy an immediate-instant experience, the growth and the sharing, and move on to the next one. Move forward along with time in the here and now, without being encumbered by any egotistical weighty baggage to your experiential journey. When others are ego-bound, and must be right on an issue, let them be so, by providing them with an egotistical hatch through which to escape: "Perhaps you are right on that point, and now how about we think of what we are going to do together tomorrow."

## Finding a mutual path of progress

The very word 'communication' sounds rather cold and pedantic. In your social and family environment, connecting and gelling is not just about talking, and even talking clearly, it is also about being involved in a current issue or mini-experience, and having enthusiasm for it. We are emotional beings, and emotional intelligence (the appreciation of your feelings and the relationships between those and the feelings of others) is emerging as a fundamentally important way forward for any individual in the modern world.

Showing enthusiasm and really being involved in a current activity is about being focused, listening and acknowledging what is being said with verbal introjections as well as expressions and gestures to indicate that you are on board with the deep essence of the conversation or the activity. You are there up front, with a smile and some wit to show that you are surfing the current social wave of interaction.

This being at one with another, the sharing, is really about finding a solution together. The point is that finding solutions, even tiny, contemporary ones, is immensely satisfying, as that is how our psyche works. Finding solutions is a reassurance of our capabilities and therefore a confidence builder.

Finding solutions together is social and familial embroidery for a mutually better life. Effective communication using all its facets is a psychological caress that is essential for good relationships, whether within an item, a family or among close friends. It feels good to solve and progress together.

These feelings of oneness not only satisfy the lower chakras, but also open the way to the higher chakras. This is because as more base issues, yet so necessary for our survival, are fulfilled, there is then spiritual room for higher development.

## Respect in a relationship

Let us return to the concept of respect, as this is an important companion of spiritual development. It has two levels, both of which are important and interlinked. There is outer respect and good manners in the home environment and in the outside world. Manners are, by definition, expressions and gestures required to prevent another person becoming offended or angry. Outer respect is also about respect for privacy as appropriate. We all need quiet times, whether to reflect or engage in personal physical activities. Violation of well-deserved privacy is immensely disharmonious, and so it is crucial to always be aware of, and actively respect, someone else's privacy. This is also about emotional intelligence and kindness, both of which underpin the giving of true love.

The other level of respect is the inner one, the one of truly thinking and believing in respect, over and above simply carrying it out in terms of physical manifestations. The superficial 'I' in some people, particularly those who enjoy power, often likes the shallower, manifestation level of respect, and that type of respect is well known as fawning. In contrast, for those who are becoming more highly attuned spiritually, it is deep respect that is important. Besides, it automatically leads to mutual respect, warmer communication, increased feelings of harmony, and more genuine love.

## Truth in a relationship

Hand in hand with that deep respect is being truthful. This is not just being truthful in deed and action, but also in feeling. Being truthful also brings your inner beauty to the fore, and puts the ego in the background. This inner truthfulness is the fine tuning of emotional intelligence, and part of the path forwards and upwards to higher consciousness. Such truthfulness with oneself, and with others, is a foundation of essential goodness necessary for finding love, harmony *and* happiness. There cannot be these without inner truthfulness.

Being unequivocally truthful from within is part of the process of active growth. This is because of a strange reality. Often, we do not know whether we are being absolutely truthful or not. This is because the ego plays with it for its own ends. We then sometimes find it hard to decipher whether it is the ego bending the truth relative to the immutable truth of our inner being.

It is also easy to be economical with truth, whether via the tongue or the heart. To be magnanimously truthful emanating from within the heart is immensely difficult, and requires much reflection, practice, and inner harmonizing. A path to finding this inner truth comes from the mental and actual giving out of love, the doing of love from within and without. This is a growth process that must be given time and devotion, focusing all the while on reflection and then more practice. It also requires bravery, as only the very bravest can tell the absolute truth.

The more that love is given, the more truth becomes apparent, and the more there is increasing enlightenment leading to inner contentment and happiness. This contentment and happiness is then not an endpoint, but a feedback cycle into the giving of more love for all around you, and a feeling of even greater happiness.

This feedback cycle and upward growth, via truthfulness and inner appreciation, into the realms of the higher chakras, has an important element that is part of the nature of all things. Whether star formation, evolving life on earth, or spiritual growth, they all go through alternate phases of consolidation and expansion. There may be long times of reflection or wrestling with inner thoughts and feelings, and then there are moments of great insight and growth, a satori. These are moments of enlightenment, of understanding, of wonder. From these comes joy, and a feeling of harmony with all around, often coupled with a sense of intense beauty.

Sometimes these moments are small, but sometimes they are huge and life-transforming. Then afterwards, the ego tries its hardest to disharmonize and cause regression, so that there are inner conflicts leading to inner and outer power struggles, competition and disappointment. These manifestations of the ego can be instantly recognized as deviations away from the path to love, harmony *and* happiness. The fighting back by the ego can be dissolved by immediately performing acts of loving kindness, not questioning anything, and feeling intensely the oneness and the power of your inner being, with its beauty and connectedness throughout the cosmos.

## Prosperity and your financial comfort zone

Financial prosperity is not of itself at loggerheads with spirituality. Greed is a different matter. Prosperity is partly about physical well-being. It need not necessarily be about the individual, but about a wider social context. A town or an agricultural area may be prosperous when its inhabitants have enough resources for a good diet, physical comfort and security.

As there is one certainty in this world and that is change, it means that there must be preparedness for the lean times when physical resources are short. Many animals do this anyway, whether it is a squirrel storing nuts or a bear putting on weight for winter.

As humans, we often forget to cater for the lean times. One of the reasons for this is that whether we go back to our savanna origins or we consider our lives in the ice ages, there was always a plentiful supply of protein, so long as we were astute enough to seek and procure it. There was no need to live beyond our resources because it required such a great deal of effort to do so. But today, at least for many people, there are so many temptations in our modern world, and theoretically at least, it takes no effort but the click of a keyboard or the swipe of a credit card to get, or try to get, what we are tempted and taunted to acquire.

We are not biologically equipped to deal with this ease of procurement, and so it is inevitable that we will overshoot thresholds of potential happiness by falling foul of creditors. We are even doing it globally, with repercussions on many business and sustainability sectors.

What this means is that we must be more like the squirrel and think more in terms of saving nuts. This is not easy, because not only are human egos given to competition, but we are virtually compulsive neophiliacs, lovers of new things. We must do and be seen to be doing better than our neighbors, which also means having to acquire new things on a regular basis, and so running on the treadmill of retail, which is not retail therapy but retail addiction.

This new-is-better mentality is part of our mental make-up of continually wanting to move on, which originally enabled us to conquer the globe within a matter of just a few thousand years in environments as different as those with permafrost to those with tropical rainfall. Yet ironically, neophilia does not move us spiritually upwards. This is precisely why there has been so much unhappiness. This unhappiness results from disillusionment through our egotistical 'I' masking the message coming from our inner being.

The antidote to this materialistic treadmill begins firstly with appreciation. The wellspring is to start with appreciating being alive in this beautiful world and this exquisite universe. Just think for a moment how wonderful it is to see, hear, taste and touch, and to feel the world around you. Having such awareness is a truly wonderful gift that we have been given.

There is no need to punish ourselves with thoughts of ego-hassles, of dwelling on the excessive materialistic in life, and on the competition. Those thoughts can all be dumped. Then your inner being can be called upon to override all that internecine egotistical I-ness. Embrace and enjoy every moment in life and the world around you.

Appreciation through a little twist of alchemy becomes love. As you give love and warmth, so planning for difficult times becomes more feasible. Love enables contingency planning. It does this through connection with a much wider array of people around you, leading to safety in a network. This is a fundamental feature of nature but not easily seen on an everyday basis, but is felt the more you love those and the world around you.

As you network with love, the more the addiction of neophilia will fade, and the more secure you will feel. This is because gross materialism is a manifestation of insecurity and lack of confidence. Then as you begin to feel more secure, the more obvious becomes the way forward for planning for physical and spiritual prosperity.

## Your beliefs

Believing is being human. Even the most dyed-in-the-wool scientists are believers. They believe in the scientific method of objective investigation and finding new avenues of exploration from within the cell to the deepest reaches of the ocean and of the universe. No one method is right and another wrong. All have a place in this phenomenon of being human. A scientist may consider it irrational that there are human cultures who divine rain. But then it is easy to see it as irrational when sitting in the comfort of the ivory tower of a university. When your family depends on rain coming soon, it is in the fortitude of the human spirit to call upon the heavens to bring rain. We have to believe to make sense of the world in the context of our survival.

There is such a tragedy among faiths. Faith is really a personal issue, but has a social context. It has an important function as social cohesion among the harsh realities of making a physical living. Faith is for you, but morally it is not for you to impose on to others. By all means impart it where someone is in need of faith. In reality, each person must find their own faith, and one that enables them to weather the storms of everyday, physical life. To believe is to gain strength, and this strength comes from feeling not alone, and to feel connected. You and your faith is a node in the whole magnificent network of life and living.

The vehicle of faith is prayer. Prayers are the messages that pass throughout the network of being. What you truly give in prayer you will likely receive, especially when followed by positive action. Giving thanks will network the universe and link with receivers who appreciate that thanks. There will then be returns of appreciation which will give you well-being.

Prayers that seek guidance for your well-being, embedded in the well-being of all living things, will reverberate around the universal network, and solid visionary advice will be returned. Prayers *are* the giving out of love and harmony. A spiritual path forward then opens up. It is no good asking for a physical thing because the universal network of love does not understand this request. If you pray to win the lotto, you might just as well ask a frog.

If you believe that God holds this universal network, and that this network is God, then that is a belief for you personally. You may not believe in God, but there is still the tangible cosmos. Whatever the case, it is essential to have *your* belief, and it is your individual right to believe as such. The more you love God or the cosmos, the more that God or the cosmos will love you, and the more harmony and happiness you will experience. This does not mean being simply passive to receive, but rather it is the seeking of insight to make positive plans and then to actively engage in making those plans happen.

The more you love the wonder of life and the wonder of cosmic evolution, the more you will feel enraptured by it, and the more love, harmony *and* happiness you will experience. Of course though, you must always *act* upon this wonder, and thoroughly enjoy the upwelling of *spontaneity.* As you think, as you feel, as you do, as you inspire, so shall you be.

* * *

***Loving Family and Friends*** Empathy is to really appreciate what it is like to be in someone else's shoes. Engaging intuition and rich imagination is essential for empathy, which in the end, is really the ultimate communication and connectedness.

Empathy is an important component of emotional intelligence, the recognition of our own feelings and those of others. Emotional intelligence is, in turn, an important motivating force for us and for others. Empathy requires courage, as it is the harnessing of our deep inner being, irrespective of ego, and responding sensitively to someone else's feelings.

This caring and loving process also has other ingredients, especially trust, honesty, transparency and humility. It also means having good verbal communication. This may involve overcoming differences in gender tongues, with the man carefully listening to and interpreting what the woman is saying, and the woman seeing any point or issue from a man's perspective.

During this conversation, it is necessary to give undivided attention and firmly side-step the ego. It is essential to accept what is being said without judgment, so that the subconscious can process it and be able to return goodness emanating from our inner being. This does not mean that we must agree on everything that is being said or proposed. Instead, we assess its value for our and for others' well-being and spiritual growth.

Caring also means taking action. In a domestic setting, this means for example doing little things around the house, without asking for praise. Doing with love can create defining moments.

All the while, we are exploring our partner's sensitivities, thoughts, aspirations, doubts and anguishes, so that we can almost predict their reaction in any situation. With the growth of love, we can address all these. While treading only softly and sensitively on our partner's dreams, we are also growing in absolute love as we let more light shine through from our inner being.

We are always giving encouragement and support, and having enthusiasm for our partner, so as to inspire. We create variety and novel perspectives arising out of our intimate mutual communication. We also honor our partner, and we stick to our promises. Should we slip on these demanding dimensions of goodness, we need only know that we are all fallible, and a sincere apology followed by positive action may be needed.

Any differences that arise at home between loved ones must be resolved and let go. This means being alert to what is a sincere issue that needs resolution as opposed to the tyranny of the ego making a statement. All this means making a constant effort to improve communication, which is not just verbal, but visual and tactile too.

While we reach out with good and encouraging words, we need also to do so with facial expressions and hand gestures. Besides, good communication leads to feelings of sharing, companionship, cohesion, kindness, excitement, healthiness, intimacy and sexiness. Effective communication also means knowing how your partner likes to be loved, and overcoming all the barriers. It also means communicating clearly and unambiguously using kindness, verbal understanding, gentle touches and warm expressions, and then consolidating these with little but actual gestures of doing something loving. In a long-term relationship, re-affirmation of your feelings of love is crucial.

This good communication also includes a smile and some humor, both of which are effectively a little touch of imaginative thinking. All this communication is to take steps, seize defining moments of goodness, where our inner being has free rein to engage in emotional intelligence. It is about giving out love, and feeling harmony. This often arises when we find solutions together, as this dispels loneliness. Besides, it simply feels good to share, and especially to share in the decision making.

This sharing does not necessarily mean that physically we are crowding each other, with respect for each other's space also being important. It is like appreciating the space in a cup as well as the cup itself. It is to know when to be quiet and be scarce, as well as to know when to be present.

Any good relationship must have truth. This is not always easy, because sometimes we are not sure of what the truth is, even within ourselves. Where we are not sure, then we must explore. Sharing our thoughts and feelings with our loved ones helps define that truth. Genuine communication overrides the ego, and seeks out the truth, which is another expression of harmony. The ego will try to disharmonize by causing power struggles, which inevitably encourage dishonesty. Openness and honesty must be left to outshine the ego.

Financial prosperity is not in conflict with spirituality, although greed is. It is a question of having enough resources to maintain physical well-being and survive lean times. The real problem stems from the fact that we tend to forever want new things, making us neophiliacs. While this is good for exploration, it is not good in terms of greed.

Wealth is not a bad thing of its own, so long as it is shared for others' well-being as well as our own. We are all connected, and sharing is part of making that connection work for the common good. To share means that there is appreciation and well-being among those we love. When we share our good fortunes, whether physical or spiritual, there will be an ever increasing sense of togetherness, connectedness, love and harmony, leading to happiness.

Having faith is being human. We are made to believe. It helps us make sense of the complexity and vastness of the world, and helps take away loneliness, and to survive difficult times. Real faith is a personal matter, and the morally right course is for everyone to find their own particular faith.

The consolidation of faith is through prayers, a time of quiet and of giving thanks for well-being and harmony. Prayers are not vehicles for asking for something, they are for imparting feelings of well-being and love to all. The more we love God or the cosmos, the more God or the cosmos will love us, and the more wonder and joy there will be in our lives. Also, as we develop a sense of wonder for life and for cosmic interactions, the more we feel enraptured by it and the more we feel love and harmony followed by a deep sense of happiness.

There is great joy to be had in having a great sense of wonder about the world. The aim then is to *act* upon this sense of wonder, and thoroughly enjoy the upwelling of spontaneity. As you think, as you feel, as you do, as you inspire, so shall you be.

* * *

# 14

# Traveling your path

## The unfolding of your path

Let us now review how we should be traveling our path to feel the wonder of life, and to find love, harmony *and* happiness. A crucial first step is to decide that you do in fact have such a life goal, and that it is crystal clear and you feel full enthusiasm for it. This goal is one of fulfillment and dedication, so that you can reflect back in your old age knowing that you did it. You are no longer stumbling along spiritually blindfolded, because you have decided that you *will* find love, harmony *and* happiness. But you also realize that you cannot even begin on this path unless you resolve to *give* love, compassion and affection, and that harmony is an essential ingredient in that process.

You have also realized that happiness is not a goal but a reward stemming from the process of giving from the depths of your heart. All the while you are not naïve either. You stand firm on what you know is right and good, and appreciate what harmony is with a warm, passionate and giving life.

That is your overarching, universal goal. Now there are the practical, everyday goals that are the steps along your path towards wholeness. The practical steps involve everyday giving of love, compassion and empathy to a partner, friends, family, other fellow human beings and other life forms. After all, we are all on this journey together. Then there are your immediate survival goals such as earning a living, training for a vocation, and finding prosperity without greed. There is also your physical world of the senses, of sight, sound, smell, taste and touch, all of which are delicious.

To these ends you aim to give not simply 100 percent, but 110 percent. This comes about because the instant you give and you achieve, the bar is immediately set that little bit higher. It is a positive feedback cycle where the power of the instant is also an instantaneous launching point for higher understanding and deeper feeling. This is the growth of your emotional intelligence. This is the unfolding of your path, which you now see clearly in front of you. There is no longer a fog of indecision and fallibility, but a definite way forward that is opening up for you as the energy in the network of the universe returns its spiritual rewards to you. And it is all divinely beautiful, truly awesome.

### Love and time

Time really is of the essence, not within the universe, but in your life. Your three score and ten plus-years are a blink in the record of life, and you need to steer them for maximum engagement with universal harmony. Yet time is not really something tangible that we can use, any more than we can grasp thin air with our hands. For spiritual growth, there is only the one experiential moment, the present one, which compacts, opens up again and becomes infinity.

The way to feel this moment, this infinity, is to give love, especially through seeing beauty with intense joy. The universe rewards this giving of love with happiness, through the vehicle of harmony. Yet this harmony is not, as we normally perceive it, a constant, like a wave form from a tuning fork. Harmony is swaying with the dance of change that is forever taking place throughout the universe. Contradictory as it may seem, harmony is as much about spontaneous excitement and passion as it is about peace and calm. Real, deep, true love is *feeling* the dance of universal being. Time gives us thinking and feeling space to enable us to understand this dance. Time is the universe's way of making sure everything does not happen at once, and so it enables experience. How we make the most of that experience and enjoy it is up to us. And that means being able to truly laugh as well.

In effect, the universe has given us time as a tool for being able to understand and practice universal love. Yet love itself is not time bound. Love is scalar, starting close to our physical bodies in the form of touch and sensation with our loved ones. It then expands out to our community, our region, our planet. Love continues to travel timelessly, and it has no beginning and it has no end, it is simply 'as is'. This means that during our life *time* on this planet, we must *seek* time, not *spend* time, so as to convert it into *timeless* love.

Our world is full of possible parallels. While we are doing mundane tasks at home, or negotiating in business, we can still be giving out love that resonates to our loved ones and expands through into the universe. The exquisite beauty in the universe is based on a framework of clean mathematics. This outer beauty also resonates with our inner beauty, so that we feel an inner and deep oneness with all around us. The more you feel this ineffable beauty, the more it seems that time stands still. We could put this simply by saying that we seek time so as to be able to love more.

## Balancing goal setting with enjoyment of life

Converting time into experience and then, through love and harmony, into happiness is one of the most challenging currency changes that we all face. Part of meeting this challenge is to set our everyday physical goals. We must eat and sleep, earn a living, fulfill our roles in society, and look after our family. We must then know where we aim to be in practical terms. This does not of course mean that we will not be flexible and change our goals as time unfolds.

A mind is for changing, while a heart is for growing. This means that in reality you will be honing your goals as experience accumulates, and also as your connection with universal love develops. In practical terms, this alignment also means balancing your goal setting and attainment with enjoying life to the full. Really enjoying life then only comes as the feeling of love inside you begins to develop and grow. Your inner being is not about growth as it is what it is and is already universal. What needs to grow is your consciousness through aligning and feeling more attuned with your inner being.

A life plan pulses between growth-with-focus on the one hand, and having enjoyment on the other. Yet these two are not mutually exclusive. The challenge of focused growth of your consciousness has immense and lasting satisfaction. This is not the same as the short-lived satisfaction of winning a prize or buying a new car. This is because the one is alignment with the immutable and alchemical beauty of your inner being, and the other is identity with the pressures from the ego. We may view this as inner growth versus superficial satisfaction. Both are intrinsic to us as individuals. They are arguably necessary facets of our lives for everyday survival, and it is important to recognize this, as long as we are able to read and interpret the difference between them. For practical reasons, it may well be necessary to purchase a car, which is fine, but this will not lead to fulfillment or to happiness per se. It may though, be an enabling tool to visit someone to express and give love. The point is to know the difference.

## Organizing your life, your day

Practical organization of your life brings us back into the realms of appreciating the essence of time. Time management is an extraordinarily valuable tool for spacing out activities for, in the end, maximum spiritual growth. It is valuable to recognize the activities that can indeed be done in parallel. A yoga session or a long soak in the bath is not only a wonderful way to switch off from the day's ups and downs, traumas and joys, but is also a good time to reflect and plan. Ah, but that reflection and planning is not living the present moment you may say! That is the value of engaging in parallel activities, the wonderful warm comfort of the bath for example is the experiencing of the present moment while at the same time you are able to undertake some prioritization both for your immediate time schedule and for your life plan. The warm sensations also help open up awareness as you begin to relax, and so there is a spiritual dimension as well as a physical one.

Good organization does not mean stifling creativity or spontaneity. It simply means knowing where all your tools of life are, spatially and temporarily. You may well have a messy looking closet, but that does not mean that you do not know where things are in it. Similarly, having an apparently messy desk does not mean that you do not know which notes and papers are the most important ones to address. In this way, the best meals are often prepared, and the best paintings often come about, from a seemingly messy immediate environment. The inspired chef will inevitably spill crumbs, and the passionate painter will inadvertently flick paint. That is ok, because it is the product that is important.

Prioritization is important as it enables the urgent and important things to be done first. But therein is the catch. Which things are truly urgent and/or important? We are all familiar with the concept of quality time, giving time to loved ones to show just how much we love them. But so often we neglect to do it because we are so wrapped up in our own orbit. This means that prioritization must involve reminding yourself of your bigger mission, of giving love, and of finding love. It means pacing and spacing your life to focus on what your inner being is trying to tell you, rather than that of the ego which will continually vie for attention and to eat into your valuable inner-growth time.

## Letting go, and dumping anger

Growth is about dumping emotional hurt and ego-baggage as it is about moving along your path. Let's revisit this in the context of time. Letting go of stressful events and traumas is as much about skill and discipline as it is about letting time heal. We (actually the 'I' in us) accumulate so much negativism and angst that one wonders sometimes how we move forward at all.

There will of course, as we have already discussed, be times of genuine upset that require healing, which also often leads to growth through more compassion. These life-events are sad, traumatic and often unexpected. We 'just-must' overcome them and start to grow again. Yet there are also a whole host of what is tantamount to minor upsets that linger and feed on our inner selves through our egos. This often leads to resentment, bitterness, regret and even a feeling for revenge, which as politician Winston Churchill pointed out, is one of the least rewarding of activities. These are not healthy dispositions, and they can stunt real inner growth.

One effective way to deal with these retarding inner ailments is, in addition to thinking positively, to realize that they are a complete waste of your valuable time. Remind yourself that the clock is ticking, and every second that passes must be used as an opportunity for growth. In other words, the opportunity here is to be able to seize the second, the minute, as well as the day. This is not difficult to accomplish, but it does take practice, positive reflection, resolution, insight and belief. But it also means recognizing that time is not now a new master but a new friend that taps you on the shoulder with a reminder that time is not just immensely valuable but also holds within its essence immense joy.

Practice is simply about immediately letting go of an ugly instant, such as another driver on the road cutting in front. No need to let the ego be offended, it is not worth it. And then perhaps someone is being awkward towards you. So you reflect instantly on why that should be the case, and rather feel sorry for them than letting your ego react. Besides, reaction begets ugliness, which is not helpful for your path, and is special time wasted.

Insight comes with close observation of all the body

movements, facial expressions and eye movements of another person. It is a rapid yet comprehensive assessment of the situation, which is quite likely to be a mini-event in any case. The key for growth is to rapidly store that information in your wider mind library of experience, then let it be, and move on. The subconscious will resolve it as it harmonizes with your inner being.

Then there is belief. You do what you do because you believe in it. You have already decided that you really do want to find love, harmony *and* happiness, so in this greater personal scheme of things, you know that you will not deviate from your spiritual growth path because you believe in your inner being and its beauty and not in the reactive ego.

In short, time really is extraordinarily precious. Yet it presents some wonderful instantaneous decision trees, where you instantly choose one branch over another. Ugliness, deliberate hurt, pride, angst and other ego foibles is effectively a dead branch, and the more you go along it, the more likely is it to break and you fall.

## Overcoming 6s and 7s

Quandaries and having to make decisions can be remarkably stressful, even continually deciding whether to stop or go through orange traffic lights. We spend a remarkable amount of time and energy on making decisions, mostly small but not necessarily insignificant. Yet too much indecision also leaves us frustrated, unfulfilled and eventually despondent. So inevitably, it is important that we find ways of overcoming indecision.

It really does help when you know that your overall spiritual path is one of overall moving upwards. When there are small decisions to make, you can instantly make reference to your path, and let that help you decide. When making a decision, simply steer your thoughts to what is right and good according to the subtle message coming from your inner being. You ask yourself whether a decision made in this way contributes more love to you, your loved ones and, in turn, to those around you. You also ask yourself whether such a decision enables you to resonate more with your inner being, or whether any one decision is perhaps pandering to your ego. This is effectively making your spiritual path one of guidance for making good and right decisions.

With practice, you will see that you can make many more decisions quickly and with less stress when you relate to your spiritual path. So how does this help everyday mini-dilemmas such as stopping at traffic lights? Decide to always cruise (a metaphor for life) and be prepared always to stop (being aware and living in the present moment) rather than making a decision each time you approach a light (letting mind chatter go back and forth). Then when the lights stay green, you just carry on (you did not egotistically react but followed a spiritual path), dilemma resolved.

Of course there are many much bigger decisions that you have to make and which have major consequences for your life plan. And you need to make the decisions with the confidence that you are making the right ones. This is where *feeling* that the decision is right can also be important, over and above rational resolution. The issue often is that, while you may *think* that you are making a decision on the right information, in reality, not all the information is there, and you do not actually *know* this is the case. So instinctive, or gut feelings, become vitally important.

Furthermore, even if you do make a decision one way or another, there is the chance that outside circumstances will change, and then the decision becomes null and void. This is where praying, putting out your thoughts to the universe, gaining insight, and believing in your inner being and in the universe's decision (i.e. your subconscious), really does help. The reason for this is that there are so many interactions taking place in and around you that there is a great deal of information to sift through. This means that you need all the feedback you can get.

While praying or meditating, your subconscious is weighing up all the pros and cons without stressing your physiology with dilemmas. There is, in fact, a reasonable, insightful and rational evaluation that is taking place. Your subconscious has been engaged, which is calling upon all your past experiences and outcomes, and linking them to the best options for your future well-being. When you pray 'to give' rather pray 'to receive' these inner resolutions happen hardly without you even realizing them.

Once you have made a decision, you then should trust it. This does not mean that you must never change it, but simply digest it without any clamoring of further inner indecision. Let the decision unfold of itself. Only when further information and feeling causes a re-evaluation, do you need to resurrect the decision process. Rather take a lateral position with your decision, and overlay a feeling of love on it.

Let's imagine that you have decided to take a new job, and you have weighed up all aspects of it and that you have evaluated all the input from your loved ones and dearest friends. In addition, you need to *feel* inside that you have made the right decision. You reflect on your decision and you send it out into the cosmos for evaluation. While this may seem abstract, what is happening is that you have eased your mind and are letting the subconscious mull it over, while drawing upon its vast supply of information from past decisions and its reflection on your path of love through your inner being. After a night or two of good sleep and, if you can, a little daydreaming, you will find that your decision will, or will not, be reinforced. Here is where a little time does help. While most decisions are best made instinctively, big, life-changing decisions require a still mind, so that you can honestly say that you know and *feel* that you have made the right decision.

## Creative thinking

Imagination is a fundamental feature of being human. Creativity with all its ideas and forms is immensely enriching to our lives. We tend to think that creativity is black or white, and fixed. We tend to say that he or she is a creative person, or that she or he is not. Yet creative ability often relates more to having the inner skills to let creativity open up than it is to being innately creative or not. Also, our creative ability varies enormously from one day to the next, depending on mood, and over the longer term as we grow in outlook and change our lives.

The more that you feel the essence of love, the more creative you will feel and be. Love poems are part of that. True, there can be art arising out of desperation, and there can be art that comes from some of the deepest and darkest of human thoughts. This type of art, when good and inspired, may nevertheless be pointing out the folly of the ego, as in some war paintings.

The very word 'illumination' refers to light, like 'enlightenment'. The highest chakra, the crown chakra, while reflecting purple, is often represented by white light by some early masters. Goodness, kindness, love and harmony all ring of gentle, clear, warm colors, and the more compassion and empathy you give, the more you will see purple. When this is combined with flashes of insight, you will also see a white brightness.

Creativeness can be practiced, especially through the activity of lateral thinking. This is where you take all sorts of combinations of things or even ideas and combine them into completely novel alignments, configurations and associations. Nothing is too crazy. You want to find love, so let's toss around some thoughts and ideas. You like adventure, and so you seek a partner to go white water rafting, when perhaps you have never before actually planned to do it. You love to paint, so you do Saturday tours taking your paints with you, and next you find you are sharing creative thoughts with someone who comes up to see what you are painting.

Creativity is an adventure, and an enjoyable one. You can even practice it during your everyday activities. You see a flower, and through lateral thinking, you imagine it in the sky, perhaps dancing. This triggers the thought of a creative pilgrimage to see the colors in India. You see a smile across the room and you capture it like a photograph in your mind, and recall later the joy of a brief but poignant moment of happy social interaction. Then, see things as they really are by using a creative wellspring. Think and say 'the clouds really did bump around in the sky today', 'do carry my dreams with you', 'such a tangy aroma', 'the trees are whispering'....

Imagination does take us forward, and it seems almost that we as humans are blessed with pots of it. Wonderful times, and with our minds, there are wonderful places to go.

## Po

Beyond 'yes' and 'no' is 'po', a useful word and concept coined by the well-known psychologist and creative thinker Edward de Bono. So much of our cultural underpinning is based on the binary 'yes' or 'no'. In a court of law, the prosecution may well ask a question and demand that the answer is a yes or no. But the reality is that the world is not simply 'this' or 'that'. There is also an in between. So 'po' helps us here. It means just a minute, let me think about that. It also means let's keep the options open.

While we argued above for incisive decision making, we can only do that when we have enough information, when we *feel* it is right, when we don't need to call upon more time, and we are sure, both in our minds and our hearts. Yet we do not always want or need to be compromised into an instant decision that is one way or another. Sometimes it is good simply to say, well, my answer is pending. That way you are in the driving seat and not being coerced into a premature decision.

So what does po have to do with love, harmony *and*

happiness? Decisions need to be made with absolute clarity of mind. Then there must be a feeling that the right decisions have been made. Po enables you to poise at a decision branch without having to go along it. It is a play for time, as well as a time for play, it is valuable time, reflection time and feeling time. It embodies the concept of hovering without being forced into a corner. You hover, but not through indecision, but because you have actually decided to hover and are enjoying doing it. This gives you time to assess what is right and good, what is the giving of love, and what is harmonious. It means enabling you to make the right decision at the right time for your spiritual well-being.

## Enjoy a challenge

Loving does not mean wafting around in a world devoid of reality. Loving must have a firm foundation, which engages all the chakras if it is to reach fulfillment. This also means taking on challenges in life, yet knowing the risks. Most risks are reduced with more information and more insight. The more you know about someone, the less chance that something will go wrong in the relationship. Yet there are always wild cards.

A long-term relationship, where together you are an item, means knowing all the reactions of both yourself and your partner, and the reactions of both of you together interactively. Yet we cannot know all the circumstances that will arise in the future, and how we will tackle them. This is where imagination comes in, and making the most of time available to be able to sketch and process in your mind all possible future scenarios with your partner.

There are some basic issues that, strangely, are often not brought out into the open. This may be thoughts ranging from adopting children and the amount of time to be spent with relatives, to views on politics and whether there is an afterlife. These, and many others, all need to be discussed with absolute honesty, and as soon as possible. This may also include calling upon your most resilient inner resources by not being at all judgmental, and above all, to be empathetic.

Most challenges can be seen not as a hurdle, but rather as simple bumps to overcome in your path of spiritual enlightenment, and with minimal fretting. Challenges should be met head on and tackled without a second thought. This is easiest done when the challenges are shared, because a challenge shared is not only halved, but also stimulates bonding.

## Nothing ventured, nothing gained… together

Personal power is about doing, about action. It is also about saying no when you honestly believe something should not be done. Exploration is integral to the human spirit. We humans have been exploring since the dawn of our appearance, and we continue to do so. This urge to explore is deep within us. We explore to know ourselves, and sometimes to test ourselves. We challenge ourselves to ask whether we are brave enough to explore the unknown. One reason for this is that we do not really like the unknown. It has a spooky ring to it.

While we like to see, vicariously, other men and sometimes women, physically exploring remote parts of the earth and near space, it is essentially a social activity. Rarely do individuals explore entirely alone.

Yet we are on an inner journey as well as an outer one. We may think that this is a solitary journey of 'finding ourselves', when really it is also social, as it involves the giving of love, and the receiving of love. Yes, it is true, there are times when we need to be alone, to reflect, to recharge, to gather in all threads of information, feeling and interaction that have taken place. This is consolidation time, ready for the next phase of social exploration with a loved one, and with dear friends of a like mind.

We need to explore, whether it is our physical world or our inner world, as this is when we find excitement and we gain experience. That is when we grow. Novelty has always been good for us, and is likely to be so in the future. We work well through exchange, trading of ideas, sharing of thoughts, and developing ideas together. Indeed, one of the magic glues for a long-term relationship is to share dreams. Then, translating those dreams into reality is a major bonding mechanism, because really, it is rather personal. Nothing ventured, nothing gained… together.

## Perseverance

Dreams may morph and change, brighten and dim, give immense satisfaction, but remain a meme, a thought. Dreams require the doing of something to make them happen. Not all these doings will work out well, and the reality of the dream may sometimes be unreachable. This is where fortitude, determination, and perseverance come into play. Nothing much is achieved without trying, trying again, and trying yet again. The aim here is not 'no sweat' but 'lots of sweat'! 'Kool' is no good, while 'overcame it, did it, experienced it' is! Indeed, laid back expressions are really cover ups for social conformity and weakness through giving the appearance of not trying too hard. We really are strange beings sometimes.

We need to explore and grow, through action, with lashings of perseverance, and tweaks of spontaneity. The old adage that 'if it was easy everyone would be doing it', rings so true. Perhaps this is why so many people, despite having inner capacity, do not grow spiritually, do not find love. It is perhaps considered too much hard work.

Yet if this finding of love, harmony *and* happiness seems too much like hard work, then the dream cannot be clear enough and the motivation only at half capacity. This is where the just doing it, with enthusiasm, just making it happen, with joy, becomes so important. There are no dilemmas, no reservations, just the realization of crystal clear dreams.

Finding love, harmony *and* happiness does mean putting in some real effort, but the rewards are truly great. Diligence to the task of spiritual growth, with a sprinkling of imagination, and a bit of fun and spontaneity, will inevitably lead to happiness, as that is the only possible outcome. All darkness and loneliness, manifestations of the ugly ego, are then automatically dispelled.

## Building buffers

To be able to realize dreams, they need to be in sharp focus. However, translating those dreams into reality may turn out to be impossible, a case of lost in translation. As a result, there may have to be compromises from both partners to realize the dream. But all is not lost because the process of compromising, when done together, enables growth together. Then the reality may even turn out to be greater than the dream. For example, you may meet your dream partner, who later also becomes a really true and passionate companion.

Climbing Mount Dream will inevitably involve some hardship and much perseverance if all is to be worthwhile. But what if unexpected challenges present themselves? In such situations, you need buffers. These may be to cushion you from adverse impacts or to give you a firm foothold when the going gets tough.

Adversity may come in the form of extra challenges from work, or an old lover being a nuisance. Your dreams may also not be realizing themselves. Rather than become frustrated, you need to have distraction zones and buffers. These may be with favorite friends, or may involve going to an enjoyable place.

There is nothing wrong with occasional retreats into comfort zones. This is a perfectly natural activity. You cannot always be facing the blasts of reality and the unrelenting challenges of fulfilling the dream of spiritual growth. While retreats, whether physical, mental or emotional, are important buffers along your spiritual path of love and harmony, sometimes stoicism is also called for. This is the retreat into the wilderness, virtual or real.

Quiet times, especially over a few days can be enormously invigorating. This of course is generally easier for a man than a woman. Many men are perfectly happy to stay in a log cabin or on a houseboat in the wilderness. For women, a retreat to a health spa or a faraway relative is probably the more realistic option. Virtual retreats are also recharging, and may involve going to a concert, music club, theatre and even a cozy restaurant. Soap operas, in small doses, can also function as mental and emotional retreats, and are often sounding boards for one's own reality, a point so often missed by cynics of such programs.

The point is that we need change, we need variety. Looking at this the other way round, we are not good at dealing with sameness all the time. It saps our energy, takes away our motivation and fades our dreams. This is where just a little bit of stoicism is sometimes so rewarding. It does not matter that it is pouring with rain, still go out to the restaurant. When it is cold and dark outside, yet warm and snuggly in bed, still get up and go to the gym. These little 'let's just do it now' actions make life so much more rewarding.

The touch of stoicism on a regular basis is also part of the fiber for moving you along your path to higher spiritualism. This does not mean that you must necessarily beat yourself with birch sticks and jog in the arctic snow (unless so inclined of course), but it does mean that you will only grow when you truly make the effort. Just as being a couch potato does not firm you up physically, so not disciplining the mind to give love and find harmony will lead to spiritual stagnation. Spiritual growth comes through action, mental, physical and emotional. And of course you must also believe in it.

## Get into a positive feedback cycle

Effort is required to move anything forward. Physical energy is needed to move things, and mental and emotional energy is needed for spiritual growth. As is the nature of things, there are negative feedback cycles which sustain the world in some sort of order. Time is the thread running through this process so that at one moment there is movement, let's say, to the right, then after a while, there is loss of momentum, and feedback turns it back to the left. This then is repeated on the left side back to the right, and so on.

Then there is the process of positive feedback, where, to use our analogy, a motion to the right triggers more energy in the same direction, so that there is ever increasing motion to the right. Some chemical reactions leading to explosions involve positive feedback.

What has this got to do with spiritual growth and love? The message here is that we need small changes and variety, alongside our dreams, to trigger small interactions that grow into something larger. We need to be stimulated so that we make ever greater effort to find romance, to find love, and then to let it grow into harmony. This is a positive feedback cycle that feeds on the beauty of the relationship. Relationships grow, and they begin to blossom. But this 'explosive' growth must be funneled into controlled energy release, just as an explosion in the cylinder of an engine drives the piston for forward motion. Then to use the motor analogy, you are in the driver's seat and manage these positive feedback spiritual packages so that you continue on track along your spiritual growth path. It is like catching the surf of a wave with good positive energy and then riding it forward by steering back and forth, while all the time loving the adventure.

Un-romantic as this analogy may sound, it nevertheless emphasizes that on the one hand there can be good development, and on the other, this good can all be blown away and the relationship falls apart. It will grow when the romance is converted into the giving of love. This will be the positive outcome of a romantically magical relationship. But when one or both partners do not give the relationship a chance to grow and mature, through the giving of compassionate love, then it will fall apart.

This positive feedback and harnessing of romantic energy into spiritual growth energy has cycles of growth and of settling. It must continue like this to stay alive and well. Growth of a relationship must involve active physical, mental and emotional commitment to growth from both partners. This must be communicated clearly between each other.

Honesty and true expression helps this communication, and in turn, inevitably helps grow the relationship. But then there must be a time of plateauing of the relationship, where re-assurance takes place. Both partners must spend that valuable commodity, time, in consolidating the relationship. This is where quiet reassurances using a smile, a touch and a gentle word become so important.

This re-assurance phase must then be followed by a renewed growth phase where there is a deliberate commitment to doing new things together, whether simply a vacation, deciding to have children, building a house together, making love differently, or doing a sport together. Alternatively, there may be a need to give each other more space, more independence, knowing that the romantic thread is always there.

The key in all this, is reaching out a hand of understanding, compassion and empathy, all on a base of honesty. This growth period then needs to be followed by a further consolidation period of mutual re-assurance.

## Always end on a positive note

Sports enthusiasts know to always end a practice session on a good action, whether a fine swing or a fine shot. A good action leaves an afterglow of positive reinforcement. This is the same with relationships. Any temporary parting must carry with it an afterglow, a sense of well-being and a sense of re-assurance.

Sometimes an effort needs to be made to actually do this perhaps because of too much familiarity or because the romantic feeling is not there. This lack of feeling, even when tiny, is one of the most important telltale signs that something is not right with the relationship. This means that there must be an honest reflection within yourself and a truthful discussion with your partner at some later point.

There are various types of feelings on parting. These range from a sense of loss, a feeling of excitement for the next meeting, a necessary respite, or a feeling that something is not really right. It is important to read these feelings, and women are usually much better at doing this than men. Women, with their subtle sensitivities, which is really a detailed processing using both hemispheres of the brain, can often assess those feelings very well. This is why most relationships are terminated by the female partner following insight and assessment.

Reading these feelings is important. It is the branching of the decision tree. The first branch is to decide whether there is a fundamental flaw in the relationship which is irreparable. If not, then what are the actions needed to address this dip in feelings. Perhaps not enough was said, or there was not the sensitivity of touch. This is the time to not wait until the next arranged meeting, but create a surprise one. Use creative, lateral thinking. Use some imagination, put aside pride, and get in the car and go over and just hold each other, and say how much you love each other. Be demonstrative, be proactive, be bold, be loving, and always end on a positive note.

* * *

***Travelling your Path*** We resolve to give love, compassion and empathy, as that is the only true path to happiness. We also realize that happiness is a reward and not a goal.

We also stand firm on what we feel is right and good, and what is in harmony and resonates with those around us. This is our universal goal, with physical well-being, sensuous and heightened awareness, and a still but enthusiastic mind being integral to that path.

We also give our most to all we do, knowing that next time the bar will be set a little higher, which creates ever more joy because of growth in our emotional intelligence. It is a path that unfolds as we overcome challenges and become more attuned to all about us. We have become aware that the world is intrinsically so beautiful. Any fog and stress of indecision is lifted, as we have seen that beauty, and we know where we are going.

Time is of the essence with us packing in as much experience as possible. Yet we are in no rush. The more we enjoy and grow spiritually time becomes infinitely compressed into the present moment and infinitely expanded into the cosmos. Love and beauty become timeless, and harmony prevails. We begin to feel oneness with all around us.

Time is simply the cosmos' way of ensuring that everything does not happen at once. Yet we aim to convert our physical time into even more valuable experiential timelessness. This happens when we continue to adapt to new challenges and experiences as we increasingly align with our inner being, while overriding the time-confined ego.

This alignment comes from disciplined focus on tasks at hand and on tuning the senses so that awareness becomes total. There is superficial enjoyment, such as purchasing something new. That is fine, but real enjoyment and growth comes from becoming enlightened through giving love and compassion.

A key is for us to realize that time management is a vitally important skill to be honed and practiced on a regular basis so that we can maximize on all the physical tasks and senses while leaving time to reflect and plan for spiritual growth. This enables us to prioritize our everyday life, while exploring the timelessness of our inner being. This timelessness resonates in tune with love, compassion and insight.

Appreciating the value of actual time helps so much with life management. Practicing letting go of indecisions, traumas and offences from the ego enables us to then move on to new, positive experiences, especially those of giving love and compassion.

When real setbacks and emotional traumas come, time will heal. Yet this time can be reduced by dancing and resonating with our inner being, so that actual time is translated into experiential time. All the while, this conversion depends on overcoming the reluctance to let go created by the ego. We let go, and we move on. This letting go, combined with increasing awareness of the world around us, and the having faith in the beauty of the world, then brings us back on the path to higher consciousness.

As quandaries and indecisions are stressful, we have to practice making swift decisions based on inner confidence emanating from our inner being. We then resolve to move on, by instantly recognizing when the ego is holding us back. We develop insight based on past experiences combined with knowing and feeling what is right and good. We then trust our decisions. These decisions, especially major ones, require a still mind and a warm, resolute heart. Such a situation only comes after giving out love and compassion, being aware, and ignoring the taunts of the ego.

Imagination and creative thinking are a vital part of this making the most of our time, our life, so to reach timelessness. Love and creativity go hand in hand, with the word 'illumination' meaning to light up through creativity. It can be enlivening to have lateral and imaginative ideas, and then to share this creative enthusiasm with our loved ones.

Where we find it difficult to make decisions or to resolve

issues, no worries, we just put it all on hold with confidence, and let it rest there, so that the subconscious (cosmos) can digest it all and later inspire us with the right idea and right solution. As we think and feel, so will the right vibrations resonate back to us.

Developing awareness and experiencing spiritual growth does not necessarily mean being passive. Sometimes some strategic risks and challenges should be taken as they can be growth steps. This also means discussing and sharing with loved ones and with a fully open mind and a full heart. It is about exploration. True bravery is required to undertake this spiritual journey. That bravery is love, compassion and empathy.

Yes, exploration, discipline and growth are sometimes difficult to accomplish, but immensely rewarding. Giving love all the time is a huge challenge, because the ego's activities so often get in the way. This means that it is essential to be continually vigilant and to instantly recognize when the ego is beginning to rear its ugly demeanor. This recognition is half the challenge dealt with, while dealing with the other half is to give love, compassion and empathy, while all the time seeing beauty.

Overcoming the challenges in life requires perseverance as well as determination. It also requires some imagination and being excited. It is possible to inwardly smile and outwardly laugh one's way to illumination, enjoying all the while the great dream of being.

Diligence is not dull, it is the making the effort to feel the wonder of beauty inside and all around you on a regular basis. Translating life dreams into reality requires continual vigilance, which can be enormously enjoyable too, as the journey is as rewarding as the destination. When spiritual wheels do come off, which they will now and again, we make sure that we already have in place buffers that help us get back on track. These may be an occasional treat or even retreats into our own imagination where we can create wonderful images.

This wandering off track often happens because we need to have change and variety in our lives. Also, we often do not know where the boundaries are. There is illumination and eventual happiness on one side, and darkness and unhappiness on the other. We need to awaken to the bright and wonderful, yet defining, moments on the illuminated side. That illuminated side has our inner being as the guide to steer us away from the dark side, where the ego is trying to cause havoc. So we make actual change and have variety so as to direct us towards love and harmony.

Indeed, variety and change in our lives are essential, as that is how we are made, to thrive on novelty. We aim to turn that great need for novelty into spiritual development. This means engaging in novelty through listening to the moral compass of our inner being.

Too much routine leads to lack of imagination, and is a breeding ground for ego trouble. The aim is to find variety and novelty by sparking our imagination, and doing things for both our and others' well-being. This is the growth of love, which is what turns a gray relationship into a colorful and exciting one.

This growth in the relationship is then reinforced by honesty and trust. Re-assurance is also brought into the picture, to enable growth together through mutual decision making. This is the reaching out of a hand of understanding, compassion and empathy.

This growing of the relationship will be further consolidated when every major interaction is ended on a positive note. This means being physically demonstrative, showing love, and cultivating togetherness with spiritual growth at the same time. This harmony, when maintained through constant vigilance of the ego and development of awareness, then leads to happiness.

* * *

# 15

# A Personal Guide for Discovering the Alchemy of Love

## Life's formula

- Acknowledge that your being is a triad of three realms, representing 1) your physical being, its form, senses, motivations and wellness, 2) the selfish egotistical self, and 3) your inner being and beauty, the gateway and path to higher consciousness.
- You need to keep your physical being well, which means looking after your body and mind with good food, feeling healthy, enjoying life, having romance, having good relationships, and living life to the full. This is the wondrous 'sensing it, doing it, feeling it, and living it'.
- Your physical realm also includes having enthusiasm for life, while all the while letting go of past traumas and emotional congestion. It means that you are in the driving seat and not psychologically at the mercy of the ego.
- Time is of the essence for you in this physical realm because you aim to overcome challenges as quickly and as efficiently as possible. You are motivated to do so because the more efficiently you overcome inhibitions to your spiritual development, the more time you have for staying on the path to higher consciousness. It also means you have more time to spend with those you love, or those you wish to love.
- All the while you are alert to the scourge of the ego as it feeds on memes of competition, greed, jealousy and vanity. The ego will try to drive and coerce us to gain a competitive edge over other egos, and to make us jealous. You need to practice recognizing this temporary madness.
- Recognize that the ego tries to make us win approval through

personal, competitive achievement. Yet in reality, this separates us as individuals from others. This is because the ego is anti-love, anti-harmony, aggressive and isolationist. It thrives on unhappiness, disillusion and revenge, and spreads these memes through, among other things, the news media and gossip.

- Know that the third realm of the triad, your inner being and beauty, unlike the physical realm and the ego realm, knows neither space nor time. It is as is. In reality, it is an essence and the dynamo of love which melds with universal illumination. You have it within, all the time.
- Know that your inner being is the alchemical appreciation of immutable golden beauty of love. It builds on the well-being of your physical being, the messenger of love.
- We cannot convert the baseness of the ego any more than we can change metals into gold, but you can acknowledge your inner beauty, and through awareness and the giving out of love, let it shine with its natural brilliance and illuminate the dark recesses of the ego. The ego gets dissolved in the pure white light of your inner beauty. The ego, the 'I', has no power in the face of this unequivocal, formless, totally unselfish love.
- For this light to shine, you need to treasure your body with physically good things and loving thoughts. You think and feel kindness, modesty, humility, honesty, truthfulness, awareness, sensuousness, spontaneity, passion and discipline.
- On your foundation of physical well-being, you can focus on your path to greater inner awareness, consciousness and enlightenment. This develops as a lovely warm, delicious 'tickling' inside of you. When you feel it, enjoy it.
- You can recognize your inner being as being peaceful, affirmative, loving, compassionate, giving, enthusiastic and immutable. This contrasts with the warlike, aggressive, competitive, destructive, selfish, uncaring, demanding, vain and fickle ego.

- In reality, our lives are somewhere along the spectrum from fully ego-bound to fully enlightened. The fundamental biology in us has been honed by our desperate survival struggles in our deep past and it still lies as the primal animal within us. This means that we cannot be rid of this biology, but we can relate more and more to our inner beauty so as to tame the ego. Learn to constantly recognize where you are along this spectrum.
- Recognize the ego trying to dominate when you see selfishness, competitiveness, intransigence, cruelty, vanity, revenge and arrogance. If you let these dominate your life, it will only lead to disillusionment and unhappiness, as that is simply the way of the cosmos.
- Be aware that at the social level, this dominance of the ego has given us group identity and a sense that our group, whether a sports team or a country, must win. Wars are a manifestation of the final dominance of the ego with its terrible consequences for all.
- Give out love as a thought, a feeling, a touch or as an activity.
- Be alert to when the ego is trying to gain a foothold. As soon as you feel the dark shadow of the ego, think of the light emanating from your inner beauty, with all its glorious colors, especially purple and gold. Embrace these emanations with a thought of dance, a twirl of body, mind and spirit, which then tickles you and makes you laugh.
- Learn to be confident of your own inner and outer charisma, which is simply being aware that you have an inner, immutable being. Yet all the while you have humility, a love of all life, and a strong ability to say 'no' when you know that it is required.
- While you are bathing in this light, you know too that time is precious, and the physical realm is finite, but yet you also know that your inner being and beauty is forever. Every day, remind yourself that your inner beauty is your immutable

gold center that is forever connected with the cosmos.

- Be alert to the ego as it denies your connection with your inner being and beauty. This means at times that we slip into an ego-bound existence, mostly temporally, but sometimes more severely, which can be manifested as depression. This is a signal to reconnect with the perennial light of your inner being and its beauty, and when you get that little tickle, you know that you are again making contact with the beauty of your inner being.
- Sometimes you will have small flashes of insight, and even, when you are in a highly tuned mode, great revelations of total knowing but not-knowing the great void and all that is connected in it. These moments of great insight are satoris, which forever consolidate your path to higher consciousness. Revel in these times.
- The ego ambushes us on a regular basis, with daily actions of other egos irking us. When this pressure from the ego gets too much, it is a sign that you need to take time out to reflect, to recharge your spiritual batteries so that you can again become aware, see colors, have enthusiasm, give out love, be non-reactive and feel harmony once more.
- Enjoy traveling the spiritual awareness path, when the voice and ugliness of the ego begins to fade. Yes, it will spring up now and again, but the more alert you are, the more aware you become, and the more you are able to instantly dispel the advances of ego. When you do banish the ego, that lovely tickle comes back.
- Realize that all life is a wonder. As there is life all around us, it means that this life has survived alongside us. We are no better or no less than any other life. This has profound importance for our lives, because it lets us be empathetic to all life, be bio-empathetic. This is a joy, as we are all connected.
- Every time that you look at your skin, recognize that some of the great advances in life came about through co-operations,

known as mutualisms. Even the energy powerhouses of your cells, the mitochondria, were once free-living bacteria and are now an essential part of *you*.

- Be aware that mutualism, which in effect is love and compassion, is the only real way forward for our survival, as well as for many other life forms on our planet.
- Recognize that the mutualistic key to the future is that between your physical form (keeping it well) and your inner being (knowing that is always there to guide you). This marrying of the two takes immense courage as we are hard-wired with a strong ego, which we must continually overcome.
- Cast aside the medieval perspective of a world that is anthropocentric and earth-centric. We are an integral part of the cosmos and its awakening.
- Recognize that happiness is more elusive the more the ego interferes, because the ego thrives on unhappiness.
- Recognize that your awakening (finding harmony and happiness) is a tough path, and perhaps it is meant to be. Recognize that you need to be worthy to walk it. Your inner being has the map of the path.
- No matter what our religious or philosophical beliefs, we still all have a finite time on Earth and there is not time for us to engage in dispute. This is the time period to dispel the ego, and to celebrate your life in all its magnificence.
- You are aware that the ego has a trump card, making us fear death. Unlike your inner being, which is unknowing of fear or time, the ego will use time to preserve itself. Don't waste your precious time on it, as you fully intend to move forward and find love, harmony and happiness.
- Your physical form will dissolve on death, yet your inner being will always be there dancing with the cosmos. There in the cosmos is a great big smile and a 'tickle' that is us anyway, simply loving, and being intensely romantic.

## A Strategy for Getting on Track

- As there is no turning back the clock, reflect on how you are going to make every moment and every opportunity count. This does not mean watching the clock, but making the overall decision that you are going to improve the quality of your life. It is important to know that sometimes we feel stuck. Leave it be, while giving out loving thoughts, until the time is right. Solutions will present themselves when your frame of mind and feelings are right.
- Focus on your overall life trajectory, knowing you can and will let go of, and overcome, the setbacks and difficulties. In other words, *resolve* to move into an upward trajectory of life.
- Simply think all the time about *giving* love, firstly to your own being, and then transferring that feeling to others. It may be hard, but just do it without dwelling on it.
- As so many of our ills and frustrations have arisen through our being disconnected from nature, always seize the opportunity to appreciate nature, from appreciating fresh air to noticing a flower or a cloud. This is the wellspring of our being, because that is how our body and being were honed over the millennia.
- Happiness does not equal excessive financial gain, with happiness coming after giving love and finding harmony. You are not what you own, but how you feel inside. Simply feel the pulse of being alive and rejoice in it.
- There is only the present moment, with the past gone and the future not yet here. Reflect on the past for enhancing the present but do not dwell on it. Regret is not even in your vocabulary. Past setbacks are the learning ground for experiencing the present. They are the challenges to overcome that build us into ever-loving beings, and enable us to reach a higher plane.
- Start your upward trajectory by simply dividing your experiences into good and not so good, without magnifying the

disappointments. No need to dwell on the disappointments, just let them go, by casting them into the universe, which will replace them with wonderful feelings as you give out loving thoughts and let harmony flow.

- Finding ongoing love is *giving* ongoing love.
- Your action, and then the receiving of love, stems from how you *think and feel* in the first place.

## You are Free to Choose your Path

- Happiness is a reward, not a goal. It comes from making small corrective steps throughout your life, starting from now. It is never too late in life to take that first step.
- Life need not always be so serious. Enjoy the act of playing whenever you can. Through play, you automatically explore and discover, as a child does. Play also bonds, between friends, between partners.
- Taking the right steps along your path to enlightenment requires physical, mental and spiritual effort. This requires discipline and focus. The more you have this, the easier it becomes to do it. Always think in terms of giving that little bit extra. Enjoy exertion, it is always rewarding. Always put in your greatest effort, and just a little more.
- When idle, your mind will quickly be filled with thoughts that dwell on the past or agonize over the future. This is the 'chatter of monkeys' and you need to avoid it, as it is the egotistical 'I' trying to pull you away from increasing awareness.
- Downers and traumas require you to think about giving out love, even if small thoughts of forgiveness and compassion. This may seem strange, but it is the path of resilience.
- The bad times are times that show us the way to grow spiritually. This is done by letting go of the downer or trauma. Just let it fall away.
- During the recovery period, eat well, walk, exercise, and see

nature in all its beauty. Opportunities will present themselves to you.

- During very stressful times, such as death of a loved one or a divorce, the body goes through a grief cycle, with certain steps. This is all perfectly natural. There will be recovery, but it does take time.
- You can release yourself from pain by identifying what you are hanging on to, and releasing those thoughts through seeing all around you and being determined to live life anew. This requires steps, one at a time, towards a renewed and expansive mind, assisted by being physically active.
- All the while focus as much as you can on the present moment. Observe all around you, hear as many sounds as possible, and see all the movements taking place as you go about your daily activities. Be aware, be tuned. Increase awareness, and become increasingly fine-tuned. Become absorbed, expansive, enthusiastic, and feel alive.
- Tune in to love and warmth by giving it out, even though you may feel down. This may involve just a simple gesture of thanks, of compassion and of service, like making a beverage for someone else.
- Reflect on the huge and beautiful space within you, where love and harmony reside. Try and feel them through your increasing awareness.
- Notice all the little things in life, the beautiful things. While doing so, never judge. Just observe, hear, smell, touch and taste, and enjoy it all. Feel a sense of profoundness developing within you.

## Finding your Life Path

- Practice imagining your life goals very clearly. Have a clear picture in your mind of you at your destination.
- Imagine yourself on the path to a more loving and harmonious life as if you are arriving at your destination, all the

while *giving out* at least a feeling of love. This visualization is a dynamic, living picture, where you can even hear sounds and smell aromas within the picture.

- This visualization is practiced and then acted upon, resolutely and with feelings of love. You give enthusiasm to your visualization so that goodness and light outshines the darkness of the ego. You actually take small actions on a regular basis to enable you to continue along this path of better and more harmonious living.
- Thinking positively is a constant in your everyday life, but you do it with a sense of loving goodness towards others. You always see the funny side of things, and in your mind, you turn a negative comment into a positive one. You also recall happy times with a smile and with color.
- You also think in terms of solutions rather than obstacles.
- Positive thinking also involves visualizing your inner being as if actually connected to the cosmos. This is brought about in part by having compassion and humility.
- Enjoy reflective contemplation now and again. Reflect on who you are, your strengths and weaknesses, and where you are on your spiritual path. This is not at all the same as the darkness of the ego letting you dwell on your competitive place in the world.
- Start with saying that you really like yourself, that you are fine with who you are. Feel delicious love inside you.
- The more you love, the more you will be loved, as your action leads to the same reaction in others.
- Recognize your talents and skills so that others may benefit from them. If you are good at something, which we all are, however small, impart it to others, and do so with humility. We don't have to be good at everything and we can enjoy and feel at one with ourselves when we enjoy talent and skills in others. The key is enjoyment, either in you or others.
- Always remember that the ego thrives on envy, fueled by the

media persuading us to consume more.

- Recognize this envy trap and know it is the ego coercing you away from your spiritual path.
- You need to have both long term and short term goals. These may be material, which will not necessarily bring happiness.
- There is nothing wrong with wealth, so long as it is shared with others and it is not made at the expense of the well-being of others or of nature.
- There are laws of the land, and to flout them generally leads to unhappiness. There are small rules too, closely related to manners, which require attention. Anger and blame, along with bad language, are simply outbursts of the ego. These need to be defused so that you can move along the path of spiritual growth.
- You are in the driving seat of your own destiny, and it is for you to guide yourself along your spiritual path. Be aware of manipulation, even from your loved ones. You call upon your deep insight to overcome these everyday pressures and trials.
- You practice recognizing when game playing by egos is taking place, and you develop your own spiritual strong mindedness. This comes about not through resistance, but through acceptance of other points of view. Your ego has no need to react. No one is able to pull your strings. You will not be put out of phase by these arbitrary intrusions on your inner space.
- Our sense of place is strong within us, but we carry our faith wherever we go. Faith is your personal religion, which may or may not include a loving God. Faith is your personal journey of belief, which includes belief in yourself.
- Your belief in resonating omnipresent love throughout the universe will underpin your sense of harmony with the cosmos and lead ultimately to a feeling of happiness.

## Becoming Aware of your Inner Being

- Aim to feel good about yourself by building confidence and creating charisma around you through firstly having thoughts of peace, love and warmth.
- Remind yourself that your body is the vehicle for feeling love. Always relate feelings of love to looking after your body with healthy food and activities, whether passive (like meditation, yoga or soaking in the bath) and/or active through exercise.
- Aim to feel comfortable about yourself physically, which partly means ignoring the pressures put upon you by the media, especially glamor magazines.
- Feeling good, physically and emotionally, enables you to get closer to your inner being, which is an attractor drawing you to the spiritual realm. Visualize this like a ball (feeling good, doing good) in a basin going around and settling in the center at the bottom (your inner being).
- Recognize that it is the ego that keeps that 'ball' of spirituality and consciousness from settling. The ego is there within us because it had great survival value for us in our distant past. Negative feelings of self-importance, jealousy, pride, material accumulation, competition and many others, keep that ball from settling. Practice seeing the ego preventing the 'ball' from settling.
- There is another reason for looking after your body. It is a resonator for cosmic life forces. Your body needs to be in good shape for tuning into the positive resonances in the universe. Practice loving as a tuning into goodness, beauty and loveliness.
- You can feel love in the universe flow back and forth the more you travel in your imagination, and as you follow the attractor to your inner being. This feeling of pure love transcends all time.
- Maintaining your path to higher consciousness involves taking time out to reflect. This is exercising your imagination

to visualize your being at one with the universe. Practice thinking about joy, and recalling the wonderful cameos of life that make you smile. This is the non-talking part of your day where you focus on all positive thoughts. See this as a horizontal process where you scan your horizon of wonderful past events, through present moment awareness of all around you, yet feel the future drawing you with enthusiasm. Be aware that is very different from the vertical chatter of monkeys where you continue to churn over useless, energy-sapping thoughts.

- There is no point at all in bottling up thoughts which only stir our emotions negatively. It is essential to think cherishing thoughts, harmonious thoughts, loving thoughts, so as to continue along the path to consciousness and to happiness.
- Life is full of challenges. Overcoming them with positive thinking and action, with love, is a joy in itself.
- Challenges need to be recognized, assessed as to their size, tackled with discipline, and then re-assessed to see that you have dealt with them. Where they are, on further consideration, clearly insurmountable or irrelevant, just move around them and move on.
- Recognize that there is no need ever to feel down in spirit, or frustrated, this is just the ego trying to hold you back.
- Often overcoming challenges is through non-resistance, letting go and finding a new direction, like water flowing through bamboo on the hillside.
- Seizing the day is to enjoy and experience special, positive and creative moments throughout the day. Also enjoy reflecting on halcyon moments. Enjoy all aspects of life and grow.
- Happiness appears as you grow along your spiritual path. This means being vigilant that you are giving out unconditional, non-judgmental love, and doing it with joy and wonder. There will be moments of intense joy, which are steps in your growth, which are part of the loop where you are

tickled by your inner being.

- Loyalty and faithfulness seem dated, but as they are rooted in our early survival, they have a firm foundation, and are an essential ingredient to finding love, harmony *and* happiness. Practicing them daily through trust, transparency and honesty are vitally important for outshining the ego with illumination.
- These positive actions and feelings give you strength as you become increasingly aligned with your inner being. After all, you are in the driving seat and no one pulls your strings.
- All thoughts of ill will must be cast out, as they create bad vibrations with your inner being, and the spiritual 'ball' cannot settle. As soon as a thought of hurting anyone creeps in, turn it away instantly and replace it with thoughts and feelings of love and compassion. Giving love dissolves badness and ugliness instantly.
- Obsessions must first be recognized. Knowing that they are a manifestation of your ego enables you to unmask them. As soon as the obsessive thought, which may lead to obsessive action, creeps in, dispel it by instantly thinking of loving, beautiful thoughts, and of giving compassion and love to someone else.
- Remorse can be dealt with by a sincere apology and by letting go. Regret is more difficult to overcome as it is the continual recycling by the ego of a past event about which nothing can now be done. Let it all go and think of the beautiful expansive beauty within you and all around.
- Know that you are always still learning, and no matter how expert you are at something, you must have humility, else the ego will isolate you from others.
- We all make mistakes, and acknowledging them, and moving on is an immense strength. It is youthful too, as it means you are still growing, which is a wonderful feeling.
- It is not easy to always be giving out love, especially when the

frustrations and intensities of everyday life are wearing you down. Recognize that this is a sign for you to take time out, relax, look after yourself, recharge yourself, and start afresh with at least loving thoughts, if not deeds. Loving thoughts and actions will then start to be returned to you.

## Love your Body

- Feel the resonance from within you as being especially strong around your heart. Practice imagining the resonance and glow coming from your heart. Then feel your inner resonance tuning into the same vibrations within the universe. Think of your body as a warm carrier of beauty.
- Focus on feeling good about yourself, which involves also dressing well and being well groomed. This gives out a message of good health and hygiene.
- Practice true bravery which is practicing resonating with your inner being through constantly giving out thoughts of love and compassion. Where possible follow these with positive deeds.
- Maintain your 'thoughts' hygiene' by keeping your thoughts pure, fresh and lovely. This ensures harmony, along with physical and spiritual vigor.
- As soon as egotistical or destructive thoughts enter your mind, immediately dispel them. Try too, to think positive, resonating thoughts, even if fleetingly, when you go about your everyday tasks.
- Imagine and feel also the positive resonances (life forces) of the universe, or chi, entering all along your spine. Yoga is specifically designed for this.
- Also imagine and feel the balance between yin (receptive, contractive, responsive, conservative) and yang (expansiveness, overtness and dominance). This balance can actually feel tangible as it is manifested through practice.
- Be alert to disharmony when yin and yang are out of balance.

- Essentially, all the chakras need to be awakened and this can be done not only through yoga and meditation, but also through thinking of pure and beautiful love on a regular basis.
- The more you give out feelings of love, the more you will feel the energy of chi flow into you, giving you enlightenment. This is circular, with the practicing of giving out love, increasing awareness, forgiveness, acceptance, compassion and enthusiasm, leading to enlightenment which then lets you feel those attributes even more.
- A good diet for maintaining your body in good shape is an essential vehicle for your spiritual development. Variety of diet is also important as we are made to need and enjoy variety. This also means enjoyment of variety of place too, so make a point of visiting new or different places which need not necessarily be far away. We must also have variety of action, so now and again move out of your daily routine and do something different.
- Do not to be tempted by this variety too much, as overindulgence will lead to disharmony. Your spiritual path, with recognition of yin and yang and the chakras, is the essential foundation for expansive love, around which you can build physical variety in moderation.
- We are made to enjoy little treats, so enjoy them now and again. Men should think in terms of giving their partner small heart-felt gifts forever, and sometimes spontaneously. Women must appreciate these gestures, even if the gift is not the perfect one. This is an essential part of giving variety in our lives and cementing companionship.
- Attractiveness is about keeping well and looking well. This involves impeccable hygiene, which, for deep biological reasons, is sexy.
- Men are deeply responsive to women who are able to mollify them by enhancing their neotenous features, such as

increasing the size of the eyes with makeup, emphasizing full lips, blending in the nose, maintaining fresh, soft and smooth skin, and maintaining a soft voice. These are all instinctively highly attractive to a man.

- Maintain shiny, voluminous hair, a message of vigor, as well as sensuous body language.
- As a woman's hands are very beautiful to a man, their care is essential. Well-groomed nails are a sign of good health and good disposition, and are magnetic for a man. A man's strong hands and arms, in turn, give a woman a feeling of being protected.
- Bear in mind that when a man looks at a woman, he sees a portrait of the upper body, especially the eyes, lips, breasts and neck. This portrait is enhanced by jewelry, with a man generally being highly responsive to a well-groomed, decorative woman with charismatic body language. You do not have to do this, but this is simply inherent biology.
- Do not wear too much lipstick as this is inhibitory to a man, especially when it is very red. The message is extroversion and too much yang. Choice of lipstick needs to be subtle.
- Be aware that a man is highly attracted to partial exposure of a woman's body, such as décolletage and calves, or back and calves, or belly and arms. Too much from too many parts of the body (breasts, back *and* belly), unless on the beach, are generally more indicative of a woman's strong ego than her portrayal as being attractive.
- Good legs and buttocks are always attractive in both sexes, as they emphasize the qualities of bipedalism, one of the great advances of humankind.
- While women often think that big buttocks are not desirable, what catches a man's eye is the ratio of waist to hips (ideally 70 percent circumference), and not whether there is an extra pound or two.
- Maintain a good body posture as this is attractive, as it too

relates to bipedal skills. When combined with energetic activities, good body posture is immensely attractive to both sexes as it is such an evolutionarily advanced feature.

### Feeling Beauty and Finding Enjoyment

- Practice breathing well and deeply, as this allows efficient exchange of oxygen and carbon dioxide, and allows the life force, chi, to flow. When you breathe deeply, imagine that you are also breathing through your sacral dimples at the base of your back, through the region between your shoulder blades, and through your arms. Try to do this deep breathing three times a day.
- Be aware that water is sensitive to your thoughts, with ice crystals and snowflakes becoming distorted by bad or hurtful thoughts. In contrast, loving thoughts are felt by the water as being harmonious. This is because we are mostly water. Ensuring loving thoughts harmonizes our bodies and those of others. This harmonizing also helps keep away harmful pathogens that would otherwise cause disease.
- As our DNA is also bathed in water, it is not difficult to see a possible link between bad thoughts, disharmony and diseases arising from adverse influences on the processing abilities of your DNA.
- Bear in mind that water is our life. Enjoy it, and respect it. Enjoy bathing and splashing in water. Even physical loving, from kisses to orgasm, has a strong dependence on water. And give thanks when you drink water.
- It is important to feel youthful, as it has amazingly and literal rejuvenating effects. Even as an adult, still play, as it is creative, and it will resonate with your inner being.
- Do daydream as it is a powerfully harmonizing activity which freshens up your feelings. Through its creativity, daydreaming also resonates with your inner being. Daydream whenever you can, whenever it is safe.

- Always treasure nature, whether wild nature, or a plant or a pet animal. Life is special. It deserves special treatment in its own right. Life also harmonizes our thoughts and feelings.
- Laugh and feel good, as it is a creative activity. Laughter stimulates the right body chemistry for well-being and resonates inside us.
- Smiling too, is good for you and for others, so long as it is a genuine warm smile and not a superficial grin. We all enjoy a lovely smile from the eyes and heart as well as with the teeth and lips. Smiling is an antidote to the ego.
- We all have an enormous number of small chores to do. Just do them without a second thought, while at the same time enjoying good body posture, spiritual thoughts, and cameos of happy past events that make you smile inside.
- 'Just making it happen and doing it' reduces dilemmas in life. When you just do it, a huge amount of stress is taken away. So make snap decisions whenever you can and then just get things done. When next you complain, remember that it will be even more peaceful when you are dead, so don't complain, and rather rejoice in life!
- It is well known that putting off doing things magnifies them. Procrastination also causes extra and unnecessary stress, because small amounts build up. So again, just sort it out now and make it happen.
- When doing a task, focus sharply. Sharp focus temporarily increases intelligence, and therefore ability to undertake a task more efficiently.
- Be fascinated by all around you, as it gives you a much richer perspective on the tapestry of life. Fascination is rejuvenating and balancing for the mind because the ego is being ignored. When you couple this fascination with enthusiasm, you are moving along your spiritual path to happiness.
- Continue to dissolve your own bad thoughts, and deflect any bad intentions that come towards you. Show non-reaction,

and just chill.

- Walking in nature is inherently therapeutic. While doing so, look at all the beautiful complexities of nature, the colors, forms, spaces, and movements.
- Swimming is good too, as so many muscles are being exercised and the medium of water is so good for us. The sound of splashing also scrambles intrusive vertical thoughts that spoil our feeling of well-being. If you can climb, or at least scramble, do so, as you are exercising and exploring through your hands as well as feet, many wonderful textures of nature. The same goes for gardening.
- Have a 3x8 rule: 8 hours' sleep, 8 hours of work, and 8 hours' interacting with life.
- Get your beauty sleep. If you wake up or can't sleep, it is because of an overactive mind. Know this and then use your imagination to dissolve it. Write down tasks you have to do or troubles to resolve, even in the middle of the night. But don't try and solve anything. Then make a warm drink, and get thoroughly comfortable. Then let colors appear and disappear in your mind. See them morph and swirl, and really enjoy all these wonderful colors, shapes and interactions.
- Perhaps color-imagining doesn't work for you. Then enjoy a good novel, and be absorbed. As your vertical thoughts are distracted, your eyes will close, and you will gently drift off.

## Senses, Passion and Motivation

- As we don't generally explore our primary senses of seeing, hearing, smelling, touching, and tasting to the full, we need to practice using them, especially at the same time. Really and truly focus on the sensations. Treat them as never ending exploration.
- Additionally, use these sensations to paint pictures in your imagination. Practice seeing a sound, tasting a sight, hearing

a touch, and all other combinations. Enhance these visualizations with thoughts of love and compassion.

- Experience nature as often as you can, and absorb it holistically, especially with all its sensations. This fine tunes and hones the senses.
- Choose to be with enjoyable, harmonious sounds that trigger good, loving thoughts, whether the lovely sounds of nature or of music. Combine this with a soothing atmosphere, with soft sights and wonderful aromas.
- Have candlelit dinners as often as possible as they are so enjoyable and sexy. This is because they create calm, make us feel secure, and give us the time and space to focus on each other. These dinners also bring out the yin in a man, making these times romantic.
- For a good and lasting long-term relationship, caress with your sensitive fingertips as often as possible as this stimulates release of pheromones, or skin hormones, which play an enormous role in attraction and pair-bonding.
- Choose food by its color as well as by its aroma as the selection is often indicative of your body needing certain types of nutrition through fine-tuned awareness.
- Choosing certain colors, especially of clothes, accessories and make-up, can be vital for relaying subtle yet important messages. Choose the color and hue to match the mood you would like to get into, rather than the mood you are in, and certainly not just because you think that you should color code.
- As a woman's skin, whether light or dark, is exquisitely beautiful, keep it always glowing with good nutrition and positive, harmonious thoughts.
- Lipsticks and their color convey strong messages. Light red and lip gloss is appealing for passion, and pale lipstick for tenderness.
- Eye make-up and especially eyelash extensions are highly yin,

and is a call for affection and warmth, through some balancing yang. These are not necessary, but can be considered enhancements.

- While all this physical attracting may seem base relative to your spiritual path, it is actually a firm foundation arising from our deep biology. To ignore its strength is to ignore your base chakra, and to skip a part, and an exquisitely beautiful part, of your upward path.
- Making your body physically attractive is a call to receive romantic, physical love, to balance your chi, which then travels up your spine towards enlightenment.
- You can use your senses and your physical adornments to enhance your well-being. This also helps you resonate with your inner being and beauty, which then resonates with all in the cosmos.
- On the one hand we need peace and calm, and on the other, we also need passion. Enjoy passion. Its intensity is what spurs on spiritual development through enthusiasm. The intertwining of physical passion and spiritual enthusiasm is to dance with the cosmos towards higher consciousness.
- The physical passion of romantic love has a distinct set of biochemical reactions associated with it. An essential key for finding true love, harmony *and* happiness, is to channel this wonderful passion, which usually has a finite life, into the giving of love and of compassion.
- Passion can be like a spinning top, easily becoming unbalanced, especially by pranks from the ego, which can create such feelings as doubt and jealousy. This passion addiction must be dissolved so you can move into the realms of comfort and security. In this zone, you can then openly give out love, and comfortably enjoy receiving it. This is the maturing of a truly romantic relationship into a truly fulfilling one. It also leaves you with spiritual space to grow.
- Should the passionate romantic relationship not work out,

still find comfort and security, heal, and still grow spiritually.

- During development of a romantic relationship, appraise its growth relative to the development of your path to higher consciousness. Is your new-found love enabling you to grow, or is it causing you to wobble? Then make a decision one way or another, cultivate it or leave it. Be firm.
- Your path to higher consciousness requires the fuel of motivation, which can be converted into spiritual growth through intense and focused enthusiasm. All the while you need to feel motivation so as to change your life and to grow spiritually.
- You are always in the driving seat of your own destiny. You can achieve in the physical world, but when you do, be careful of the ego, and so make sure you have humility.
- Keep up your motivation by having regular breaks and small changes. Pack a lot of different things into your day.
- Discipline for efficient practical living and for spiritual growth is essential. There are always ups and downs, but all the while you make sure that you continue on your long-term mission, which is to find love, harmony *and* happiness.
- With discipline, motivation, and enthusiasm, as well as other attributes, you will inevitably grow. This will require saying 'no' at times, and it will always require focus. But focus is not excessive perfectionism. All the while you are focusing on the bigger picture of growth, enjoying it, and not being put out of phase by any minor setbacks.

## Tuning into your Subtle Senses

- Always take the opportunity to develop your 'sixth sense'. This means becoming acutely attuned to all around you by using all your senses to their fullest.
- The more that you are mindful of all around you, the more that you feel that you understand the world around you, enabling you to embrace it.

- Your senses become even more finely tuned by feelings of joy and by knowing that within you is an expanse of infinite love which resonates with all in the cosmos.
- Be prepared as you practice developing this awareness. There will be occasional flashes of intense awareness, insight and a feeling of apparent deep knowing. These are known as satoris. They are an instantaneous and joyous celebration of life. They enable you to see and feel all life's connectedness, as well as the resonating of goodness beyond space and time. View a satori as a dream but not a dream, knowing without knowing, and seeing without seeing. Words have no currency for understanding it, as it is pure beauty. Feel it.
- The essence of higher consciousness is to revere, respect and love all around you. Enjoy doing this. It is the iterative process you experience when you *give out* reverence, respect and love. What then happens is that they wrap themselves around and within you in a wonderful white light of being. You will feel the joyful essence around your heart in particular. It also enables you to see the madness that the ego causes in our everyday lives.
- Enjoy the process and discipline of letting go, which is the warm antithesis of the worry of accumulating things and holding on to them all.
- Feel the balance between your receptive yin and expansive yang as you enthuse and give compassion and love. Feel this balance as a divine light along your spine, which is helped by imaging colors which will arrive as you think and feel harmony and love.
- Imagine red, associated with the base chakra at the bottom of the spine, and strong on yang, so as to give you physical vitality, motivation, stability and spontaneity.
- Then imagine orange, associated with the sacral chakra, which stimulates creativity, enthusiasm, optimism, pleasure and productivity.

- Follow on with yellow, associated with the solar plexus chakra, and which goes with open joy and fun, creativity, as well as the lateral power of humor and intellectual crispness.
- See the green of nature in particular. This is an association with the heart chakra, and represents balance, harmony, true love, acceptance and sociability.
- Feel also blue, as in the sky, and associated with the throat chakra. It is in the realm of yin, and represents freshness, peace, calm, kindness and humility.
- Appreciate indigo or navy blue, as it is associated with the brow chakra of the forehead. It is deeply yin, and represents inner peace, trust, loyalty and honesty.
- Experience violet and purple whenever you can. It is associated with the crown chakra at the top of the head, and integrates physical and spiritual energies. It also represents intuition, imagination, great creativity, meditation and resonates with cosmic consciousness.
- Bear in mind too, the tones, white and black, which are also influential in our lives. White is yang, bold, confident, clean, fresh, and harmonizing. Black is yin. It is the tone of blending in, retreating, and about vast distance. Nevertheless, black and white in contrast are a bold statement of yin and yang looking for dynamic balance. Yet a total mix of the two, gray, represents impartiality and detachment, like fog, but can be lit up with a bright splash of color.
- Gold is a truly high octave and represents cosmic awareness and the ultimate wisdom of knowing but not knowing. It is absolute love, compassion, reliability, grace and respect. As high as it is, not surprisingly, it is counterbalanced with a strong down side associated with self-gratification, greed, deception and ultimately downfall. Gold can only be handled by those who have reached a high level of consciousness as it is so strong.
- Other hues for you to consider include beige which has the

power of our primeval savanna roots, while rose is a strong balance of physical energy with a strong spiritual component.

- As such a huge amount of information flows into us from sensory input and is then integrated, trust your feelings and instincts about a person, a place or an action. Believe in your hunches, insights and intuitions, as they are the result of being highly aware and attuned physically to what is around you and its significance, as well as to the no-space, no-time resonances.
- You will find that you will be more attuned to these inputs the more you are at peace with your inner being and beauty. You can also further perfect this synthesizing ability through practice. This information is also integrated and resolved while you are dreaming, hence the value of 'beauty sleep'.
- You can also develop an awareness of what coincidences mean, and how they can change the direction of your life. This awareness to coincidences helps you make decisions with more insight than usual. When this insight is combined with a feeling of true love, a decision is likely to be the right one.
- You will find a sense of profound beauty and clarity will come as you cultivate your subtle awareness. As you fine-tune your awareness capabilities, colors begin to have real meaning, and a sense of harmony with the cosmos develops. This leads to a feeling of the cosmos making the right decisions for you. You will have feelings of deep peace, of a wonderful nothingness, like a delicious excitement, inside you. Once you are in this realm, many aspects of everyday life, where the ego reigns, become banal.
- It is an honor to feel the resonant kisses of the cosmos, and it is important to give deepest thanks for it. This can be done through prayer. The giving of thanks is the true function of prayer.
- While we may have satoris and we grow, we must also always

stay alert and tuned. You can do this partly through always feeling the radiance of your inner being and its beauty. Simply let your inner being, with its strong radiant non-reaction, outshine the ego. This is 'feeling the essence of beauty'.

- There needs to be time for reflection during your spiritual growth. This means not listening to the chatter in your head. Simply see, hear, smell and touch with no-thoughts of absolute nothingness. Release the chattering monkeys.
- As you become tuned into the cosmos you will see colors or auras around people. Different people and at different times have different colors, but these are not for you to judge or comment on, just to observe. This has nothing to do with 'psychic powers' which are an ego-phenomenon, it is just your heightened awareness and your attunement with the resonances of the cosmos.
- You will also see these colors all around you at different times in your day, and they are strongest when you are most aware. As your path to higher consciousness develops, you will increasingly see purple, which swirls and morphs like a pale mist all around you.
- Sometimes you will feel that something ominous is going to happen. This is not to be confused with 'psychic' powers. It is simply your highly tuned body letting you know that your practical reactions and judgment (through temporarily disharmonious body rhythms) are not at their best, or quite right today, and are warning you to be extra careful, say with driving.
- Be aware of just how often many people engage in psychological game playing. Identify the motivations and reasons. Often these games aim to get sympathy, show power, to prove a point, and dominate you. They are a whole string of coercion techniques that are common and easy to spot. "I thought you were going to call me" for example, really means "My ego is here, and right now it expects your attention, and all the time,

no matter what you are doing or how you feel".

- This widespread game playing is easily dispelled through a combination of awareness (being attuned to all that is going on around you), spontaneity (having the freedom to choose and express your feelings) and autonomy (riding in a higher plane above the mundane grayness of unfruitful game playing). All this requires constant alertness tempered with an inner smile.
- Fear comes from programming in the past, often from family scenarios on the young mind. Dealing with fear comes firstly by recognizing it and identifying it clearly. Trace it back to when it started. Then parcel it up as if it is irrelevant and let it drift into the cosmos on a wave of love. This takes practice and persistence but not trying too hard. Think of bright colors to wash away the gray of fear, and feel the pulse of nature and beauty around you.
- Optimism is not just about a half-filled bottle. It is the refilling of it with awareness, spontaneity and intimacy, with love and harmony.
- As we depend on a wide array of support networks to ensure our survival, it means that there is now an ethical foundation for giving out love on a universal basis. The more that people in societies do this, the sooner we *all* will be on the right spiritual track. This is the development of global consciousness.

## Finding your Partner

- It is essential that we look after our bodies and think and feel positively and harmoniously, so that we increase our chances of greater longevity and increased spirituality.
- We need to be aware that bad and selfish thoughts, driven by the ego, disharmonize us and disrupt the harmonious link with our inner being. This is why it is essential to recognize and dispel the ego's game playing. This means linking with

your inner being of expansive love, both for physical well-being and for moving to greater spirituality.

- As you let these harmonious vibrations take place, so will people resonate with you. Your good vibrations bring out love in them which improves their physical well-being as well as helping them along their spiritual path. This will also draw a potential partner to you.
- Where your love is not received or not understood by a potential partner, accept the joy of having given it, wish them well from your heart, and move on.
- Seeking a partner means being clear on what type of relationship and what lifestyle you wish to have. You know that you are always growing spiritually, and now the search is for romance leading to a deep relationship where there is both passion and compassion.
- Be *prepared* in your mind and heart every moment of the day to meet the right person. A happy chance encounter, perhaps out of the blue, may well occur. One couple recently married after having first met while exchanging license plates following a vehicle collision!
- By all means think positively, but do it with sincerity and love. Only with true and good feelings will you attract the right person.
- There are practicalities to consider that increase the chances of a good relationship developing. Among these, is being in the right environment for both of you. Meet where your interests meet, at an art gallery, doing a particular sport, having a particular pastime etc., with a similar passion. This is not prescriptive, as there are many successful relationships where partners' interests are different, but where there is a difference, do be prepared to work towards understanding how each other ticks.
- Internet dating, while exciting, misses all the subtleties of truly personal interaction, which are so essential for weighing

up the potential for a romantic relationship. Often it is the ego on the internet, not the real person. Bear in mind that electronic communications move much faster than good sense. Nevertheless romances do work out via the internet, but they arise from careful selection.

- When first meeting, consider your 5 vital Cs: confidence, conversation, communication, charisma and chemistry. This means being at ease, having something meaningful to say, being well groomed, glowing, and exuding the right body messages.
- Just breeze into a conversation, all the while focusing on the potential partner. Use the word 'you' but not the word 'I'. Think of conversation as a gentle volley of thoughts, ideas and fun. Throw out conversation hooks on topical and interesting subjects, and those of interest to all of us, like cuisine, travel and interesting ideas.
- During an initial conversation, make good and sincere eye contact, and smile from the heart. Feel that you are exuding love. No need to go on talking about yourself. Rather listen and pick up on little nuances of your potential partner's comments. Add a little wit and humor too. Enjoy your path of discovery.
- Eye contact, along with a smile from the eyes and heart has great connecting value. A man derives great pleasure from intently watching a woman. He enjoys her complex body movements, associated with facial expressions, neck movements, as well as wrist and finger movements. A man is usually mesmerized by highly feminine body expressions and body language. While a man thinks he is in control, it is really the woman who is.
- For a woman to capture a man's attention, she needs to have presence all the time. This means thinking and feeling that you would rather be here and interacting like this than doing anything else in the world. This is not being insincere,

because to be really present, means putting aside the ego. You also need to be fully aware of your body posture and expressions as well as engaging in scintillating conversation. Building a conversation is also asking about how the other person *feels* about a particular topic. Also, be a little provocative on some topics just for the fun of it.

- Any woman or man needs to understand that there are differences in the way communication takes place, known as gender tongues. A woman is generally less direct in her comments than a man. This means that she needs to be more explicit when talking to a man than when she is talking to another woman. Conversely, a man needs to read more into what a woman is saying and feeling to a greater extent than if he were talking to another man. So also be prepared to have gender ears as well: listen and interpret what your potential or actual partner is *really* saying and feeling.
- Relationships have layers, from superficial first exchanges to deeply personal thoughts and feelings. Regularly assess where the relationship is at and where it is going. This is so often forgotten, leading to misunderstandings with unfortunate consequences.
- You cannot actually *expect anything* from a relationship, only what you can give it. Perhaps it is best just to stay friends, or perhaps you can cultivate it into a beautiful romance, all according to how well you have assessed the relationship and have responded accordingly.
- You cannot just leave your relationship to grow in its own wild way, but this is not to exclude the joy of spontaneity. A good, long-term relationship must have two-way trust, openness and honesty, where you share desires, dreams and even anguishes. There is no game playing here, no ego interference, because those are not part of your growing a good relationship.
- As you cultivate and cherish a relationship, touch each other

and do little things that actually show that you really care, and re-affirm your care and even your passion.

- When your new relationship is growing, know that there needs to be space as well as contact. Learn to feel the intimate dynamics of the relationship.
- As your relationship grows, develop your own special means of communication to emphasize a sense of 'we', which may also involve you both sharing some intimate sayings as well as feelings. All the while, this communication is very much in the present moment.
- Your physical passion is in tune with your base chakra. This passion is as much about thoughts as it is about intimate physical contact. Sex is largely fantasy, and daydreaming about it is highly creative and restorative. This creative and restorative aspect is related to your developing spiritual awareness, through thoughts as well as intimate and delicious physical interaction.
- Sex is so powerful because it dispels loneliness through forming families, mindfully, emotionally as well as physically. It has to do with us being warm, cuddly, sexy and committed beings. When you share these things, the rest of your life largely comes together.
- Yes, men do think about sex a lot, but despite what women often think, this is not usually their priority. Men are hard-wired to hunt and procure protein for their families, and this is usually the number one priority i.e. career, but for his family.
- Men see sex as a way to emotional commitment, whereas women generally see sex as a result of emotional commitment.
- Men fall asleep after sex to recharge physiologically and because they are content, and not because they are uncaring.
- Why do men like exotic underwear and erotic features? Because they are made to be attracted to variety. A woman

who regularly changes her looks will have the attention of her man much more than if she looks the same all the time, as this has a strong fundamental biological underpinning.

- If your romantic relationship should not work out, know that any feeling of upset is about the ego crying and not actually your inner being. Although you may feel unloved, still make the effort to give out love and harmony, and a new relationship will unfold in its natural good time. As you think and feel, so will it happen.

## For Men only

- We need to realize that men and women in the past and today have complementary biological roles. Now we have to fit those roles into our complex, interactive and large society.
- Men in particular do need to reflect. This reflection comes during a quiet time such as going fishing, watching or doing a sport, tinkering with something mechanical, or watching television for a while.
- But be alert to the fact that a woman in contrast likes to talk things through, to verbalize her circumstances. As a man, do not offer interruptive solutions. Simply listen, especially when a woman is expressing her feelings. Remember that a woman can chat and think things through at the same time much better than a man, so she needs you simply as a passive sounding board.
- Be aware that women are much more sensitive to all the physical and social interactions going on about her than you are. Women notice many subtleties of facial expressions, body language and relationships, whereas men are more focused on a particular task. This includes the total attractiveness of a woman because his mind, stemming from high levels of testosterone, is focused on seduction.
- Remember that a woman can usually predict a man's move, and men generally don't understand how that works because

that is not how their neural system is organized.

- A kiss, which to you as a man is a step in the process of seduction, is a special activity for a woman. A kiss helps her assess a man's health, genetic vigor and his level of commitment.
- Think why women spend time with men. The point is that a woman's psyche is made to be seen and admired, recognized for worth, cherished and made to feel special. You must give a woman for whom you care your undivided attention.
- Bear in mind that a woman's sense of self is closer to herself than is the case for you as a man. Recognize that a woman is thinking of her appearance, her bearing, her relationships and her immediate environment. It is critical that you pay attention to, and admire, these facets. This is a different perspective from what you as a man have, where the ego is more associated with your position (career), possessions, territories, toys and dominance.
- Given the substantially different agenda for women and men, nature has devised a powerful plan for ensuring long-term relationships. This is through a potent biochemical brew for 'falling' in love, then another series of bodily reactions that give a sense of well-being and balance, bringing about the triad of yin, yang and balance. Remember that a woman is rapidly assessing your worth, health and commitment at this stage, and will rapidly break off the relationship if these factors are not seemingly perfect. Bear in mind that three-quarters of all relationships that do not pass this stage are ended by the female partner. A woman is highly selective.
- During this 'in love' phase, you as a man are subconsciously assessing a woman's worth as a potential mother of your children by assessing such features as waist to hip ratio, quality of legs, beauty of speech and elegance.
- Think of a relationship from a woman's point of view. The convention of marriage (legal or common law) has been put in

place to ensure long-term security for mother and child, and so consider a romantic relationship from this perspective. Bear in mind that during this phase, the biochemistry will be functioning optimally to ensure conception and healthy growth of the fetus.

- Consider a prolonged courtship, with mutually acceptable depths of intimacy. Letting the courtship phase pass too quickly is one of the reasons for so many unsatisfactory relationships and break-ups. Courtship enables ongoing evaluation and re-evaluation of a relationship, as well as an assessment of where it is headed. This lets you both steer the relationship into a mutually fulfilling, ongoing and growing experience.
- Always recognize that a woman's hands are incredibly important to her, hence all the nail parlors. A woman's hands also carry many personal messages. Jewelry is also more personal than a man normally thinks, as it is close to the skin and adorns parts of the body which have strong emotional messaging. This means that in your search for a long-term partner, it is essential for you to read a woman's rings as worn in public.
- Taking the left ring finger as a standard for representing marriage or at least a long-term relationship, a single ring denotes commitment, while a double ring means very strong commitment. When the ring is large, for example with a big stone, this often signifies commitment to another cause, especially a religious one, with or without a husband. Sometimes a woman will wear a simple ring on this finger which is not a regular wedding band. This suggests that she is not really seeking a partner, but would form a bond should the right man come along.
- A single ring only on the ring finger of the *right* hand (i.e. on the opposite hand to the wedding band hand in our example here) signifies a longing for a deep romantic relationship

leading to a long-term commitment, especially marriage.

- A ring on both the ring fingers of both hands signifies a strong feeling for romance and may also indicate a tendency to an extra-marital affair. If your woman has such a ring array, she should be carefully cherished.
- Rings on the middle fingers, especially when large, indicate great physical sensuality, and often great passion and high sex drive. A single ring on this finger on either right or left hand, or both, but no other rings, indicates sensuality with independence.
- A ring on the middle finger along with a marriage band on the left ring finger indicates a highly committed sensual marriage, which you should treasure. A ring on the index finger signifies a liking of authority, strength, precision, and non-negotiation. The message being given out here is not one of feminine tenderness.
- A ring on the little finger, especially with a large stone, indicates a tendency to power and authority. A woman with such a ring alongside a strong wedding band enjoys the power conferred on her through marriage.
- A ring on the thumb is a message of extroversion, self-confidence and strength.
- A woman's hands without any rings are quite simply a declaration of independence, confidence, self-security and often intelligence. A ring on every finger is often a lack of self-confidence, but signifies a committed and sensual relationship.
- Notice too, that earrings are also strong message bearers as the ears are highly erogenous. Large earrings denote bearing and confidence, with round ones denoting sensuality, and pendulous ones, power. Small point-type earrings signify liking to be fully dressed, while large point-type earrings signify an enjoyment of authority. The wearing of no earrings, like no finger rings, indicates independence, confidence, and self-security and often high intelligence.

- Remember that necklaces are generally not overtly sexual even though they may draw attention to the breasts. Rather a necklace is reflecting a woman's being, her heart. Short necklaces send a message of peace and calm, freshness and warmth, with a hint of strong passion at times.
- Ankle chains are highly feminine and say come and hold me and kiss me.
- No need to be envious of the single man. Those that are single are determined to be so. If you are a family-man but single again, you will not stay single for long as your natural status quo is to have a romantic partner.
- Women love to be understood and appreciated, made to feel special and romanced. As this list is so long, suffice to say that it is essential that you are courteous, attentive and empathetic, and of course passionate. This means translating the gender tongue. "Can I trust you?" means "If you flirt you are in deep trouble", and "Do you love me?" means "Are you sure that there is no other woman that appeals to you; if so, you are in deep trouble". Notice that these are rhetorical questions.
- You must touch a woman gently, hold her firmly, and kiss her with warmth, and this is not just when you want sex. This is all the time.
- If the relationship is young, and you adore her, kiss her beautifully, first time and every time, because a lovely kiss is really important to a woman. Remember too to be reliable, because a woman likes the man who gives her security and solidness.
- Remember that a woman's hormones have a cycle (which as a man you are not tuned into). In the middle of her month, her testosterone levels (which are of course much lower than yours) are a little higher, making her feel particularly sexy. During this time of the month a woman often likes to be treated with firm muscle and chin. This does not mean being unkind in any way, but rather treated with firm demonstra-

tiveness followed by attentiveness.

### Loving Family and Friends

- Whomever you meet, greet with a sincere and loving smile.
- Smile with the family too, as we often forget!
- If a relative stranger does not return a smile, no need to let your ego affront you. Warmly continue to greet the next person you meet and they will probably return a smile as warm as yours.
- Always put yourself in another person's shoes and try to feel what they are truly feeling, as this is a high level of communication, and an important part of your spiritual growth.
- Always recognize subtle feelings and insights, and combine these with rich imagination. This then enables you to connect with other people through empathy.
- Develop your sense of empathy as it is an important part of developing your emotional intelligence, which is recognition of your own feelings and those of others for motivating yourself, and for good management of emotions both within you, and in your relationships.
- Learn to listen attentively to what someone has to say as it is an important component in the development of your emotional intelligence.
- Expressing and showing another person how you are feeling with facial expressions and appropriate gestures of touch are important additional components to empathy.
- To reach inside another's feelings you need to harness your own deep emotional feelings and understanding. Your ego will not help you but your inner being will. You can listen to the message of your inner being by showing humility. Only the truly brave can do this.
- While we all like exciting relationships (because we are neophiliacs, lovers of new things), deep down we all need an ongoing, caring and intimate relationship. A relationship

deepens as reciprocity with another person starts to develop. You give, and they give. Keep it fresh with spontaneity, that is, say and do happy chance things now and again. After all, the growth of a deep romance is a nascent family.

- As a meaningful relationship develops, all the while you are thinking in terms of respect, honesty, understanding, trust and acceptance of your partner as regards all facets and knowing their true character. A really good spiritual relationship deepens as these mutual attributes grow between you and another person. This does not exclude having passion, excitement and fun, as long as the outcomes feed into your spiritual growth and that of others.
- Loving understanding between partners comes about through good communication, which means accepting differences in gender tongues. This means appreciating how a woman or a man thinks and expresses according to gender differences.
- Listening is such an important art that when well-developed could be considered a gift. Always make sure you give your partner focused undivided attention when they are communicating with you.
- There is never any need for you to be defensive in the face of hurtful comments. Just let them flow past you on the wind, knowing that your inner being is not interested in such negativities. To react is to let the ego get the upper hand.
- There will be some differences of opinion in a relationship. That is alright, because you have both agreed to disagree on some points.
- Relate to your true friend or partner on their thoughts, feelings and securities. Say kind words, and make little gestures, especially suggestions for doing something together.
    - This is especially true for a long-term relationship.
- Just doing something thoughtful and kind, out of the blue, can create a special little glow in a relationship.
- How well do you *really* know your partner? Do you know

their dreams?

- Encouragement is a powerful facet of love. You will be showing true love when you show encouragement.
- When considering a life-changing event, go away somewhere else for a while either singly or together and let your subconscious help you make the right decision.
- Real love, harmony *and* happiness are about knowing that your inner being is the foundation for your spiritual growth. Yet, your inner being is not isolated. Your feeling of fulfillment only really comes about when you connect with other inner beings through your deep empathetic relationships. You feel what they are feeling.
- There are some everyday rules for maintaining this connection with others. Among them is standing by your promises alongside absolute honesty.
- When you do make a mistake, which we all do, simply apologize without dwelling on it, and do so with total sincerity. Follow this with some positive action of reconciliation.
- Always maintain your dignity in its traditional sense of worthiness, elevation of mind and character, as it is another important guideline for maintaining your connectedness with all based on practical action.
- Honor in its real sense is traditional dignity with spiritual development. Also, as you attain higher consciousness, so honor has more meaning.
- Time is short as we have only one wonderful life, so no need to let the ego rule. Think of having written on your tombstone 'She/he found love, harmony *and* happiness', which says it all.
- Life is tough enough, so no need for battles at home. Turmoil must *always* be resolved, now. The terrible twins of anger and blame are two of the strongest bites coming from the ego. When they start to surface, rapidly connect with your inner being and its ego-dissolving power through patience, caring,

compassion, humility and humor. Simply remind yourself that anger is actually a waste of your valuable one-life time.

- Always aim for good communication, as it is critical for a good relationship. It involves discussing, chatting, touching, expressing, relating, and letting go. These all lead to feelings of sharing, companionship, cohesion, kindness, excitement, healthiness, intimacy and sexiness.
- Good communication is also about asking your partner how they would like to be loved.
- There is a long list of why we fall short of good communication, especially when emotional issues are concerned. Vital for good communication is the interpretation of feelings, in addition to the content of the message being conveyed.
- Communication is not only verbal. It also involves facial expressions, gestures, touch, and of course, a kiss.
- Good communication is about clear replies, as well as a clear opening message.
- Loving is doing. It is about actually doing things purely for someone else. Strange, isn't it, that we don't do it more often? And of course say 'I love you'. Be spontaneous with your actions.
- Kindly and constructive criticism is so important for keeping the practical side of a relationship on track. Careful how you do it, because the ego is highly polished and hates to lose its shine through criticism.
- As a meaningful relationship is about finding a mutual path of progress together, grow your emotional intelligence. This involves sharing and showing enthusiasm for a common dream. Find solutions together as this activity is amazingly reassuring for both partners in a relationship. With this foundation of shared positive action, it is easier to move along your path to enlightenment.
- Always have respect for a partner, friend or family member so as to maintain good connectedness. This also means appreci-

ating another person's occasional space and little privacies.

- Always try to speak and practice the truth for a harmonious relationship. Yet truth is not an absolute. We do not always know the truth about ourselves let alone be able to always tell the truth. The problem lies with the ego distorting the truth. Learn to recognize when this is the case. To be magnanimously truthful from within the heart is very difficult, and requires much reflection, practice and inner harmonizing. Real absolute truth resides within your inner being, emphasizing the importance of continually relating to it, especially through humility and compassion.
- Finding this truth comes through giving out love, having immense enthusiasm, having a sense of wonder for all around you, and seeing beauty, even when at first it does not seem to be there. When an untruth starts to appear, just do something with loving kindness. In doing so, you will instantly connect with your inner being and beauty as well as with the beauty of the cosmos.
- Spiritual development is not averse to financial prosperity, but it is to greed. The path to higher consciousness as regards financial prosperity has two things to say: have resources for lean times, and share your prosperity with others so that they may grow too.
- Your antidote to the greed treadmill, which is driven by the ego, is to appreciate the exquisite beauty of the universe, and enjoy seeing, tasting, touching and feeling from within. Your appreciation of, and feelings for, beauty concerns all in the cosmos, where there is no ownership. Have empathy too, and use your wealth to be well physically and to grow spiritually by helping others.
- You will find that true appreciation, through a little twist of alchemy, becomes love. With love, the rest is easy.
- We must all have faith to be fully human. We have to believe to make sense of the world with its complexities and in the

context of our survival.

- Faith is a personal issue in a social context. Your faith is for you, but not for you to impose on anyone else, although do impart it if someone else is in need.
- As you believe so you will gain in strength, and this strength comes from a feeling of not being alone, and of feeling connected.
- Your vehicle of faith is your prayers, which send out a vibration of thanks into the cosmos. You are giving thanks and not asking for anything.
- If you believe in God or the cosmos, then that is your belief for you personally and it is your individual right to believe as such. The more you love God or the cosmos, the more they will love you, and the more harmony and happiness you will experience, as long as you actively do something distinctly positive based on the intuition and insight that you receive.
- The more you love the wonder of life and cosmic evolution, the more you will feel enraptured by it, and the more love, harmony *and* happiness you will experience.
- You will find that the more insights you receive and the more intuitive you feel, the more spontaneous you will be. This is the creative side of your humility, compassion and empathy, the glory of the alchemy of your inner being and beauty.

## Traveling your Path

- For your path of love, harmony *and* happiness to unfold, you need to decide that this triad is your committed life goal. You resolve to give love, compassion and affection so as to resonate with your inner being and all its beauty.
- You have already realized that happiness is not a goal but a reward. It comes to you only after being fully aware and giving out love, compassion and empathy.
- You are *not* naïve. You stand firm on what you feel is right and good, and what is harmonious and lovely.

- Giving out true love is also about having empathy for a partner, friends, family, fellow human beings, as well as to all other life forms. It is having kind thoughts and making kind gestures on a regular basis.
- Beyond your everyday survival goals, such as earning a living and finding prosperity without greed, you also regularly appreciate your physical world of the senses, which, when tuned, help link your inner beauty with the beauty around you, giving you that delicious exuberant and exquisite tingling feeling inside.
- When you give, you do so 110 percent, so that the bar of attainment is set increasingly high, enabling you to continue to grow through a positive feedback cycle. This growth is particularly important in the case of your emotional intelligence, where empathy is a significant component.
- There is no longer a fog of indecision and fallibility, as you are constantly alert to the artfulness of the ego.
- Your inner beauty is increasingly vibrating with the energies and resonances in the universe. The more that you practice tuning into the world around you by simply being aware, the more you feel that all is divinely beautiful, truly awesome.
- Time is of the essence for you to engage with cosmic energy during your lifespan. You pack in as much love and sincere positivism as you can, as there is really only one shot at it on this current earthly plane.
- Yet for spiritual growth, there is only the one experiential moment, the present one, which compacts and opens up again to become infinity.
- We can feel this moment and this infinity by giving love and seeing awesome beauty. The universe receives the giving of love by returning happiness through the vehicle of harmony.
- This harmony is not a constant wave form but rather the dance of change. Real, deep, true love is you being able to feel that dance of being alive through the medium of the subcon-

scious.

- Time enables you to understand this dance, through letting you live your life and practice spiritual development, with satoris and flashes of beauty coming to you along the way.
- Bear in mind that time is simply the universe's way of ensuring change and manifestation, while not letting everything happen at once. Time gives you space to grow.
- The universe has also given you time as a tool, a gap, for understanding universal love.
- This means that during your lifetime on this planet, you must seek time, not spend time, so as to convert it into timeless love.
- In practical terms, this also means no matter what you are doing in terms of tasks or activities, you can always be giving out love.
- Converting time into experience and then, through love and harmony into happiness requires patience, practice and persistence.
- This means that your everyday goals must be well honed so that you have optimal time to engage in loving activities. These goals become clearer with experience and with greater connection with the cosmos. This is a way of saying build your confidence through the power of your subconscious.
- Enjoyment of life comes with the feeling that true love is growing. In other words, it is alignment with your inner being and its beauty rather than with the ego.
- It is important to recognize the difference between superficial enjoyment and real growth. Superficial enjoyment is when the ego is getting satisfaction, while inner, deeper growth, which is true enjoyment, comes from experiencing love.
- Good time management is a valuable tool for you to space out actual activities for maximal spiritual growth. This is because enlightenment is about doing activities as well as it is about feeling and experiencing illumination.
- You will also find that good time management also gives you

more opportunity for creativity, because everyday tasks can be done efficiently, leaving you more time to focus spiritually.

- Prioritization of tasks is not all about just doing things for you. It is also spacing your life so you can resonate with your inner being and to be able to give out love to those around you. One way to do this is to convert ego time, such as dwelling on pride, status and material possessions, into valuable spiritual growth time.
- Your growth is about dumping emotional hurt and ego-baggage while you are moving along your path to illumination.
- Letting go of stressful events and traumas is as much about skill and discipline as it is about letting time heal. You need to think in terms of letting go of the hurt, angst and negativism accumulated by the ego. Even though you may feel that you need love and compassion, it is essential that you try your best to give these out. We 'just-must' overcome negative and heavy thoughts and start to grow again.
- One effective way to deal with ego afflictions such as competition, greed and pride is also to realize that they are a complete waste of your valuable time, which can be put into more profitable spiritual growth. You need to seize the second, as well as the day.
- You can overcome with practice, positive reflection, resolution, insight (knowing that there is ego interference, and so you are going to be more aware) and belief (you are going to get over this through resonating with your inner being).
- Dominance, deliberate hurt, pride, angst and other ego foibles make up a dead branch, and the more you go along it, the more likely it is to break and you fall.
- Quandaries and having to continually make decisions, even small ones, are remarkably stressful. The point is that a lot of small ones add up to big frustrations, as well as irrational

thoughts and actions, and when severe, even to major traumas.

- To overcome these accumulated stresses, know that your inner being is with you and that you are on a good path. Always steer a decision into the zone of your inner being by recognizing where the ego is interfering. Let go of mind chatter, feel the power of your subconscious, relate to the goodness of your inner being, enjoy its beauty, and make a good decision.
- Where the decision is life-changing, the *feeling* that a solution will present itself really does help. Pray and put your thoughts out to God or into the cosmos while thanking it for helping you with support, for all which is good. Sleep and daydreaming also helps you make the right decision.
- Once a decision presents itself, trust it. Yet all the time, you decide to reserve the right to change your mind should further information and insight become available.
- Imagination is a fundamental feature of being human, with creativity being immensely enriching of our lives. Creativity often comes through taking time off from arduous tasks and even from the continual giving out of love so that your mind can wander all of its own accord, especially while daydreaming.
- The more that you *feel* love the more creative you will be. Love poems are an expression of this.
- Creativity is closely linked with seeing and feeling colors, from fern greens to serendipity pinks. You can even feel lovely warm colors when you think of goodness, kindness, love and harmony.
- You can be as creative as you like, by having some totally lateral, even seemingly crazy, ideas. You can use lateral thinking to link seemingly completely different things, thoughts, ideas, and recombine them into new, even fantastic ideas. With regular and creative ideas, you will find that love comes to you automatically, because to be creative is the voice

and paintbrush of your inner being and its beauty.

- Never feel pressed to give a 'yes' or 'no' response when you are not sure. You simply say 'po' which means your decision is pending. It also means that you are perfectly happy in that suspended state for a while, until a decision presents itself.
- A commitment to a long-term relationship is about having sufficient information on which to make a sound decision. It is also about having the feeling and insight as to how your potential partner might react to various circumstances in the future. This is where using your imagination to sketch all possible scenarios in the potential relationship is valuable. This includes some important issues which are often not fully discussed, such as the possibility of adopting children, how much time to spend with relatives, views on politics and whether there is an afterlife.
- Developing a sound relationship is about sharing challenges and even personal setbacks as well as enjoying each other.
- Harnessing your personal power is about doing, about action. It is also about saying 'no' when you honestly believe something should not be done.
- Explore whenever you can, as it is stimulating. As exploration is essentially a social activity, it is best done with a partner.
- Our journey to discover the immense beauty within us is not a solitary journey but a social one, as we are all connected. The more deeply and more expansively connected you are, the less lonely you will feel. This means that the more you give out love and harmony the more you will connect, and the less lonely you will be.
- We sometimes need time to be alone, to have space. This is part of your spiritual path which is not at all lonely because there is love and beauty all around you. We just have to see and feel it.
- This spiritual exploration is a bonding activity. Nothing ventured, nothing gained... together.

- Whatever we do we must persevere. To make physical and spiritual waves, is about lots of sweat, not 'no sweat'. An essential underpinning is that your dream must be crystal clear.
- Diligence to the task of spiritual growth through love and harmony, with some imagination and a bit of spontaneity and excitement must inevitably lead to happiness.
- With real enthusiasm, sometimes the reality turns out to be bigger and more exciting than the dream.
- Part of planning for growth also means that you must have some contingency plans should surmounting any particular step to greater enlightenment not happen. You must have some comfort zones, both physical and emotional, to which you can retreat. This may involve being sociable with a partner or friends, but it may alternatively be the peacefulness of a health spa or a visit to a faraway relative or friend. This is because we are made to need variety, and are not good with sameness all the time. This is where the 'let's just do it right now' activity plan is so important. A little hardship can give great joy. You will grow when you make the effort.
- This 'making the effort' has immense rewards through positive feedback. The more you do, the more you achieve, the more you grow, the more loving you feel, and the happier you become.
- Where this positivism leads into an intense romantic relationship, the passion is fine, but it must be coaxed into safer and more secure ground by turning feeling and biochemistry into giving love as well as being in love. This is a critical transition, the alchemy of converting passion into compassion.
- Spiritual growth has spurts and then times of settling. Steering this growth within a relationship means having a physical, mental and emotional commitment to developing this growth together.

- For the relationship to grow healthily, it needs expansion phases and then consolidation phases where there is re-assurance and re-affirmation of commitment to loving each other.
- Planning physical activities together and improving your lifestyle through emergent properties of togetherness are important. Enjoy the see-saw of passion and plan, ecstasy and empathy.
- Whenever you temporarily part, end on a positive note. Re-assure each other that you love each other, and always be demonstrative, bold and proactive. Happiness *will* arrive.

# Notes and references

## 1 How this book came about

Quote from Jonathan Black (2007) The Secret History of the World, Quercus, London, UK.

## 2 Life's formula

Quote from Jonathan Black (2007) The Secret History of the World, Quercus, London, UK.

## 3 A strategy for getting on track

Two very good general books based on sincere thought and practical advice are: Richard Carlson (1997) Don't Sweat the Small Stuff. Hodder and Stoughton, London, and Eckhart Tolle (2005) A New Earth: Awakening to your Life's Purpose, Penguin, London.

**Better to have done it than never tried**

Meeting and overcoming life's challenges, and learning from personal setbacks, is enshrined in Buddhist thought. An excellent introduction is Damien Keown (1996) Buddhism: A Very Short Introduction, Oxford University Press, Oxford, UK.

**What sort of person are you, really?**

Reflecting on your past does not necessarily mean delving deeply into every traumatic event in your past but applying Cognitive Behavioral Therapy, described by Christine Wilding and Aileen Milne (2008) Cognitive Behavioural Therapy, Bookpoint, Abingdon, Oxon, UK, as the 'psychology of common sense', where emotional and behavioral activities are channeled into a positive cycle rather than a negative one.

Living for the present moment is enshrined in several ancient philosophies (see Yatri (1988) Unknown Man: The Mysterious

Birth of a New Species, Sidgwick and Jackson, London, UK. This is a truly astounding book) and is the main thesis of Eckhart Tolle (2005) The Power of Now, 3rd Edition, Hodder and Stoughton, London, UK, an excellent read.

**Our deep roots**

One of the most important feel-good compounds of the body is serotonin, a neurotransmitter, biochemically derived from the amino acid tryptophan in our diet, and mostly found in the gastrointestinal tract, blood platelets and the central nervous system. Yellow fruits such as papaya and banana have high levels of tryptophan, as do some other foods with appetizing colors, such as dates, salmon and turkey (http://en.wikipedia.org/wiki/Serotonin).

**The Mexican fisherman**

The author of this story is unknown, and various versions can be found on the web. The story is similar in spirit to a story told by the Chinese philosopher Chuang Tzu (see Burton Watson (1964) Chuang Tzu: Basic Writings. Columbia University Press, New York).

Dan Baker and Cameron Stauth (2003) What Happy People Know, St. Martin's Griffin, New York, give some very good examples of where financial wealth per se does not beget happiness.

**Beauty, and passion too**

We are not just thinking beings but emotional ones too and that is part of how we are made and is not to be denied. Thoughts and emotions are deeply interconnected, with emotions arising out of our thought processes, so feeling good comes from positive, constructive and loving thoughts (see Christine Wilding and Aileen Milne (2008) Cognitive Behavioural Therapy, Bookpoint, Abingdon, Oxon, UK).

**What we can learn from Helen Keller**

There is an excellent summary of Helen Keller's life on Wikipedia. See also Dorothy Herrmann (1998) Helen Keller: A Life, Knopf, New York.

**The '50 percent Rule'**

This is a starting point so as to get on a positive feedback loop. The positive 50 percent enables you to experience positivity, while the negative 50 percent is to practice letting go of negativism. If the positive is greater than 50 percent, and it increases, then it is so much the better.

## 4 You are free to choose your path

Quote from Damien Keown (1996) Buddhism: A Very Short Introduction, Oxford University Press, Oxford, UK, p. 37.

**Time of ages**

Peter Lemesurier (1991) The Great Pyramid: Your Personal Guide, Element Books, Salisbury, UK.

**Who said life is easy, or even fair**

For background on this topic, known as Foraging Theory, see D.W. Stephens and J.R. Krebs (1986) Foraging Theory, Princeton University Press, Princeton, New Jersey, USA. An application of it to humans 3000 years ago, see K.J. Gremillion (2002) Journal of Anthropological Archaeology 21, 142-164.

See a) S. A. Miller (2010) Social-cognitive development in early childhood, in R.E. Tremblay, et al. (eds) Encyclopedia on Early Childhood Development, Centre of Excellence for Early Childhood Development, Montreal, Quebec, Canada. b) J. Sattelmair and J.J. Ratey (2009) Physically active play and cognition: an academic matter? American Journal of Play, Winter 2009, 365-374.

**Dealing with downers**

Dan Baker and Cameron Stauth (2003) What Happy People Know, St. Martin's Griffin, New York, point out that there are four 'Happiness Traps', collectively they call VERBs, Victimization ('poor me'), Entitlement ('I deserve to have these things'), Rescue ('please help me'), and Blame ('he is responsible for making me unhappy'). Dwelling on, and falling prey to, the VERBs will constantly steer you away from finding deep happiness.

**Big knocks, small steps forward**

Exercise exerts its effect on the brain in several ways, including improved mood and nerve cell growth (neurogenesis) and endorphin release. Endorphins are neurotransmitters produced by the pituitary gland and the hypothalamus and lead to a feeling of well-being. They are thought to be responsible for the so-called 'runner's high' or 'endorphin rush', which is a feeling of exhilaration brought on by pain, danger, or other forms of stress. In effect they mask pain while giving a sense of well-being. They can also be released in a state of profound relaxation.

**Living the moment**

Living for the present moment is equivalent to developing awareness i.e. being aware of all around and of wisdom within, with no resistance or judgment. This is fundamental to Zen, which arose out of Buddhism. It has been well articulated in modern times by Eckhart Tolle (2005) The Power of Now, 3rd Edition, Hodder and Stoughton, London, UK.

For a very interesting discussion on relative aspects of time, see Stefan Klein (2006) Time: A User's Guide, Penguin, London, UK.

Susan Blackmore (2005) Consciousness: A Very Short Introduction, Oxford University Press, Oxford, UK, gives a very illuminating account of meditation relative to what we currently know about consciousness.

**Experiencing love from giving love**

The loving of oneself and the experience of giving love is fundamental to all established religions. It is also believed to be leading to the development of higher consciousness in humans in general (see Yatri (1988) Unknown Man: The Mysterious Birth of a New Species, Sidgwick and Jackson, London, UK) possibly through the process of morphic resonance (Rupert Sheldrake (1990) The Rebirth of Nature, Rider, London, and earlier books) which is, as yet not scientifically proven, self-organization found in systems at all levels of complexity and is, according to Sheldrake, a feedback mechanism between particular forms making the existence of a new similar form possible. Memes, which are cultural equivalents of genes, and manifest as habits, behaviors, skills, individual beliefs and stories, are copied from one person to another. Memes are not chemical components like genes but are units of information that pass through spoken word, media, literature, works of art etc. Groups of memes form memecomplexes which change our culture through religion, viewpoints, science, art and technology, and may be important in the future for developing a collective higher consciousness among humans. For discussion on memes, see Susan J. Blackmore (1999) The Meme Machine, Oxford University Press, Oxford, UK.

**Never too late**

Making an effort, i.e. discipline, may seem to contradict the concept of 'letting go'. The difference between the two is what we call today 'frame of mind'. This is where wisdom comes in, which is recognizing the difference between the two. On the one hand, thoughts of resistance, anger, judgment, self-pity, and entitlement need to be released into the universe. This comes about as you become aware of the present moment when combined with warm and loving thoughts. Making the first step is choice, and choice is freedom. Then the next step is to turn being aware into a habitat practiced anywhere at any time.

## 5 Finding your life path

### Having a clear picture of your spiritual goal

There are really two issues here, static visualization and dynamic visualization. Static visualization is like looking at a photograph with all its details ("One should really use the camera as though tomorrow you'd be stricken blind. To live a visual life is an enormous undertaking, practically unattainable. I have only touched it, just touched it." Dorothea Lange: photographer and photojournalist of the Great Depression, and quoted in Dorothea Lange: A Visual Life by Elizabeth Partridge (1994) Smithsonian Institution Press, Washington DC, USA). Dynamic visualization is about seeing an image and morphing the image as your feelings and aspirations change.

Eckhart Tolle (2005) A New Earth: Awakening to Your Life's Purpose, Penguin, London, UK, in his inspiring book, points out that the word 'enthusiasm' comes from ancient Greek 'en' and 'theos' meaning God, and relates to divine inspiration and revelation.

### Positive thinking with sincerity

Quote from Isabel Allende (2004) Kingdom of the Golden Dragon, HarperCollins, London, UK.

Positive thinking per se may not necessarily take others' feelings and welfare into consideration, which is selfish positive thinking, and will not lead to long-term harmony and happiness as the 'love' ingredient is missing.

Susan Blackmore (2005) Consciousness: A Very Short Introduction, Oxford University Press, Oxford, UK, points out that most of what goes on in the human brain is largely outside the realm of consciousness, that is, the realm of us actually realizing that we are perceiving and processing the information.

Most of the activity of the billions of our brain's cells does not make it into our consciousness or awareness but remains in the realm in our subconscious.

Positive affirmation by repeating with sincere belief is part of harnessing the remarkable abilities of the subconscious mind (see for example Joseph Murphy (1963) The Power of Your Subconscious Mind, Prentice-Hall, Englewood Cliffs, New Jersey, USA). However, practicing this must be for the good of others as well as yourself, or else long-term happiness will be elusive.

For information on subtle sensitivities associated with brain activity, see Richard Wiseman (2011) Paranormality: Why We See What Isn't There. Macmillan, London, UK.

**The envy trap**

For a discussion of the diversification of mammals after the mass extinction of the large dinosaurs see Springer, M.S., Murphy, W.J., Eizirik, E. and O'Brien, S.J. (2003) PNAS 100: 1056-1061. For a general account of the history of life and the mass extinctions, see Richard Fortey (1997) Life: An Unauthorised Biography, HarperCollins, London, UK.

For a discussion of envy see Victoria C.G. Greenleaf (2009) Envy: A Survey of its Psychology and History, Cypress House, Fort Bragg, California, USA.

**Being in control of your own destiny**

Wayne Dyer (1978) Pulling Your Own Strings, Arrow, London, UK, engagingly articulates the importance of not being a victim and taking control of your life.

**Your beliefs are important**

For recognizing when your life is getting 'stale' and you need a change, you need then to anticipate change, adapt to change quickly, enjoy the change, and be brave. This is discussed through parable by Spencer Johnson (1998) in his book Who

Moved My Cheese, Vermilion, London. However, there have been counter arguments (e.g. Amy Coffin http://www.thebookhaven.net/Z_who_moved_my_cheese.html) pointing out that change is inevitable, and where deliberate change must be made which involves others, it must be done responsibly without hurting those others.

R.E. Davies and R.H. Koch (1991) All the observed universe has contributed to life. Philosophical Transactions of the Royal Society, B 334: 391- 403.

## 6 Becoming aware of your inner being

Quote from Yatri (1988) Unknown Man: The Mysterious Birth of a New Species. Sidgwick and Jackson, London.

### Your universe

For a stimulating discussion of attractors, as well as other concepts such as morphic resonance see Rupert Sheldrake (2012) The Science Delusion: Freeing the Spirit of Enquiry. Hodder and Stoughton, London, UK. A truly astonishing book.

## 7 Love your body

### Appreciating the chakras

Quote from Jonathan Black (2007) The Secret History of the World, Quercus, London, UK.

### All things in moderation

For a discussion of captivity ennui, see Michael J. Samways, Melodie A. McGeoch and Tim R. New (2010) Insect Conservation: A Handbook of Approaches and Methods, Oxford University Press, Oxford, UK.

Lyall Watson (1989) Neophilia: The Tradition of the New, Sceptre (Hodder and Stoughton), London, UK.

**Little treats**

Quote from HH Dalai Lama and Howard C. Cutler (1998) The Art of Happiness: A Handbook for Living, Hodder and Stoughton, London, UK.

**Your physical environment**

For general discussion of the mathematical laws of physics and how they pertain to life, see Paul Davies (2006) The Goldilocks Enigma: Why is the Universe Just Right for Life? Penguin, London.

For a fascinating, illustrated account of proportions in nature, see Priya Hemenway (2005) The Secret Code: The Mysterious Formula that rules Art, Nature, and Science. Evergreen, Cologne, Germany.

Quote from HH Dalai Lama and Howard C. Cutler (1998) The Art of Happiness: A Handbook for Living, Hodder and Stoughton, London, UK.

**Vive la difference!**

Desmond Morris (2004) The Naked Woman: A Study of the Female Body, Vintage, London, UK.

Elaine Morgan (1985) The Descent of Woman, Revised Edition. Souvenir, London, UK.

Fritjof Capra (1991) The Yin Yang Balance, in The Best of Resurgence, ed. by John Button, Green Books, Bideford, Devon, UK, pp. 185-193.

## 8 Feeling beauty and finding enjoyment

Quote from Meher Baba (1955) God Speaks – The Theme of Creation and Its Purpose, Dodd, Mead and Company, New York.

**Water love**

Quote from Masuru Emoto (2005) The Secret Life of Water, Beyond Words Publishing and Simon and Schuster, London, UK.

Elaine Morgan (1985) The Descent of Woman, Revised Edition. Souvenir, London, UK.

For details of number of words used by women and men see Matthias R. Mehl et al. (2007) Are women really more talkative than men? Science 317: 82. This study was conducted on university students in the United States and Mexico, and there are likely to be differences among other social groups, cultures, and ages, as well as between individuals.

### Think young

For an excellent discussion of valuing nature, see Holmes Rolston III (1994) Conserving Natural Value, Columbia University Press, New York, USA.

### Laugh and feel good

Quote from Jonathan Black (2007) The Secret History of the World, Quercus, London, UK.

### 3 x 8 rule

I thank Mark Wattrus for elucidating this rule.

## 9 Senses, passion and motivation

### Seeing, hearing, smelling, touching and tasting

For information on the Divine Proportion, see Priya Hemenway (2005) The Secret Code: The Mysterious Formula that rules Art, Nature, and Science. Evergreen, Cologne, Germany. The quote in this section is from the same book.

This acoustic clamoring for attention is what Susan Blackmore (1999) The Meme Machine, Oxford University Press, Oxford, UK, would call meme competition. In effect, the units of information, the memes, are in competition with each other, with the most successful ones lodging in your mind, and you passing them on to others, even by simply buying the product being advertised.

**Colors to enhance your life**

Quote from Desmond Morris (2004) The Naked Woman: A Study of the Female Body, Vintage, London, UK.

As well as Morris' book, see also Elaine Morgan (1985) The Descent of Woman: The Classic Study of Evolution, Souvenir, London, UK.

Vatsyayana/Sir Richard F. Burton (translator) (1994) The Kama Sutra. Penguin Popular Classics Edition. Penguin, London, UK.

For details on color standards, see the classic: Andreas Kornerup and Johan Wanscher (1967) Methuen Handbook of Colour, Methuen, London.

**Motivation**

Quote from HH Dalai Lama and Howard C. Cutler (1998) The Art of Happiness: A Handbook for Living, Hodder and Stoughton, London, UK.

## 10 Tuning into your subtle senses

**Mysticism**

Quote from Yatri (1988) Unknown Man: The Mysterious Birth of a New Species, Sidgwick and Jackson, London.

For an introduction to mysticism, see Alexander Roob (2006) Alchemy and Mysticism, Taschen, Cologne, Germany.

**Sacredness**

Quote from D.H. Lawrence (1980, reprint) Apocalypse, Penguin, London, UK.

**Chakras and color therapy**

An excellent introduction is Frank Don (1987) Colour Magic: Learn to Use your Personal Colour Power, The Aquarian Press, Wellingborough, Northants, UK.

**Colors, tones and hues**

For an interesting fictional account of the significance of white, among other things, in traditional Chinese culture, see Lisa See (2007) Peony in Love, Bloomsbury, London, UK.

**Rapid appraisal**

See Malcolm Gladwell (2005) Blink: The Power of Thinking without Thinking, Penguin, London.

**Realizing your intuition**

James Redfield and Carol Adrienne (1995) The Celestine Prophecy: An Experiential Guide. Bantam, London, UK.

**Seeing behind you**

These auras may not necessarily be emanating from another person but be generated by your own visual activity combined with your heightened perception generated as a feedback process between you and another person.

Richard Wiseman (2011) Paranormality: Why We See What Isn't There. Macmillan, London, UK, discusses the subtleties of perception (and deception).

There seem to be criminal cases which have been solved by so-called 'psychic detectives' but the mechanism involved is uncertain.

**Fine-tuning intuition**

Quote from Eric Berne (1964) Games People Play: The Psychology of Human Relationships, Penguin, London. This revolutionary book is well worth a read.

**Releasing fear**

Quote from John Matthews (1989) The Elements of the Arthurian Tradition, Element Books, Longmead, Dorset, UK.

**Feeling what is right and good**

For a fascinating discussion of resonances in the universe see Rupert Sheldrake (2012) The Science Delusion: Freeing the Spirit of Enquiry. Hodder and Stoughton, London.

Quote from Yatri (1988) Unknown Man: The Mysterious Birth of a New Species, Sidgwick and Jackson, London.

## 11 Finding your partner

**Striking up a conversation**

Quote from Dan Baker and Cameron Stauth (2003) What Happy People Know, St. Martin's Griffin, New York, USA. This is a truly excellent book, with many examples of how people changed their lives from being very unhappy to becoming very fulfilled and happy.

Quote from HH Dalai Lama and Howard C. Cutler (1998) The Art of Happiness: A Handbook for Living, Hodder and Stoughton, London, UK.

An excellent book on the topic is Leil Lowndes (1999) How to Talk to Anyone, HarperCollins, London, UK.

**Body harmony and touch**

Helen Fisher (2009) Why Him? Why Her? Finding Real Love By Understanding Your Personality Type. Oneworld, Oxford, UK, gives a very interesting discussion on subtleties of physical interactions relative to personality types.

**Growing a relationship**

These comments refer to the social and family situation and not to the workplace. In modern commercial society, where equity is a central issue, there is a moving to the center by both genders. This may have been the case in pre-historical societies, where one can imagine that both men and women explored and discussed options when moving to new geographical locations for better or safer resources.

## 12 For men only

### It is ok: we *are* biologically different!

An interesting and engaging book on this topic is: Linda Papadopoulos (2009) What Men Say: What Women Want, Arrow, London, UK.

### What women really want

It is easy to simply categorize men and women into different camps when in reality it is not quite that simple, with much overlap in outlook and approaches to communication. See Rebecca Cutter (1995) When Opposites Attract, Bantam, London, UK for a thorough discussion.

### Reading the rings

This discussion refers to the message being given out and is not a judgment on personality type.

### Message from other jewelry

For a stimulating discussion of women's body adornment, see Desmond Morris (2004) The Naked Woman: A Study of the Female Body, Vintage, London, UK.

### Fallacy of the fantasy of being single

See discussion in Rebecca Cutter (1995) When Opposites Attract, Bantam, London, UK.

### Understanding a woman

Helen Fisher (2009) Why Him? Why Her? Finding Real Love By Understanding Your Personality Type. Oneworld, Oxford, UK.

## 13 Loving family and friends

### Empathy

Rebecca Cutter (1995) When Opposites Attract, Bantam, London, UK. This is a very perceptive book on human communication, especially between the sexes.

Daniel Goleman (1998) Working with Emotional Intelligence, Bantam, New York.

**Home harmony**

Rebecca Cutter (1995) When Opposites Attract, Bantam, London, UK.

## 14 Traveling your path

**Creative thinking**

See Edward de Bono (1967) The Use of Lateral Thinking. Penguin, London, UK.

**Po**

See Edward de Bono (1973) Po: Beyond Yes and No. Penguin, London, UK.

AYNI
BOOKS

"Ayni" is a Quechua word meaning "reciprocity" – sharing, giving and receiving – whatever you give out comes back to you. To be in Ayni is to be in balance, harmony and right relationship with oneself and nature, of which we are all an intrinsic part. Complementary and Alternative approaches to health and well-being essentially follow a holistic model, within which one is given support and encouragement to move towards a state of balance, true health and wholeness, ultimately leading to the awareness of one's unique place in the Universal jigsaw of life – Ayni, in fact.